Dreams, Nightmares and Dreams Again

by
Angéla Szepesi

White Mountain Publications

Dreams, Nightmares, and Dreams Again
©2000 by Angéla Szepesi

A Division of White Mountain Investments Ltd

Box 5180
New Liskeard, Ontario P0J 1P0
Canada
Visit our website:
http://www.nt.net/~wmpub/index.htm

Cover Design: Deborah Ranchuk
Front Cover: From the original watercolour by Angéla's mother, **Aranka Széll** portraying Angéla at the age of three, on the bank of the Tisza River, by the village of Tiszaúg, Hungary.
Back Cover: Angéla Szepesi, 1996 in New Liskeard, Ontario, Canada.

Canadian Cataloguing in Publication Data

Szepesi, Angéla, 1920-
  Dreams, Nightmares and Dreams Again

ISBN: 1-896331-03-3

1. Szepesi, Angéla, 1920- . 2. Bahá'í Faith. 3. Bahá'í women –
Canada – Biography. 4. Hungarians – Canada – Biography. I. Title.

BP395.S93A3 2000   297.9'3'092   C00-931010-X

ISBN: 1-896331-03-3
Printed in Canada

Dedication

I dedicate this book to the memory of my parents: Aranka Széll and Brunó (Schmidt) Szepesi and my spiritual mother, Valeria Lamb Nichols; and to my long-suffering and still loyal children: Tip, Sandy, Kathy and Teri.

Angéla Dear:

True friend for many years; courageous, lover of justice wherever it leads even in the face of great challenge of body, mind and spirit — and even in close relationships with others....

Audrey Robarts

Acknowledgments

My thanks are due to too many people to be able to list them all. I am specially grateful for the steady support of the National Spiritual Assembly of Canada and the guidance given by the Association for Bahá'í Studies, in Ottawa. Member of the Universal House of Justice, Ian Semple and Counsellor Hartmut Grossmann of the International Teaching Centre, in Haifa, Israel, read the first version (the part that was easy to recount, entitled *Sooner or Later*), and their encouragement and warm interest throughout gave me courage to proceed. In the writing of the first version, Phoebe-Anne and Bill Lemmon gave me their warm support. The Polyvalent School of the Transcontinental in Sully, specially Gilbert Labonté, helped me greatly by letting me use their computers. The same generous help was extended by Onil Dupuis, at École St-Pierre, Rivière-du-Loup, and the Polyvalent of Cabano, Québec, where I am specially grateful to Hilaire Ouellet and Gaetane Pelletier. Also very great is my indebtedness to the school in Campbell's Bay, Québec, and to Susan Sloan for her patient help. Bruce Filson, Larry Rowdon and Linda O'Neil gave invaluable moral support, and Enid Wrate's selfless offer to edit the messy manuscript was an assurance I needed and appreciated immensely. In the often painful but always fruitful process of maturation as a Bahá'í, I want to thank Douglas Martin, Ed Muttart, Hussein Danesh, Bill Hatcher and 'Abdu'l-Missagh Ghadirian, who – each in his own way – all played important roles in my life. The last person to thank is my publisher, Deborah Ranchuk and her family, who gave me an unforgettably warm week in New Liskeard, where, with her expert co-operation, the book received its final polishing. To all of you, and to all my beloved spiritual children and friends, all over the world: God bless you!

Angéla Szepesi

Table of Contents

From the Publisher

Presented here is the amazing story of a life lived in times of great upheaval, for the world and the author, spanning World War II and formative years of the Faith. Written from an intensely personal perspective, this book is presented as such; it does not pretend to be an official statement about history of the Faith, its institutions, or even her family. It is about a personal relationship with her family, God, and the Bahá'í Faith, none of it a smooth pathway, but a journey worth taking and now, through this book, observing.

Without the diversity of perceptions and opinions recorded in these early days of the Faith, future scholars will receive a view of these days that will lead to the conclusion that these early days were easier than they really were. History deserves better.

Rather it is hoped that the operation of the Faith and God's Will at work in life will inspire readers to ignore their own shortcomings and persevere as Angéla has done: simply continue to live, pray, love and teach, and let God operate through us especially when we do not understand where it leads. He knows.

Deborah Ranchuk
White Mountain Publications

Foreword From the Author

It was in Portugal and I was in my twenties when friends started saying, "Angéla, you should write a book about your life!" I tried. When I did, my life changed so drastically that I had to drop the pen and reach for *skyhook*. *Skyhook* is a strap that hangs from the roof of streetcars, buses and underground trains in Budapest. When the road is rough, you grab it to keep you from losing your balance.

When I first tried to write about my life, everything changed in it so fast that I had to get hold of the skyhook, hang unto it and wait till I found the ground under my feet. Totally new ground; without the help of the skyhook, I would have been lost, bewildered. Bewildered I was, but the security from Above held my hand, assured my heart.

Now I am old, still holding on to the skyhook. I needed it all along, through a difficult life. That life could have easily ended in a car accident two years ago. Why did God not take me? The accident turned into a blessing, healed old wounds, gave me renewed courage.

I want to tell about that life, share the lessons I learned. There were some horrible things in it that I should have avoided, that should not happen to anyone. There were also very beautiful events. Some of what I lived is of historical significance. Most of it is only personal, of human interest. I do not want to take the lessons I learned with me into the grave. My intention is not to entertain, shock or commiserate. I only want to say, "You are not alone."

Coming from a Hungarian background and having been a Bahá'í for most of my life, I might use words and names that are unfamiliar. To explain them, I add a Glossary at the end.

Angéla Szepesi

Hungary
1867-1928

I was born in Igló, county Szepes of Hungary, below the Tátra Mountains of the Carpathians. By the time I was baptized, the town was called Spisska-Nova-Ves and the country was the newly formed Czechoslovakia. My family was of German origin like most of the Hungarian families of that region. Most of my ancestors arrived many centuries ago.

The last member of the family to emigrate from Germany was my father's grandfather, Peter Schmidt. He came from Hofheim in the Taunus Mountains near Frankfurt where the Bahá'í House of Worship stands today. He left Germany because he was a Nazarene who did not believe in war and in touching arms. Peter came to Hungary to be able to live up to his convictions, but he arrived at the wrong time. The War for Freedom (1848-49) broke out because Hungary wanted to become free from Austrian domination and declared her independence on March 15, 1848. Austria replied with a war of repression. Peter Schmidt was so inflamed by the tyranny that he devised an efficient cannon to help the cause of the oppressed. For his conversion to the cause of liberty he passed

9

a few years in the prison of Kufstein. After his release he reverted to his former beliefs and died a peaceful man.

A cousin told me that our grandfather was born in prison. Apparently Peter Schmidt was taken prisoner together with his wife, who was expecting a child. According to the tale, she heard hammering, climbed up on a bench to check out what was going on outside. She fell and gave birth to our grandfather. In the courtyard, Count Batthyáni, for whom the scaffolding had been prepared, was led to his execution.

The war for freedom was lost and a period of deep repression followed. It ended in 1867, the same year that saw the birth of Canada as a nation, with the pact called the Compromise, which created the Austro-Hungarian Monarchy, under Emperor Franz Joseph, and his beautiful wife, Emperatrice Elizabeth.

My grandmother, Ilma Scholtz, whom we called "Imu" for Ilma-nagymama, was five at the time of the Compromise. Her grandfather was the mayor of Igló. There was a big celebration on the main square of town. The mayor delivered a speech in Hungarian, and his brother, representing the region at the Court, spoke in German. They were followed by a town councillor speaking in Slovak.

Although Imu was only five years old, she could recall the event clearly and wrote it down for me. An only child, she grew up among adults, and would listen and observe more than other young children. She had a look of radiant happiness when she talked about that early memory. It became increasingly important for her to remember and to talk about that afternoon of great happiness in 1867, the reconciliation of two nations, with the participation of three cultures. After the First World War, two-thirds of Hungary were divided amongst the new nations of the Little-Entente. Great animosity developed amongst the groups speaking different languages. Imu would remember that afternoon in 1867 as the promise for a better future to come, certain to come one day.

My great-great-grandfather, the mayor of Igló mentioned above, had a brother called Otto. Ritter Otto von Klein, or as we used to refer to him, Uncle Otto, was the most romantic male figure among our ancestors. He was an aide-de-camp to Joseph Bem, beloved Polish leader of the forces fighting for Hungarian liberty. He went into exile to Turkey when that cause fell, but was soon forgiven by the emperor, called to Vienna and became an aide-de-camp to Archduke Albrecht of Habsburg. I do not know how long he stayed at the court, but he left very suddenly. The story goes that one night a fire broke out in the castle of Schoenbrunn and my uncle saved the life of a princess. The embarrassing part was that they were both in their night attire. Uncle Otto never married. He died rather young and his diary was buried with him. In the 1920s the family crypt had to be renovated and his remains transferred into a new coffin. The family was disappointed to find that the diary had decomposed with the body. We younger ones were glad that he took his secrets with himself. It is much more romantic this way.

Imu, my grandmother, was very dear to me. I never saw her walk, she knew only how to run. She was small, thin, wore silent shoes, flowing skirts and a round piece of lace on the top of her head. She had very little hair and she loved to have me comb it. While I combed her hair, she asked me to sing old folksongs. She was close to 90 when she wrote that she hoped to hear me sing to her again. Whenever I happen to sing Hungarian songs, I remember her and know she hears me.

Imu was my father's mother. My other grandmother, Grandmother Széll, was dignified, energetic and I was afraid of her. I remember her presiding over coffee in that old house where I was the last of the family to be born. It had many rooms, an inner courtyard with cobblestones and arched terraces all around the whole house. That house, called the old Széll house then, is called today *Galeria Umelcov Spisa* (*Art Gallery of Szepes*).

11

My grandmother Széll would sit very straight, with her big white bun on top of her head like a crown. I admired her hair and I loved the cakes she served with the coffee. I would walk around the house on tiptoe. Between the rooms there were often a few steps which I found very strange. The front of the house was on the main square, the garden ran down to the river. The water was cold, with bloodsuckers clinging to the mossy rocks, but I loved to bathe in the Hernad River. I loved grandmother's garden with the sweetpeas, gooseberry bushes and a little summer house where she would doze on warm afternoons.

I never knew my grandfather Széll because he died long before I was born. But I knew my grandfather Schmidt and was rather awed by him. He was a manufacturer and publisher. Imu was his second wife. The first one was Ludmilla Akilova, daughter of a Russian aristocrat. My grandfather was in St. Petersburg, representing Hungarian publishers. He saw this beautiful young lady come into a library looking for serious books on agriculture. That amazed him and made him ask questions. It did not take long for them to fall in love. Her family did not approve and disowned her when she eloped with the strange Hungarian. She gave Joseph Schmidt three children and died of tuberculosis, then called "consumption".

My grandfather Schmidt and my grandmother Széll were rich, authoritarian citizens of Igló. They were people who competed against and hated each other. The love affair between their two youngest, Brunó and Aranka, was a kind of Romeo and Juliet story.

Brunó, who became my father, was a very handsome young man, with dark eyes and an aquiline nose. He was a fine sportsman, mountaineer, skier and a brilliant scholar. The family was rich, steeped in the finest European culture. Brunó could decide what and where he wanted to study. He went to Graz, then Geneva and Paris. His sister, Gizella, my beloved Aunt Gizi, shared his tastes and talents. They studied together. Aunt Gizi became the first woman in Hungary to

12

have a doctorate in French literature. Yet her real fame stems from introducing trousers for women who went mountain climbing. When she first exchanged the crinolined skirts and huge hats distinguished young ladies were supposed to wear for the breeches she borrowed from her brother, a tourist magazine carried an outraged report about her brazen behaviour. She calmly answered that the long skirts were rather dangerous when climbing. It took her a year to win her point. She had time to get her doctorate before the First World War broke out. Her brother, a year younger, did not finish before he enlisted. He was made an officer of artillery, was sent to the Serbian front.

Brunó and Aranka fell in love while climbing the Tátra Mountains and became engaged during one of Brunó's leaves from the front. He was wounded in Bosnia, more wounded in his soul than in his body. They married when war ended. I never knew him as the dashing young man; the experiences of the war on the Serbian front wounded him for life. He would never speak about the war. "Noblesse oblige," we do not talk of our sufferings. I learnt it from him.

Aranka, who became my mother, had scarlet fever at the age of six which affected her hearing. At times she would hear quite well, at other times she could only lip-read. I have a portrait of her as a young woman. The intensity of her eyes betrays her deafness. She grew into a fine painter and teacher of fine arts.

I was born as Angéla Berta Ilma Schmidt, on April 9, 1920, in the country now called Slovakia. The Austro-Hungarian Empire was finished, my family's wealth was gone, and my father was somewhere in what remained of Hungary. My mother picked up a few pieces of furniture and moved into a railway cattle car to find her husband. Aunt Gizi and her baby daughter shared the exodus with us. This was specially good for me because my mother had little milk, and Aunt Gizi would take me to her breast after her baby daughter was satisfied.

13

Angéla as a child.

After a few months of shuttling between towns and stations, as four of the two million displaced souls, we found Aunt Gizi's husband in Eger where he became a notary public. My father was also in Eger, first teaching philosophy in the famous old college; but he committed a grave error, if we realize what it did to his career. Hungary had a Communist government in power for a few months. My father told his students that one has a right to speak according to his convictions. When the Communist era ended and Admiral Horthy came to power, my father was considered a radical and unreliable person, who had to be punished. The promising young philosopher became a teacher of German and French in a high school in Kecskemét, in the heart of the agricultural lowlands.

When our train drew into the station of Kecskemét, my father noticed a pair of baby legs in a cattle car and that's how he found us. He took us to our first home, a nice room on the third floor of the Lutheran Palace. Three storeys high, it was then the tallest building in Kecskemét. The apartment belonged to a painter, a teacher in the college on the other side of the main square. Uncle Domby became our friend. I can still see his wife and my mother sewing a pink silk dress for me. It had frills on the skirt, which were let down each time I grew out of it.

14

When my mother became pregnant with her second child, we moved to a bigger place, into Mrs. Good's house. We shared her courtyard with a fruit merchant. Mrs. Good was a kind lady but the courtyard was crawling with cockroaches. I learned to run by trying to kill the cockroaches shouting, "Bug! Bug! Step! Step!" Of course I did not say it like that, in grown-up English. I shouted, "Bogyáj! Bogyáj! Tapo! Tapo!" in baby-Hungarian. Whenever my father wanted to use an endearing term for me, he would call me Bogyáj, or "Little Bug". From there we moved into a house, with a garden and an orchard of our own. My father's father and my mother's mother made a temporary truce to help us out. From what was left of their wealth, they gathered enough for my parents to buy the house where I grew up. It was out of town, my father had a long walk to school, but he preferred walking to living in town. He was a gentleman farmer at heart and I grew up to learn to tell apart chickens from cockroaches. Later I learned to garden, to find fruit as it ripened on the trees, and forgotten grapes in late fall when everybody thought that everything was gathered and gone.

My brother, Ákos, arrived soon after we moved to our own house. A second brother arrived for my eighth birthday. Of the birth of my first brother I remember tugging at the cord of the blinds in my mother's room because I wanted to let in the light for the doctor. It may be that this memory resulted from hearing about it often, as I was only a year-and-a-half old. But the memory of Attila's birth is definitely my own.

My mother organized a party for my eighth birthday. In the middle of it, as we were playing hide-and-go-seek in the garden, a carriage arrived and my mother asked a friend to take over for her as hostess. She said that she was going to get my best birthday present, a little brother or sister. A few hours later Father came home and announced that Attila was born. I was happy but Ákos must have felt differently; he made a deal with one of his friends to sell Attila for 20 pengoes!

15

I was in second year of elementary school. My teacher was an excellent teacher and we loved each other. Young student teachers practised under Aunt Ilonka's guidance. School was fun, so was the garden. My mother planted snowdrops, violets, lilies, lily-of-the-valley, iris, phlox, petunias, cannas and roses. Her roses! There were small bushes, tall tree roses, climbing roses, white, pink, red and yellow, pale and dark. There were forsythias in early spring like golden rain, pink-mauve smoke trees, dark pink Japanese quince and white jasmine. An alley of acacias led to the well and the fragrance of the blooms still linger.

In my memory, my early childhood is set in watercolours. I remember carrying a picnic basket while my mother carried her easel and paints among fields of wheat, red poppies and cornflowers. I remember her seated on a three-legged stool, painting a big willow tree in a green field, children playing in its shade. I recall her painting me with a big red and white polka-dotted ball in the garden in summer, posing for her by the big green majolica stove in winter. She painted me on the banks of the Tisza, with the church steeple in the background, its reflection, like a bridge of bright light, on the water of the river. That painting is reproduced on the cover of this book.

I remember her waking me one morning:

"Close your eyes!" She picked me up and carried me to the window. Setting my feet on the sill, she said,

"Open your eyes!" Outside the garden was covered in virgin snow.

One day my schoolmates told me that it was not the little Jesus and the angels but our parents who brought the tree and the gifts for Christmas. I had to verify. When Anyuka said that she was closing the door to the dining room because she had to help the angel decorate the tree, I went outside and climbed up on the ledge under the dining room window. What I saw is still plainly before my eyes. I saw her hanging a silver star on a high branch and above her head there was an angel hanging a white bell on a higher branch. The angel was
16

the same size as my mother but instead of standing, she (or he?) was horizontal, like a flying bird. Or like a flying angel? I remember my mother reading *Heidi* to me in her bed. That wonderful story of mountains, goats, rough but kind old men, loving grandmothers and warm friendships, was at that time not translated into Hungarian yet. Anyuka held the book in German and told me the story in Hungarian. Her bed was warm.

She gave me her faith, her firm conviction that God is strong, He loves us and watches over us at all times. She took me to light candles on lonely graves on All-Saints Day and sent me with a basket of sweets to a family with many children at Christmas. She taught me to garden and showed me which were the flowers and which were the weeds. But that summer, after Attila was born, I did not help her in the garden. I spent that summer in Igló, with my grandmother, Imu. On the morning that I left, Anyuka was not feeling well. She did not come to the terrace to wave good-bye. She watched me go and waved from a window. I can still see her smile and her waving hand.

Imu's garden was big and beautiful. It was not like ours in Kecskemét. Some of the trees were old and very big. There were hazelnut and raspberry bushes and an apple tree on a hill by the wall on the street side. Lots of rotten apples were on the ground and I gathered some and started aiming them at the flat hats of the Czech soldiers passing in the street below.

At that time Hungarian children were taught patriotic songs at school. The feeling was very high about the unfair treatment meted out to our country in the Treaty of Trianon. I learned the word "justice" in the patriotic slogan "Justice for Hungary!" Czechs and Romanians were called thieves and other ugly names. Now I mixed the fun of childish games with the emotions of righteous patriotism as I aimed the rotten apples at those flat soldier hats. The fun came to an end when I lodged a full hit with the softest, biggest, rotten apple. The officer whose hat got hit banged on the gate and I had to promise I would never do it again. When he left, the lady who owned the garden next to Imu's called me to the tiny gate connecting the gardens and gave me a big piece of chocolate. It was a bar of milk chocolate and tasted very good. She was also a Hungarian.

One morning I was playing in the back of the garden when I heard my mother calling my name. Her voice was coming from the house and I ran up to look for her. Imu came out to the terrace and asked what I was doing.

"I am looking for Anyuka."

"You know that she is at home in Kecskemét."

"Yes, but she just called me."

She stared at me, then said, "You heard her calling you? Come, we shall pray for her." Imu was a Theosophist and believed in contact among all God's worlds, that the soul is stronger than the body, and that prayers are the most important things in time of need.

The telegram came in the afternoon saying that my mother, Anyuka, died that morning.

I went back to the garden to pick branches from the cypress tree to make a wreath, as Anyuka taught me to do. Two days later I placed the wreath on the wooden cross above the fresh grave.

In the years that followed I passed many an afternoon sitting by that mound as it settled and then became covered with ivy. I don't remember ever crying by her grave. I just sat there close to my faraway mother who was now on the other side of the Gate. I did not feel that the Gate separated us. It just left me alone on this side. It changed our relationship; instead of being my mother, she became my perfect friend who went ahead. She brought eternity home to me.

Ever since then I feel that I belong to two worlds, one here where we act and evolve, and one for which we develop. This feeling is specially strong when I am happy. When I am exceedingly happy, I tend to cry out, "Now I can die!"

2

Kecskemét
1928-1938

Oh, how I wish my mother could have stayed just a few years longer, to guide me a bit further! With her death began my long, tragic battle with Apu, my father.

A hazy memory kept on coming back again and again. I could not have been more than four or five. Anyuka arrived from Budapest, from the Spring Exhibit where some of her paintings were shown. Her big folder was under one arm, and a beautiful pot of pink cyclamens in her other hand. Apu came out from the house, and as she mounted the steps of the terrace, he tore the flowers out of her hand and threw them out into the garden. The pot crashed, broken to pieces. Anyuka's favourite flowers! Dead!

After the funeral they found him wandering in a park near the cemetery. He seemed out of his mind, and was repeating, "I killed Aranka." I never said it, but I also thought that he was responsible for my mother's death. She was not happy and could not fight to stay alive any longer. The doctors said that it was not a serious case of paratyphoid fever. I was convinced that she did not want to live, because he was not good to her. So when she died, in my heart I also blamed Apu.

One day soon after she died, I was crying on the bench in the garden by the well. Apu came by, and asked what I was crying about. I told him that I was crying for Anyuka. He became angry. Now, when I think about this, I can understand that he would become upset, that he was not angry at me but against himself, for his inability to bring her back. But I was eight and I felt that he was angry with me.

The most unhappy moment of my childhood is connected to Apu. There was something I did wrong and I wanted him to forgive me. He was going towards the gate and I ran after him but he just kept on going and I could not reach him. I ran and ran and called him till he was so far far away that I gave up, fell into the grass. I cried until my dog, Gypsy came. She lay down next to me, looked at me with her warm, compassionate eyes, and this comforted me.

A memory of the most complete well-being is also connected to my father. Apu found the river to replace his Tátra Mountains. He bought a boat, named it "Breeze" and made the river his happy place. Anyuka was still alive. I was six when he taught me to swim. He put his palm under my belly and was telling me how to move arms and legs. I was intent on doing it right and did not notice when his hand was not under me any more. When I did, he was laughing whole-heartedly at me from quite far away. I was swimming on my own! I became master over a new dimension! We had to take a train to get from the boathouse to home. That evening I fell asleep in the train. When we reached Kecskemét, Apu put me on his shoulder and carried me home. The most complete sensation of security and comfort of my childhood is the memory of dozing on his shoulder. The slight sunburn kept warming my still-sandy skin and his rhythmic steps were rocking me to sleep.

After Anyuka died, Imu stayed with us for two years until my father married again. We always had maids to do the housework, but Imu's chores were still not easy. She was 66 and her son was not very gentle. He would snap at her when he heard her sigh, "Mutter, don't keep on sighing like that!" And we children were not an easy bunch either. I was eight, Ákos six-and-a-half, and Attila was just a few-months-old baby. I always loved her deeply, but I must have given her a few difficult moments too. I can still see her standing under a very tall tree at the corner of the house, calling me to "please come down." I was high up in the tree, swaying back and forth on the thin branches, back and forth, in the wind.

I was ten years old when Apu married again. Our new mother was one of three daughters of our next-door neighbour.

When my parents bought our villa, they bought it from a pharmacist who divided his time between his apothecary and his garden. He was a botanist of rare skill, crossed plants and developed new varieties of herbs and fruits. In our orchard we had 32 different kinds of table grapes growing. The oldest daughter, Margit, was in charge of the family pharmacy. The next daughter, Rózsa, was a teacher until she became Apu's second wife and my stepmother. The youngest one, Piroska, was still in high school. Aunts Margit and Piroska taught me to play bridge.

I celebrated the wedding by coming down with pneumonia. It was so bad that somebody announced at school that I had died. The black flag was waving in the wind until the two teachers, who were dispatched to bring flowers to my body, arrived back with the news that I was alive and sitting in bed. I can still see their faces as they walked up to the terrace, slowly, sadly. Then they saw me through the open door of my room, welcoming them!

I asked Apu one day that, if I ever got better, would he allow me to take piano lessons? When I was well again he registered me in the music school. I was sitting, excited, waiting to start my first piano lesson. I heard ugly noises coming from the room; a rough female voice. Then the door opened and out came an 18-year-old girl whom I admired. Behind her came the teacher, still berating her. Then came my turn,

21

with shaking knees, and my heart beating in my throat. My fear of the teacher only increased with the weeks of trying to cope. Finally I faced my father and asked him to please allow me to have another teacher. Apu was not in a good mood, "This is the best one. If she is not good enough for you, you won't have any piano lessons." He paid the tuition for the whole year, and took me out of music school. This left me with a yearning that stayed with me for life.

Our new mother, Rózsamama, was quite different from my mother. My mother was very sensitive, sometimes moody, but always tender. Rózsamama had nerves of "wet cord" as Apu would say. Those wet cords kept the family alive and relatively well for the 25 years of their marriage.

In summer we often slept on the terrace. One warm summer evening I could not fall asleep and was crying in bed. She noticed, leaned over and kissed me. A few days later she saw me cry again and came over to ask why I was crying. I said that I would like her to kiss me. She went into the house and a short while later Apu came out and told me not to make Rózsamama ridiculous.

That night I had a dream. I dreamt that I was in a forest, sitting on a rock in a green grassy clearing. In front of me a group of fairies, in long white gowns, were dancing to the sound of a flute. It was a most beautiful melody, and the graceful, sweet dance made me calm and happy. After that, whenever I felt unhappy and could not fall asleep, I made myself recall that dream, and it always made me able to fall asleep.

In the fall of 1931 two gentlemen, speaking German, came to see my father. There were such visitors at that time all over Eastern Europe where people of German origin lived (We called that the "Drang nach Osten" – "the Push to the East"). The two gentlemen were sure that "der Herr Professor Schmidt" will want to work for the Vaterland, meaning Germany! Apu's face was very angry as he showed them the way to the gate. He promptly applied to have our name changed from Schmidt to Szepesi. This was a logical choice, as we came from the county of Szepes. The "i" at the end of the name means "coming from" or "belonging to", just as it does in Persian.

So, by the time I was 12 years old, I had changed country and name. My mother had died and another took her place. By the time I was 12, I should have known what it meant to be a young girl nearing puberty. But I knew nothing about that. Soon after Anyuka died, something awfully important happened. I saw a boy urinating. This was a simple discovery. Strange that it should have been so late before I saw an intimate part of a boy's body, when I had two younger brothers. I never saw Akos without his pants, and never changed Attila's diapers.

So, when the son of the family who took care of our orchard nonchalantly peed into the sand, I saw something never seen before, and later said to Apu, "It's strange how different Lajcsi is from me." It was really a question to which I needed an answer.

Apu did not take it that way. He grabbed me by the shoulder and shouted, "What did he do to you?" This scared me thoroughly and made me think that I should never ask anything about the differences between boys and girls. This became a taboo, a field of questions where I was not to ask. I closed it off as dangerous. This was, of course, a dangerous attitude for a growing girl, and had very serious consequences.

In the early spring of 1932 it was announced that schools in Nuremberg, Germany, were organizing a student exchange with the high schools of Kecskemét. I told Apu that I would like to take part. He said that we did not have money. We were at lunch. I turned around and pointed to the piano and asked whether the piano, which was my mother's, was now mine. Apu said, yes, it was. "If I sell it, may I go to Nuremberg?" "Yes," he said with an expression that said, "If you can catch that bird, you may eat it." I went to the instrument dealer in town and sold him the piano for 100 pengoes,

23

the price of the student exchange. Apu honoured his word and I went to Germany. Thus started the road that led me to become a political scientist.

The family, in whose house I lived for a month in Nuremberg, was called Gosstorffer. A daughter, Sophy, was specially sweet to me. They lived in Otto Strasse, by the beautiful old city walls. They were very kind and proud to have a real Hungarian *Engel-Bengel* live with them. My name means "Engel" in German. If one adds *b*, it becomes "Bengel" which means a small devil. They enjoyed telling everybody what a typical Hungarian I was. I never had the heart to admit that the year before my name was Schmidt. That month in Nuremberg was of course full of interesting things: boat rides on the Dutzensee; visiting fine Gothic churches; a full day in the Albrecht Duerer House. Those weeks brought a string of wonderful discoveries.

Our hosts organized parties where we met all the host families. At one of these festivities held in a big hall – called Sternthor – I sang for the first time in public. A boy several years older, Laci Révész, accompanied on the piano. I sang two old Hungarian folksongs, a very old one, called a "Virág Ének" or "flower song", and a patriotic song of a peasant uprising. The flower song is still one of my favourites:

Szól a kakas már, majd megvirrad már,
Ha az Isten néked rendelt, tiéd leszek már.
Várj, madár, várj, te csak mindég várj.
Ha az Isten nékem rendelt, enyém leszel már.
Várj, madár, várj, te csak mindég várj...

A "flower song" always starts with a picture from nature to foretell the mood of the song. This one says:

The cock is crowing, dawn is coming,
If God created me for you, I shall be yours one day.
Wait, bird, wait, you just walk and wait!
If God created you for me, you will be mine one day.
Wait bird, wait .... you just always wait!

If one listens only to the words addressed to the cock, one would think that the waiting is an endless, hopeless one. But the first line gives an assurance of fulfillment: "Dawn is coming." I guess that it is because of that assurance, in spite of apparent hopelessness, that I like that song so much.

From my window on the third floor, I had a good view of the road surrounding the old city walls. On the road, called the Ring, groups of young people marched back and forth. They carried flags, sang songs, and shouted slogans. There were groups carrying flags with arrows, and others with swastikas. They seemed determined to prove that the groups with different flags were wrong and that they would fight to show them. It was the summer of 1932, and Hitler was on the rise.

I watched the marching troops, heard the hatred in the voices. Pigeons came to settle by my window. I fed them small pieces of Lebkuchen, typical honey cookies of Nuremberg. Down on the Ring the tragedy of Europe was burgeoning, while up on my window sill I fed the birds of peace. For the price of my piano, my education and my choices in world politics got underway.

Next year a little sister, Viola, arrived. This gave me a delightful month away from home, because I was sent to a boarding school where some of my classmates lived.

I loved to be with people, old people, young people but I didn't feel lonely by myself either. I read a lot, all sorts of books: historical novels, science fiction, romantic tales, poems, books written by Hungarians and translations from the literature of the world. I would read in my room, on the terrace, in the garden. My favourite reading place in summer was in the Emperor pear tree at the back of the vineyard, far from the house. The tree was old, with a wide trunk and fat branches. I built a seat among the branches and passed hours and hours reading, with Gypsy, my dog, sleeping under the tree. I would read in bed, sometimes late at night, with a small lamp clamped to the book, my head under the blanket so Apu would not notice.

My favourite book of those years was Merezhkovsky's *Leonardo da Vinci*. It can be disappointing to read a book that was a favourite in youth. Reading it again, I was afraid I would find that its charm had vanished. But a friend gave it to me recently and I found that I approved fully the feelings of the young person I was then and could well understand why that book had impressed me so deeply at 15. Leonardo da Vinci is one of the people I would like to meet when I go to the Other Side of the Gate.

A book by Dostoevsky, on the other hand, I was never able to read to the end. I could not digest gloom and goodness together. To me goodness, strength, and success have to go together, at least potentially, as with Tolstoy. I cannot waste time with hopeless, senseless gloom.

In 1987 I was teaching English to young adults in Kecskemét. I asked them to report on some interesting event or a book they enjoyed. One of the boys told us of the pleasure he had reading Dostoevsky's *Idiot*. I was delighted to hear his enthusiastic report, and told him and the class that I had been prejudiced against that writer, and how much I enjoy losing a prejudice! The class surprised me for Christmas; they gave me a copy of the *Idiot*, signed by all 30 of them.

We had a busy social life in Kecskemét, before the Second World War, with games of tennis, dancing school and parties which the families of young girls would take turns to organize. My first such party – we called it "Jour" – was in the late spring of the year I turned 15. It brought me my first kiss and the first romantic disappointment.

Besides singing and dancing, we always had games. Those who lost had to give tokens and win them back. One of the ways one could do this was called "contemplating the stars". This meant going out to the garden with a member of the opposite sex and trying to get a kiss. There was an awfully handsome, athletic boy at my party, a few years older than I. He asked me to go "contemplating the stars". I was the hostess, and I thought that this is why he asked me and ran out merrily, expecting to circle the garden and run back. But he caught me by an arm, swung me around and kissed me on the mouth. I was so surprised that I walked back to the party in a daze. Everybody could see on my face that I had had an unusual experience, and a general laughter broke out. I collected myself fast. No, there was nothing to ruffle me! After the party was over, I went back to the garden, trying to imagine how it was, feeling very romantic. Next day, going to school, I met the boy who kissed me. I was expecting something, some special communication, but he was chatting away as usual. After a while I stopped, turned to him and asked why he had kissed me. "You are quite appetizing, didn't you know?" he said. Just like that, a matter of cold fact. Even this rude awakening to the unromantic world did not stop me from being romantic. I would go back to the garden and imagine that I was Tatiana waiting for Anyegin to come and take me in his tender arms.

Other fun connected to our garden and specially the orchard was the early morning market. We had apricots to sell. Apu and I were in charge. One of us would preside over the picking and sorting while the other would go at dawn with the flat wagon carrying the baskets to the market in front of the big church. I became quite expert in getting good prices for our produce. It was a great feeling to come home after a successful morning among the fruit merchants. Some were local, small buyers, but some of our fruit was sold for export. When I was in Nuremberg, I saw some boxes of apricots marked with "Kecskemét", thus the local market gained the dimension of an international marketplace for me, a marketplace where I felt at home.

Then came two wonderful summers in Igló, the happiest summers of my youth. At home I was the oldest child, but in Igló I was the youngest of seven nearly grown-up cousins. Also, mountains were always more beautiful, pure, precious to me than the flat land. My cousins were experienced mountaineers. They taught me to notice the "second wind", that wonderful feeling which comes over one's body after a short time on the trail. One starts out chipper in the morning but after a while of going up, up, a deep tiredness invades one's body and it feels as if one could not go one step further. Then comes a new vigour, a lasting strength, as when a sailboat crosses the dividing line between a small bay and the ocean and is caught up by the wind, blowing it out onto the waters of the endless open sea.

At night Imu would wait for me with a bowl of tapioca pudding and wild strawberries. That tasted so good! To me the smell of strawberries means "affection". The bed felt good after a day in the clean air of the mountains!

One morning we were taking a train to go for a three day tour of the High Tátra. I had my foot on the step of the train when I heard the voice of my little sister, Viola. I ran back to look for her, but she was of course not there. When we returned from our excursion, I learned that she had died. A quick summer dysentery took her away. She was only three years old.

By the time I came back to Igló for the next summer I spent there, another little sister had arrived. Her name is Emese and she is a big sister of mine now. Then another sister, Hajnalka arrived. Her name means "Little Dawn" in English.

I learned a lot from Imu. She taught me to recognize and collect good herbs and mushrooms. She was a "white witch", an herbalist. She knew what herb should be taken for what ailment and she would send her herbs to whoever wanted them. She always had a sweet fragrance of herbs around her. She learned their value by using them on herself. When she was around 60, she was ailing with all sorts of problems: stomach, kidney, everything seemed to be finished in her body. The doctors gave her up, but she found a book and went on a diet of vegetables and fruit. She installed a sunning board and a bathtub in her garden, let the sun warm the water and tan and heal her thin little body.

School was also fun in those days in Kecskemét, with lots of art and music. Zoltán Kodály and his pupil, Béla Bartók, were familiar to us, and we sang many of their compositions. My greatest musical success was singing and dancing as the Prince in Puccini's little opera, *Cinderella*. Apu was not impressed by the opportunity this gave me. He did not think that I should waste my time with such silliness. I did not have money for a costume, still very much wanted to wear something really handsome. So, I went to an actor who had the most beautiful costumes. He took me through the wardrobe of the theatre, and let me pick what I liked. I wore a silk, velvet and lace suit, had a gilded sword in my belt and an ermine cap on my head and felt truly princely as I reached for Cinderella's hand to ask her to the "And you will be always mine" dance. Unfortunately, at that very moment, a "frog" made my voice slip and a shriek came out in place of the beautiful sound I was hoping to utter. I clapped my hand over my mouth and the audience burst out laughing. This ended in a loud applause. They asked me to repeat!

In 1991, I met an old schoolmate. She was in the class below mine. She told me that the girls used to think of me as their idol, the Prince. That girl went through Auschwitz, and came back able to lead a normal life. Maybe the ability to dream of princes helped her to survive.

Our teacher of singing thought that I should become a professional singer. She even gave me private lessons without pay. But Apu would not hear any of that. I really wanted to be a gym teacher. Apu did not think much of that idea either.

At graduation exams, I received Endre Ady, at that time my favourite poet, as subject in Hungarian literature. When I got the paper with "Ady" written on it, I ran out to the corridor, jumped up and down, and sang, "Köszönöm! Köszönöm!" (Thank you! Thank you!) I could talk about his pain over Hungary being torn between East and West, and, delight of delights, I could recite his "Szeretném ha szeretnének" ("I would like to be loved")!

29

3 Budapest
1938-1941

When time came to go to university, I decided to study political science and economics. Mother – as I started calling Rózsamama soon after she joined the family – said that I took political science because that was farthest from home. This was not really the reason; all possible schools were then in Budapest. My choice was not directed by the distance from home. I don't really know what made me decide. As I said, I wanted to be a gym teacher, but I was not ready to revolt when Apu objected. I think that the idea of working in the international field made political science and economics attractive. Using foreign languages, being in contact with other cultures, had always interested me.

The first subject I chose at university was philosophy. It was not compulsory, but it made accepting accounting easier. I sincerely disliked mathematics and everything that had to do with numbers and money. Economics of course had accounting and double bookkeeping as compulsory subjects. The first exam I ever failed was double bookkeeping. I had to make a big effort to open my mind's blinds to pass it on the second try. I never had to make any effort to learn languages, they just stuck to my memory like iron chips to magnet. 31

Gym was – thank God! – compulsory, and we had an athletic club with a big field. I specially liked high jumping and the tasty snacks after workouts. The best tasting food of those days was hot potatoes with sour cream, which I bought after a good swim in the Sport Palace on St. Margaret Island. The pool has two parts, one covered, one in the open. It was wonderful to swim out, through a tunnel, breathe the crisp winter air, look at the sky, swimming on my back. Then jump out into the snow, exercise a bit, swim back through the tunnel, dress and go for baked potatoes and sour cream on the way home.

"Home" at that time was a boarding house for children of teachers who came to university from all over the country. It was a fair-sized building, one wing for girls, the other for boys. In the middle were the living quarters of the director and a dining room which boys and girls shared. This was where the evening programs were held. Students going to all universities of Budapest lived there. In a way it was like a university in itself. It was a pleasant arrangement, halfway between home and complete freedom.

I shared a room with a girl in second-year chemistry. I thought that chemists tolerated odours well, but Agnes allowed me to have my favourite strong cheese only if I kept it between the two windows. We would skimp on food to buy tickets to the opera. After the performance, we would go to a nightclub to dance, to dance! Sometimes we would dance till dawn, then go for a swim in the Gellért Hotel's hot springs, snooze a while under the sunlamps, then go to the boarding house where we should have been sleeping all night, have breakfast and go to lectures. With all the fun, my pocketbook started to be flat. This is normal for students. I was not specially sorry for myself when one day I found that all I had left was 50 cents. There was a quick debate between reason and inclination. Inclination won; I bought a bunch of fall violets with my last 50 cents. I ran up to our room, put them in a dainty vase and hurried off to a class of political geography.

Our professor of political geography was Count Paul Teleki. He had an assistant fill in for him because he was at that time prime minister of Hungary. That day, at the end of October 1938, the assistant asked if anyone would like to work for a few days and nights for the Prime Minister on a rush job. I was of course interested. It was something different. I was curious what the rush job could be. Besides, he said that we would be well paid. It turned out to be connected with the conference Teleki had with Hitler, which has gone down in history as the First Vienna Award.

We prepared the documentation, graphs and charts to show the nationality and language of the population of the territories given to Czechoslovakia in the treaties after First World War. At that conference in Vienna, Hitler gave a part of that territory back to Hungary — just as it was given away, without knowing the problems, the feelings and situation of the people who were affected by the decisions. A few leaders used their power to do what suited them. This time a part of the territory taken away in the Treaty of Trianon was given back to Hungary, like playing ball...

For me what I was doing was then exciting. I had the feeling that I was involved in something great, something wonderful, something that would redress wrongs my country had suffered. When we finished and the rush was over, an assistant asked if I would like to continue working for the Prime Minister in his Institute. Teleki had an Institute for Research in Statecraft. I was of course happy to join it. I could work part-time as my classes permitted, and became part of a fascinating group of people, all men, and all older than I. They must have been amused with the ardent young girl, getting into every discussion after work, with cups and cups of coffee, sitting on desks and arguing without knowing beans about the issues. They never made me feel ridiculous and I learned a lot. From my first paycheque I bought a pair of butter-coloured shoes and from the second one, a marble tombstone for Anyuka's grave.

It was at a party in a colleague's home where I met George. He was a very good dancer and he found me a good partner on the dance floor. We danced and danced, and fell in love. He was the only son of a divorced father, often away on business. Their home became my second home in Budapest. It felt good to be close to somebody, for the first time since Anyuka died. Intimate in a warm bathtub, in a warm bed.

It was George who noticed one day that I might be pregnant. He asked me to see my father and tell him that we would like to get married. I told Apu about wanting to marry George and he said, no. George was 25, a textile engineer and he was Jewish. There was no discussion about his personality, his ideas or feelings, about my feelings, needs or aspirations. Never would Apu consent to my marrying him. I riposted by getting engaged. I would marry George as soon as I did not need my father's consent. I did not ask him why he was opposed, what he would have liked for me. I just answered as abruptly as he gave his "no".

George then went to his father and suggested that the three of us emigrate to Argentina. He was in Vienna at the time of the Anschluss, when Hitler occupied Austria. He felt the danger and would have liked to go far, far away from it. His father had a good position and did not think it necessary to give it up. George then told him that we might be expecting a baby. That was a different question! This had to be looked into. He sent me to see a friend who had a clinic. When the "examination" was over, I was no longer pregnant. I had an abortion, without being asked, without knowing what had happened, without knowing what it meant, or being able to make the decision.

Had I known what was happening, and that there should be a decision taken by myself about it, I still do not know how I would have acted. There was something that happened to me shortly before I met George. I was raped ... by a colleague who was getting married the next day. A colleague

I considered a friend. He was a member of the group with whom I went to the Opera and to dances. He knew that I was a virgin and that I wanted to keep it that way.

He knocked on the door and asked if Agnes was home. When I said, no, he entered and locked the door behind himself. That's when I realized that something was wrong. I asked him to please, go away. He did not care that I wanted to keep my virginity. He did what he wanted to do. I did not dare to call for help. And for many, many years, I did not dare to remember what had happened.

It was early spring 1939. My feelings for George changed radically. I didn't feel like being cuddled anymore or to be at home in his house. We met in tea rooms or walked around the boarding school. I talked about my studies or the work at the Institute while he told me a lot about his work. We argued at times. I felt that I could not trust his judgement any more, but wore the engagement ring when I went home at the end of the semester to pack for a summer in Germany.

The family had a friend, a doctor in Gross-Gerau, near Darmstadt and they arranged for me to spend the summer there. I was hoping to get a scholarship to the London School of Economics in the fall and a summer in Germany seemed a very good preparation. Maybe my family was hoping that I would get over George that way. In that sense, my summer was a fiasco, but I learned a lot about the affairs of Europe in the hot summer of 1939. Darmstadt was the seat of Hessen and the ruling family was going through one tragedy after another. The noonday carillon of the palace's chapel was playing a march of the Nazis, the *Horst Wessel Lied*. It sounded awfully out-of-keeping with the buildings, the gardens, the graves of the members of the House of Hessen and with most of the people who walked by. But uniformed young men marched back and forth, and those who did not like that song did not say how they felt. On a boat ride on the Rhine people were watching with furtive eyes as tanks roared down the Autobahn, the first wide thoroughfare I had ever seen. The rumbling of the tanks on the road under Lorelei's Rock became deafening over the river. I finally saw that famous rock and softly sang to myself the story of beautiful Lorelei and the fishermen who were lured to their death by her treacherous song. She just sang, combed her golden hair, and made them unaware of the whirlpools until it was too late. The loudspeaker on the boat was blaring a speech by Hitler. Parents looked at their children with anxious eyes. Some youth were boisterous, full of enthusiasm for what Hitler was shouting on the radio. They seemed eager to show the world how powerful they were.

By the time I was on my way home, trains were filled with uniformed men, blinds were drawn at night, and schedules became uncertain. Soldiers had priority over regular passengers. I found only a small corner in a corridor to put down my suitcase and sat on it. A sad-looking woman sat on her suitcase next to me and we started talking. She told me that she was going to see her son who was called up, that she hoped to be with him before he goes off wherever he was to go. When she heard that I was Hungarian she gave me a smile, the first I had seen for some time. Oh, how lovely Hungarian music is! And she asked if I knew a song about a lace-trimmed handkerchief. I started humming. Sad faces brightened. I was asked to sing louder. After a few more songs, a door opened and a handsome young man appeared. He offered to take over singing to the appreciative audience while I got a rest in his first class compartment. He was an opera singer from Belgrade and was on his way home from an engagement in Germany.

I had a much-needed rest while he took my place in relieving the gloom of the first day of the Second World War, in that train edging its way into the crowded station of Vienna. Two people from two opposing sides of the "Justice for Hungary!" battlefield: Milos the tenor from Belgrade, Yugoslavia and me from Budapest, Hungary. Two young people who wanted to ease the anxiety of a sombre night, we parted at the station of Vienna never to meet again. Neither of us knew how fast both our countries would be engulfed in the conflict that started to rage then.

I found George, in Budapest, very gloomy about the events. He did not pursue his ideas about Argentina any further, and sounded rather depressed. I was busy with the beginning of my second year at university and the work at the Institute, besides I could not grasp the concerns George had of being a Jew in Europe in 1939. In late fall, I became ill. First it was a sore throat, then an inflammation of the joints and finally it turned into a general septicaemia. By the time my father arrived, the director of the Rókus Hospital had to tell him that my condition was hopeless. There was no penicillin then and my blood did not respond to the treatment by sulpha drugs.

"And if she gets a transfusion?" asked my father.

"Weakened as she is, that would surely kill her right away."

"She is dying, is there a chance that a transfusion might save her?"

"One in a million," was the prognosis.

At that time transfusions were done vein-to-vein, full force. My father was on a stretcher next to my bed. They took blood from his arm and transferred it into a vein in mine. I started shivering, then jumping up and down on the bed, sweating profusely.

After a short struggle, I became motionless and heard the nurse say, "She is not suffering any more, and it won't take long."

Standing at the foot of my bed, Apu was crying. I never saw him cry before, not even at my mother's funeral. He would rage but not cry. Now he was crying, he was crying for me. Apu wanted me to live! And I had a wonderful experience. I was warm and comfortable and I was not alone. I sensed rather than heard, "They are crying because they do not know."

This was the first time I heard a Voice from the Other Side.

Then I opened my eyes and asked for a glass of beer. They did not give me beer, but I got a lot of attention. The hospital seemed to whisper when I started walking in the corridors. Everybody wanted to see the one "who came back".

George came to see me every afternoon on his way home from work. Soon I was well enough to go home to convalesce. The evening before my departure George asked when he could come to see me in Kecskemét.

"You know how much our relationship upsets Apu. Maybe we should wait to see each other when I come back to Budapest."

"It is time for you to choose between your father and me," said the foolish boy. I took off my engagement ring and placed it in his palm. He put the ring in his pocket, took his black overcoat, put his black homburg on his head and went out of my room. A short while later he phoned.

"Is your decision final?"

"Of course it is," I said and replaced the receiver.

The maid found George by the open telephone, dead with a bullet in his head. Had I not banged down the phone, I would have heard the revolver discharge. George's father tried to see me next morning but was not allowed into my room. I will never know whether he wanted to accuse me or to share his grief, our grief.

They took me home to Kecskemét and I started a long convalescence. I was hoping to get a word from George and when nothing came, I took out the letters he wrote to me to Germany during the summer. He knew so much that I wanted to learn, I wanted to ask him all the questions I would have liked to ask my parents. He was my friend and I wanted to know him well. Mother saw me reading his letters and asked if I really meant when I said that I broke off with him. I said, of course I did.

"Then you shouldn't keep his letters. When one breaks off an affair one should destroy the mementos." I did not want to look weak so I opened the door of the stove standing in the corner of the room and put the whole package on the fire. Mother pointed to the necklace I was wearing. It had a small golden locket with a tiny photo of George in it. I opened the locket and sent the photo after the letters into the flames.

Spring arrived and I was well enough to walk to town to visit friends. I saw people on the street who looked like George and thought that maybe he would appear on the next corner. One day I visited an old schoolmate. When I arrived home I felt exuberant and burst into the drawing room where Mother was sitting at her desk. I chattered away.

"Piri was always a great gossip but today she really outdid herself. She asked if it was true that George killed himself!"

I expected Mother to laugh but she did not. She looked at the wall above her desk. I went into my room and sat down on my bed. That's the last thing I remember doing for a while. About a week later, I came out of my room and went on convalescing as if nothing had happened. I never talked about George's death with anybody, not even to myself.

The rest of that spring and summer was spent in getting strong to go back to school in the fall. I spent many an afternoon sitting on the bench by my mother's grave, or gardening or picking flowers for the house and for the cemetery. Or I would visit the people who lived around our villa who used to be my friends before I went away to university. There was a village nearby, where I knew an old woman whose son emigrated to America. She showed me letters and pictures received from him. The girls told me about joys and heartaches they had. It was good to be with those simple people who spoke with affection of Anyuka and transferred their affection for her to me. This was so welcome that summer!

Then fall came and I went back to university. This time
I took an apartment with two cousins. One was Piroska, my
beloved Aunt Gizi's daughter, whose milk I shared when we
were two baby refugees. I called her *Bocs*, which means "Little
Bear". She studied library sciences. The other was Eta, one
who took me mountaineering. She studied pharmacology.
They both knew George and were very kind about him. At
university and at the Institute nobody referred to him, as if
he had never existed. I behaved also as if nothing had happened to me of importance. I went to the opera, and to formal balls. At the Institute the work was becoming more and
more interesting. They sent me on missions to check the
progress towns were making in urbanization. This gave me a
strange position: a young girl, asking town councillors and
mayors how they fared on the plans the Prime Minister expected them to execute!

But things started to become tense as the war was
progressing. Teleki prepared an exhibit to show the need for
agrarian reform. Diagrams showed recent changes in owner-
ship of land which made it evident that members of the German minority were buying land at a great speed. The plight
of the peasants living around the big properties owned by the
aristocracy or the church was quite visible on our charts. It
was also clear that the land owned by small peasants produced
much more than the big landholdings did. Teleki opened
the exhibit which was an instant sensation, heatedly discussed
by the press. A few days later he had to order it closed. The
pressure from Hitler was too much.

One morning in April as I was walking towards the
Institute, I heard the newspaper boy shout that Count Paul
Teleki had died, having killed himself in his office during the
night. And during the same night the armies of Hitler invaded Yugoslavia, the country with which Teleki had just concluded a non-aggression pact.

For a long time I did not believe that Teleki had actually pulled the trigger of the gun that killed him but object-

ing to Hitler's plans was surely suicide until, in 1989, I was talking with Maria Ormos, the historian, and learned that Teleki personally handled the monies spent by the *Hungarian League for Revision* on the campaigns of "Justice for Hungary!" This made me see that for him there was no other out but death. He knew exactly who had received support from the funds. He also knew the results were tragic, not what had been intended. And he could not go back and remedy his fatal mistakes.

I liked Count Paul Teleki. He was the Chief Scout of Hungary, whom I first met at the 1933 jamboree, where I learned my first English word *change* meaning "I give you something, you give me something and we both will be richer". I knew him as a kind and intelligent man, a firm believing Catholic, not one who would be likely ever to do harm to others or to kill himself.

His death of course meant the closing of the Institute and that I was out of a job. There was anxiety, excitement at the university. The political atmosphere was heating up, marches were held with torches, with flags in honour of men who symbolized Hungary's sufferings. Then came the jubilation for another piece of land being handed back to us by Hitler.

Soon I found a new job. I became secretary to a man whose name was carried on one of the flags showing our sufferings. His name was András Tamás, and he was one of the secretaries of the *Hungarian League for Revision*. The brother of a colleague at school told me about him, a romantic, interesting person. He was born in Targoviste, Romania, near Bucharest. (The same town where Nicolae Caucescu and his wife were caught, tried, condemned and executed in December 1989.) His parents were Hungarians, his brother Paul became a Catholic priest, András a fervent Hungarian nationalist. He was 17 when he was caught as a saboteur who blew up bridges, trying to stop the Romanian armies that invaded Hungary at the end of the First World War. He was condemned to death but, because of his age, they put him in solitary confinement instead of executing him. Later he was exchanged for Romanian political prisoners held by Hungary and was brought to Budapest in a triumphant train ride. His train stopped at every town to allow people to see the hero who suffered so much for our country. His teeth were knocked in and his nails were pulled out during interrogations but he never gave away any secrets. I was anxious to meet the man whose career started in such a heroic fashion. He needed a secretary who spoke German and hired me at the first interview. His greying hair was combed flat on top, and he was smoking a pipe.

4   Zagreb and Berlin
Summer 1941

"He needs me," was my first thought when I caught sight of Bandi Tamás. "He needs me to teach him how to comb his hair more attractively." The way it was now combed, flattened down on top and sticking out over the ears, made his rather low forehead look really low over his slanting eyes and the high cheekbones. Otherwise he was an attractive middle-aged man who received me cordially and told me right away why he wanted to hire me. He had to send somebody to a conference in Berlin in a few weeks. That gave me just enough time to become familiar with his work, to learn what my job entailed. He took me along the same evening to hear him talk to a group of students. Tamás spoke about the obligations of people who work for our country. The one who wants to serve the interests of his country has to ensure that his private life is blameless. Then he can – must be prepared to – lie, steal and kill for his country. He has to be selfless, he has to give himself wholeheartedly to the cause. This sounded very noble and uplifting to me then. The audience was enthusiastic and I felt proud to be trusted by such a great patriot.

His office in Geneva, on rue Kermely, was run by his secretary as he was asked to leave Switzerland. He was sent there to try to convince the League of Nations to revise the Treaty of Trianon, which affected Hungary so severely. When this did not succeed, a plan was devised to awaken the countries who were signatories to the treaty, and force them to redress the wrongs. As the reason evoked for the changes was supposed to be the interest of minorities, helping disgruntled minorities seemed to be the first step to take. Tamás got in touch with people like De Valera in Ireland, Ante Pavelic in Yugoslavia, the leaders of the Basque nationalists in France, revolutionaries in Italy and extremists in Bulgaria, to see how to help them, and in that way help the cause of Hungary. He had to know what was said at a conference in Berlin but could not go himself because he was declared *persona non grata* by Hitler. How fascinating!

Then came an invitation from his friend, Dr. Ante Pavelic, who had become the ruler of Croatia. Tamás was asked to visit him in Zagreb. The German occupation of Yugoslavia had not quieted down yet, there were fierce battles in the mountains, but Pavelic wanted his friend Tamás to see him in his glory, installed by Hitler as the *Quisling* of Croatia (*Quisling* was the name given to leaders who, such as *Quisling of Norway*, agreed to co-operate with the occupying Germans).

We were driven to Zagreb by an officer who drove a fast car. That was the first time I sat in a car going at 140 kilometres per hour, and I found it exhilarating. Pavelic received us as soon as we arrived. He was sitting at a huge desk. Behind him stood a high-ranking German officer. Pavelic's eyes were warning Tamás not to say anything that could be compromising. Then he stood up and greeted us with profuse friendliness. I don't remember what he said. Those wary eyes at the beginning told me the whole story. I did not envy Pavelic at all. He extended an invitation to a dinner in Tamás' honour that evening and we left him. The dinner was sumptuous and there were speeches congratulating everybody on

44

the splendid work they had accomplished for the cause of freedom and progress in Europe. At the end of the dinner Artukovic, Minister of Interior and of Justice, paid me a special tribute. He called me a symbol of the friendship of young Croats and young Hungarians and gave me a kiss in the middle of my forehead. He told me to share it with all brave Hungarian youth. The guests were delighted and applauded loudly. We left in a warm glow to pass a restful night and prepare for a fast return to Budapest.

As our car was nearing the hotel, a big black van passed. It slowed down in front of a big gate. The gate opened, the van entered the dark passage and disappeared, and the heavy gate was lowered. In my dream that night I saw that van again, in slow-motion, entering the gate and disappearing. Who were in it, I wondered. And what happened to them? Did they ever come out that gate? In May 1986, Andrija Artukovic, 86, was extradited by the United States where he lived in hiding for 36 years. He was brought to Zagreb, tried and condemned to be shot for the murder of thousands of Jews, Gypsies, Serbs and many Zagreb families. The Canadian newspapers referred to him as "the butcher of the Balkans".

Back in Budapest preparation for my first assignment abroad progressed well. I was to be an "independent student observer" at the three-week conference organized by the Auslands Institute in Berlin. Thirty friendly nations were to take part, to be informed of the successes of Hitler and to prepare for the final assault against the Allies. I was to report to the Hungarian leadership and to the Japanese embassy on my return.

When I came back, I reported that, according to me, the Germans had already lost the war. What made me say that?! I explained that I saw German officers drunk on Berlin's streets, dead-drunk while wearing their uniforms. I concluded that the morale of the army was not good.

"If they behaved like that in their own capital, how would they behave in the occupied territories?" I asked. The second ominous sign I mentioned was a simple question. After a talk assuring everybody about the complete support for Germany, a young Swiss farmer asked,

"This is all very beautiful, but how about our frozen credits?" He received no answer.

The greatest proof of Germany's impending defeat, for me, was the speech given on the last afternoon by Dr. Schacht, director of the National Bank of Germany. He said, among other things: "With God's help, we have on our side our greatest ally, Russia, who supplies us with three-fifths of our needs in raw materials."

I gazed in disbelief at Bandi Gellért, a Hungarian journalist sitting next to me. He motioned to keep quiet. We both knew that the war between Germany and the USSR was only a question of time. Did Dr. Schacht not know it? Or did he want to mislead that audience, supposedly composed of friends? I could see no way out but a defeat and reported so without worrying whether others would think me crazy for saying this at the height of the Blitzkrieg.

There were a few other events at that conference that made me form my judgement. The most amusing one was a quick exchange with an Italian participant. He was a professor of economics at the university of Naples and presented economic proofs about the invincibility of the Hitler-Mussolini alliance.

I met him in the elevator the evening following his talk. He winked at me and asked, "Did you swallow all the crap I had to dish out this afternoon?"

After my report was received and considered, I was asked whether I would like to be sent abroad for a three months assignment. I was interested. The preparations for that assignment were progressing, but there was lots to do in the meantime. A part of Transylvania had also been handed back to Hungary and Tamás wanted to visit the places connected with his trial of 1917. He took me along to Kolozsvár (Cluj in Romanian) to visit the monastery where priests had hidden him for some time before he was caught, and to the courthouse where he had been condemned. I walked in awe on the stones of the courtyard of the monastery. The statue of St. Francis of Assisi and his small white lamb stood in the centre, in prayerful silence. Christ's head with the crown of thorns looked down from the window of the chapel.

Window of chapel.

There were less emotional things to do, such as accompanying a group of Swedish journalists on their discovery of Hungary. They wanted to see the famous Hungarian *puszta*, the plains where herds of snow-white cattle with wide horns graze. The visit of the Swedish journalists gave a chance for my father to meet Tamás, because Bugac puszta is next to Kecskemét. Several notables of town who knew me came to greet the visitors and I was delighted to introduce my friends to each other and to show the visitors the council chamber of the City Hall, with the superb paintings of the chieftains of the Hungarian tribes as they arrived in the country more than a thousand years ago. It was in that chamber, with the paintings looking down, where I delivered my first public talk when I was 17. In front of the City Hall, our school, on March 15 every year, commemorated the day of freedom in front of the statue of Louis Kossuth. He was the statesman who learned English in middle-age and, after coming to America, became

47

known as a fine orator for freedom. It was in front of Kossuth's statue that Tamás asked whether I would like to be assigned to Lisbon, and report to Hungary significant news from the English-speaking press.

Lisbon was one of the three neutral spots where news was easily available about both sides in the war. It was important for the leadership of Hungary to have unbiased information.

Although my work with Tamás became much more interesting than my studies, I still attended most of my lectures. On the afternoon of December 7, I was climbing the stairs to our apartment after class. My cousin was waiting at the door. She held her hand in front of her mouth and whispered, "Tamás is in there, sleeping on your bed." She was awfully embarrassed, but her embarrassment was nothing compared to Tamás' when he woke up and explained what had happened.

His friend, Joshinaka, the Japanese military attaché, had called and sent a car for him, because he wanted to tell him himself that Japan had entered the war. To end on a festive note, a glass of saki was brought in and emptied, with the greeting, "Banzaj!" When Tamás, who was not a drinker, got in the car to be driven home, he could not remember his own address, only mine. He gave it to the chauffeur. Reaching our door, he could only stutter, "Sorry, I have to lie down."

Next afternoon he did not feel like working. It was an unusually warm December afternoon and he proposed a walk on the mountain overlooking the Danube. He was rather silent for a while, then asked me to go with him to a Transylvanian Ball where he was one of the patrons. I wore a white lace blouse, inherited from my mother, with a long black taffeta skirt. He wore a well-cut dinner jacket. By that time his hair was attractively combed and I felt that we were a somewhat odd but good-looking couple. We were dancing a tango to the tune of "Si, si, si" when he asked me to marry him. This time Apu said "yes". He was impressed with Tamás who was

48

only seven years younger than himself and three years older than Mother. The engagement in the Pannonia Hotel was also our good-bye dinner because my appointment as reporter and Tamás' appointment as unofficial diplomat in Portugal, with the mission to establish contact with the Allies, was to take effect as soon as the Germans gave us space in one of their planes.

There were speeches at the table, wishing us happiness and success in all the services we were to render our beloved country. Apu was deeply moved. He was relieved to know his daughter was on the right track to a successful life after all. But, at our parting he really blew it, as far as I was concerned. My poor father who never hit me with his hands did it devastatingly with his words of farewell:

"If you ever have an argument with him, don't come to me because I know that he will be right."

5 Estoril, Portugal
1941-1945

To travel to Portugal from Hungary, we had to pass through Berlin and the tickets had to be ordered and approved ahead of time. Our demand for passage was handed in and we looked around for the papers that would be needed to be married as soon as we get to Lisbon. Our tickets arrived sooner and the papers took longer than we expected. On the morning of December 23, we were informed by *Lufthansa*, that two places were available for us next morning and that, if we did not take them, we could get no tickets before the end of January. We quickly packed and took the plane next morning, hoping that the necessary papers would follow soon.

Christmas Eve in Berlin was not happy that year. Although Christmas decorations were everywhere, the holiday dinner ended with a dessert topped with artificial whipped cream. It was white and sweet but it had nothing to do with the cream that comes from cows, just as the festivities had little to do with the religious holiday being celebrated. Next day we left for Barcelona and two colourful days in Spain. The trip between Barcelona and Lisbon was bumpy. The small

Spanish plane felt every air pocket over the plateaus and I wondered at times whether the sudden drop in altitude would even out before we hit ground. This was my first travel by air and I enjoyed it, even the bumps. The sun was shining over the clouds and I held my face close to the window, to be warmed.

Our embassy in Lisbon was expecting us, and the press attaché organized a luncheon of welcome. The first Portuguese meal I had, in the restaurant Aquarium, was a royal introduction to the Portuguese kitchen. One course followed the other, one better than the previous, and when I thought that every possible space must be filled in every one of us, a huge platter was placed in the middle of the table with a horrible looking mountain on it. The mountain was composed of something like insects, pink and revolting. Had I not been brought up by a severe disciplinarian, I would have made a grimace and would have stood up in protest. But Apu taught me never to show any sign of repugnance before what anybody offered me to eat. So I just looked around to see how others behaved. They reached out, picked up one of the insects, took off the heads and shells and ate the worm-looking thing. I reached out and did likewise. That is how I tasted my first shrimp.

The Hungarian ambassador to Portugal was Baron Andor Wodianer. He received us warmly but could do nothing about the fact that we had to be married in front of a Portuguese judge and that this required documents translated into Portuguese. We were innocent enough to think that an embassy had the right to marry people and that our papers written in Hungarian would do.

While waiting for our documents to be translated in Budapest, we learned the language and customs and met with other journalists and diplomats. My work was with the English and American press, so I found all the available publications at the newsstands of Lisbon and learned fast which parts of the papers had most interest for us, what I had to forward to Budapest. I also learned what would not get through the censors in Germany. When I gave news unwise for Budapest to hear, Berlin would cut in and say: "Atmospheric conditions are bad, we have to cut the connection."

Tamás Bandi and Angéla in Portugal – 1942.

I learned that if I wanted to report on the advance of Leclerc's armies behind Rommel's line in North Africa, or some other success of the Allies, I had to do it on Sunday afternoon, when the censors in Berlin did not understand Hungarian. The story of the building of the Alaska Highway was among those that I had to sneak in when Berlin was not quite awake. With the thrill of learning so many new things, I was not overly concerned about the delay in our wedding plans. Back home Apu started to worry. I got a letter saying that if Tamás had changed his mind about marrying me, I should have the courage to tell him. Fortunately, the same mail also brought the last missing document, so our wedding could proceed.

Our ambassador was my witness and the consul's wife was Tamás'. A reception followed at an elegant restaurant. When I gave the details of the wedding to my family, Apu answered by one of his typical letters. He wrote, "Your letter

53

with the photo on which you look like the daughter of a jani-
tor, with that cigarette in your hand, gave me much joy." Poor
Apu was not very good at building my self-esteem.

We found a lovely villa in Estoril, the resort town outside Lisbon on the seashore, where much of the international
activity in Portugal was played during those years. Kings in
exile, spies of both sides mingled with businessmen and ad-
venturers from all over the world. Our villa was close to the
golf course and not too far from the *picadero* or riding school.
When visitors came from Budapest, we would play golf or take
them to the casino for a game at the roulette table. I enjoyed
golf. The casino was not my favourite place. I played only out
of duty and always stopped when I won enough to buy a pair
of shoes. Maybe it was because I was not interested in the
game that I had accumulated a good number of pairs of shoes
at the casino's expense. The *picadero* pleased me much better,
but I was happiest on the beach – like Apu, replacing the
Tátra with the Tisza. Big Atlantic waves wash the sand on
Estoril's beaches. The sun is strong and the smell of the salty
water reminded me of the rarefied air of the mountains. When
I had rough moments, I would take a walk along the beach or
would sit on the terrace overlooking the sea, listening to the
rumbling of the waves breaking on the rocks.

Inoue's house, Estoril, Portugal – 1942.
Elemér Ujpétery, chargé d'affaires, of Hungary, Angéla, Masutaro Inoue,
chargé d'affaires of Japan, Mme. Inoue, Bandi Tamás.

In the summer of 1942 our work took on a new dimension. Tamás had a good friend, Colonel Ian Kowalewsky, representing the Polish government-in-exile in London. He wanted to meet one of our friends, secretary of the Japanese embassy. The next time, the American military attaché joined the two and secret peace talks between Americans and Japanese started in that villa by the golf course in Estoril. Next to our villa lived two German journalists. One night, while we were away at a dinner party, our house was broken into and everything was turned upside down. A neighbour was at the dinner and we had the distinct impression that the other one wanted to see what he could find in our house. There was nothing that would give away anything about the talks but we looked for another place to live.

The house we found was the first villa on Rua Dr. Oliveira Salazar, right behind the casino. It was in the villa next to that where King Carol, the exiled king of Romania died a few years later. When we moved in, the house was brand new. It had four bathrooms, five fireplaces and full maids' quarters. Our rent was as much as a Portuguese minister's salary. We had a cook, a maid, a gardener and gave dinners for 10 or 12 people. I would push the button under the table with my foot to tell the kitchen when the next course was due. We placed the guests according to rank and language. Tamás spoke only French, so we placed the French-speaking guests at his end of the table. As soon as I began understanding the jokes coming from the other end, I started reading a book translated into French from Hungarian. When I finished, I was ready for my real teacher in French, Anatole France. His "Thais" did my schooling in the language of Richelieu.

Bandi originally did not think of creating a family, a normal one, with children. But when it became evident that I was going to have a baby, he adjusted to the inevitable, and it did not take him long to start looking forward to becoming a father. By the time the end of August rolled around, he was so impatient that I heard him say to his good friend, Masutaro Inoue, the Japanese chargé d'affaires, "Ce type n'arrive jamais!" (This guy will never arrive!) His voice was heavy with impatience, and I found it so funny to hear him refer to an unborn child as "ce type", that I decided on the spot that the name I would call our child would be "Tip", no matter what official name he or she was given.

Tip, a healthy big boy, was born on September 8, 1943, on the day Italy surrendered to the Allies. Bandi was so excited and happy that he ran out to the street, where he saw our commercial attaché and his wife just passing, to bring them into the house to show his wonderful son. Tip's head was still somewhat American football shaped, from the effort to squeeze through the narrow passage. But he was there, breathing, yelling too, alive!

Manyusha Kowalewska, my best friend, held my hand and helped me through the mercifully short labour. Her daughter, Terezinha, became Tip's faithful, admiring big sister. Hiroshi Inoue was his best friend as he grew into a member of the human family. With a Polish surrogate sister and a Japanese brother, it was a good beginning for one, whose aim in life was to help differently speaking people to listen carefully and understand each other.

My son's arrival caused an unexpected change in me. I noticed it when I next went riding. I used to be a fearless rider, but when I sat on the horse the first time after Tip was born, I noticed that the ground was quite far, and it came to me that I had a forester great-granduncle who died as a result of being thrown from his horse. In short, I started to be afraid for my life. This was a new feeling, but it was only the beginning of a great transformation of my world. I started to ask questions about the worth of our work. I remembered the black van on the street of Zagreb, and the talks in our house started to sound more like diplomatic games than serious peace-tentatives. The high salary we received, the luxury we

56

lived in while our country was at war, while my brother was on the front, started to seem wrong. Things did not make sense any more!

One afternoon I was sitting on the terrace next to Tip's crib when the maid brought in the mail. On top was a package from my father. It contained a typewritten French grammar. Mother wrote some time ago that Apu was having problems with writer's cramp and had to use a typewriter. As I looked at that package, I had Apu before my eyes, leaning over his typewriter, typing out a personal French grammar for me. For me who begged him, in vain, to teach me, for me who does not like learning a language by grammar, for me who was able by then to hold a French conversation with anybody on any subject! My heart went to pieces as I imagined how happy it would have made me to learn French from him and how happy it could have made him to teach his own child!

I picked up the package and threw it into the waste paper basket. I did not even look into that book. I did not even leaf through to see if, maybe, he put a word of tenderness in it somewhere. I could only see the loss we both suffered and I blamed him for it. I did not see that he was now running after me to ask me to forgive him. I threw his grammar, written specially for me, into the garbage. It came too late, or, maybe, too soon.

That night we gave a dinner to an elegant group. I went through the motions of smiling, asking, answering, ordering the servants, serving cognac warmed by myself in huge glasses to guests chatting before the fireplace and saying a charming "good night" at the door. When they left I went down to the garden. It was dark. The hedge protected me from the street. I sat down on the tiled floor under the arcades and started to wail. I wailed silently, with a deep, animal-like wailing. I had no idea what I was wailing for, but it was everything. Everything was wrong. Everything was wrong in the world and everything was wrong inside of me. God! Help!

March 19, 1944 arrived, the day on which Hitler's armies occupied Hungary. The previous evening I gave the usual report to the *Hungarian Telegraphic Agency* but at the end, instead of the customary, "Until the next time," I said, "God be with you."

The man at the other end answered, "And with you too".

The German occupation of Hungary meant that we were cut off from Budapest. That also meant that our big salaries could not come any more. We had a little reserve and I wanted to move to a less expensive place, but Tamás did not take the situation seriously. He thought that he needed to carry on as if nothing had changed, because of the talks he was having with Allied circles. He believed in an eventual Allied landing in the Balkans and a peace settlement for Hungary. He was accustomed to work outside normal conditions and he did not listen to my everyday concerns.

The diplomats who were stationed in Hungary and were now considered unwanted by the Germans, landed in Lisbon on board the Swedish boat, *Drottningholm*. Then came another group of people from Hungary, the family of Manfred Weiss, the industrialist. One of this group, Elizabeth Weiss, called one evening to ask me to a movie. I excused myself saying that I wanted to draw three embroidery designs. When we hung up, I stared at the phone.

"What did I say?" I had absolutely no idea of making any designs; I had not made any designs since I left high school. Mystified, I sat down and designed three Hungarian cushions. Next day a Portuguese woman stopped by the house. She had sold me beautiful embroideries before, now she wanted to show some more. I told her that I didn't have money to spend on embroideries anymore. She noticed the designs and asked me to let her execute one. This is how my embroidery business began. It developed into a means of supporting Tip and me for the ensuing years.

While the gloom over the senselessness of our life deepened, I kept up my spirits by going to the beach with Tip and by translating a classical Hungarian drama into English. It was *The Tragedy of Man* by Imre Madách. It deals with the struggle of Adam and Eve, the eternal Man and Woman, between good and evil, between God and Lucifer. I started reading it again and felt that it should be made available for Greta Garbo to play Eve. I did not enquire whether it had already been translated. I needed to do something that seemed worthwhile doing.

Then one day I felt like playing tennis again. We went to the tennis courts a few times, but Tamás had not been brought up on tennis. He sat on the bench and watched me play with a trainer, until we gave that up. He found it strange that now I should feel like playing tennis. He said that it must be because I was sweet on the trainer. The tension that had been building up in me for months, actually from before the birth of Tip, gave way. I could not take that accusation. There is always a last straw that breaks the camel's back, they say. This was the last straw for me. I packed and Tip and I, our faithful maid Arlinda and Gypsy, a little black-and-white puppy we had bought on the beach the day before, moved out of the rich Estoril villa into an old *quinta* in Carcavelos.

6   Carcavelos
1945-1946

Carcavelos is about halfway between Estoril and Lisbon on the *Costa de Sol*, or *Sunny Coast*, of Portugal. It is an old settlement, a good change for us. A Portuguese *quinta* is similar to the villa where I grew up. It is composed of a big house for the owners, smaller homes for servants or workers, buildings for animals and storage-like cellars, a park or garden for pleasure, orchard, vegetable garden and fields.

The quinta to which we moved, *Quinta do Lameiro*, was quite old and very spacious, much bigger than our home in Kecskemét. There were two dwellings in the main building. We occupied the smaller, lower one and a family from England lived in the upper half. The house showed a strong Moorish influence, like many buildings in Portugal, with signs of the Arab occupation. It had columns decorated with spirals and the walls were covered from floor to waist-height by hand-painted tiles called *azuleijos*. The roof was covered with the typical orange, brick tiles of semi-tropical regions, the corners of the roof slanting upwards. On the terrace surrounding the house and in the corridor running from the drawing room to the kitchen the floors were paved with red tiles.

There was a huge stone fireplace at one end of the drawing room, and at the other end stood a piano. That was Tip's favourite piece of furniture. He would listen with rapt attention to the tunes coming from the keys his fat little fingers touched. To me, the music he made was lovelier than any concert. At night he asked me to sing him to sleep. His favourite tune was Grieg's *Dance of the Dwarfs.* He would say "Sing about the dwarfs walking."

The property was surrounded by high walls. The big gate was always open and between the gate and the house was the garden. It had low hedges and paths and was full of many coloured plants and flowers. The hedges were about the same height as Tip, who played with Gypsy following his every step as he pulled his little carriage puffing like a train. His head appeared and disappeared among the flowers.

The orchard had all possible variations of citrus fruit: lemons, oranges, tangerines, grapefruit. The smell of their blossoms was inebriating. My favourite fruit was the fig. This was the first time I could pick figs from the tree, and I was eager for them to ripen enough to eat. They tasted different from the ones I knew, on strings or in tightly packed boxes, with the fruit covered with the sugar that comes out as it dries. The figs picked from the tree differed as if they were not the same species at all. Both Tip and I loved them and the fig tree was the first one Tip ever climbed. It was low and had branches close to the ground, just right for a three-year-old boy.

It was wonderful to be in an orchard again and walk along the old walls with the grapes climbing on them. There was a calm relief in me at moments in that orchard. That relief alternated with moments feeling totally lost. I was afraid of what Tamás might do and also of my father's reaction. For the moment I did not even know if I still had a father and a family in Hungary, because there was no mail. News about that part of the world was bad, with fighting between the Germans and the Russians. I had to force myself not to imagine the worst.

The people I got to know well were my embroiderers. Doing embroidery designs and teaching people to execute them was much more down to earth than news reporting. The woman I mentioned earlier who made an embroidery of the first design, Doña Ilda Matias dos Santos, lived in a village nearby. She gathered a few of her family and friends around herself. Her husband, Señhor Alberto, a retired mailman, became our manager. He bought the materials, paid the embroiderers and gave me advice on how to become a good business woman. He was both respectful and straight forward. He thought that I was too soft and tried to convince me to "put some pennies into a stocking". He meant that I should be saving money for my own good. My relationship to the embroiderers reminded me of the people living around our home in Kecskemét. Different language, different climate, but the same human warmth.

Then the atomic bomb ended the war. For me, from an emotional and spiritual perspective, it felt as if it had been dropped on my head, changing my thinking, as did my child's birth. Tamás called to ask whether I wanted to go with him when the Swedish Red Cross boat, the *Drottningholm*, left with the Japanese diplomats. Yes, I wanted to say good-bye to the Inoue family. They were close to my heart, they had enriched my world. Madame Inoue served the first Japanese meal I ever ate and she would dance gracefully before their fireplace with the picture of a lonely bird on a rock above it. They gave me that picture as parting gift. It hangs now in my son's house. Masutaro Inoue once told us of his experiences on the Manchurian front, which illustrated to me the senselessness of war, more than any pacifist literature.

He was half-asleep, relaxing after a dinner at our house. I don't recall what the conversation was that brought back his memories of years before when he was an officer in Manchuria. He spoke of the beauty of meeting a human being after serving solitary duty, alone with his horse for days. I could feel the vast desert he had been riding through as he talked about his excitement noticing a small dot on the horizon.

The dot kept growing, coming closer and he urged his horse to go faster, he was so anxious to meet another human being. It could have been a brigand, a thief, an enemy. He wanted to meet him, to share his food and drink, because he had been alone for an awfully long time, starved to be with another human being. As he spoke, I saw before my eyes the newspapers showing pictures of the Japanese soldiers with huge teeth, like beasts, torturing the prisoners of war. It just didn't make sense. To me Inoue's story, his feelings, were real, and pictures of the nasty enemy were only a nightmare from which to awaken.

For me, personally, the war ended with the German occupation of Hungary. It meant that I had to start a peace-oriented occupation to earn my living. But the horror of war continued in the world, while in me the horror of being lost, of confusion was deepening. How was it possible that the war could not be ended by talks? How was it possible that it could be started in the first place? The people who met in our house would not shoot each other. Those soldiers out on the fronts were shooting their fellowmen because they were taught to hate. Children have to be taught to love. That is the role of religion. I was sure that there was a remedy to war from God. While I prepared for the first exhibit of our embroideries, I started to pray for peace in the world and peace within myself. I prayed, begged God, to show the way.

God sent me help in that confusion. He was Father Daniel Huysmans, a Capuchin priest who came to Lisbon from Budapest with the Brazilian diplomats at the time of the German occupation. He was provincial in his order for Poland and Hungary, and it was through him that we used to send news and support to the Polish underground. Once Hungary was also occupied, it was dangerous for him to remain, besides now he was more useful in Lisbon where he became head of the Allied Relief Fund for Refugees. He was a philosopher, and a truly charitable man. When my confusion grew too intense, I turned to him for advice. I was brought up as a Lutheran, prejudiced against Catholics, but Father Daniel inspired confidence in me. Talking to him about spiritual matters and what was hurting, healed all the religious prejudice I ever had. His friendship made me able to concentrate on planning a future for Tip and myself instead of nurturing my confusion.

One evening, after Doña Ilda delivered the newly finished embroideries, I spread them around in the drawing room. They were so beautiful that I felt that it could not have been I who made the designs. It was my mother who came to my help! It was she who made me say on the phone that I could not go to the movie because I wanted to make embroidery designs! Next day I had tea with Alice Turnay, a teacher recently arrived with a Habsburg family. We talked about our lives and Alice said that she had gone to the *Academy of Fine Arts* in Budapest.

"So did my mother." Alice asked me her name.

"Aranka Széll." She pushed herself back from the table.

"I was wondering who you reminded me of. She was the soul of our group."

The first exhibit of the embroideries was held in the Hotel Avenida Palace, in the heart of Lisbon. It was a complete success. The press was flattering and we sold everything and received many orders. I became known overnight as an artist with an interesting business. Doña Ilda and Señhor Alberto were triumphant. A group composed of British and Belgian businessmen then made me an offer to become directrice of an elegant store catering to rich women, selling sewing machines in one side, and ladies' finery in the other side. They asked me to fly to Paris and Brussels, to shop around for merchandise and open the store on a high note.

Paris was then, in 1946, just recovering from the war, but the life of the fashion world was already in full swing, as if people were anxious to forget the bad days and quickly make up for lost opportunities. I went to the opening shows, bought

fine dresses, hats and accessories, gained exclusive repre-
sentation and ran like mad to do everything I possibly could.
But I had to squeeze in a visit to the *Louvre*.

Just between two important rendez-vous, I put aside
two hours for that visit. In two hours one cannot see much; I
tried to get the most out of it. Some of the museum's material
was still in storage or hiding, the rooms haphazardly organized, but I wanted to see everything.

I was running from one of the rooms to the next one,
when I was stopped by a portable wall, with only one painting. From the frame of her picture, Mona Lisa was looking at
me. With that famous smile, she was looking questioningly,
right into the centre of me, as if she were asking, "What are
you running for?" I sat down and gazed up at her and could
not go on running. I had a good rest in her company and left
the museum satisfied.

Brussels was sedate compared to Paris. I felt comfortable walking among the flowers of the market and visiting
Manikin Pis. Too bad Tip could not be with me! Little girls in
Brussels don't have to wonder what little boys look like. They
can see the statue of the cheeky little boy relaxedly pee-ing
into the marble pool.

Laces of Brussels and Bruges were the reason for my
trip there. I found them exquisite. Women sat around long
tables, chattering away while their deft fingers moved the
wooden spools of fine thread among the pins marking the
pattern of the lace. I watched the traditional designs come to
life on green velvet-covered cushions in front of them.

On the return flight we crossed the Pyrenees during
daylight. I was sitting by a window and watched the mountains emerge from the clouds. Suddenly I realized that the
whiteness I saw was snow! My eyes filled with tears and my
nose recalled the smell of clean, crackling snow. I had never
noticed before that snow had a smell. The sight of uncon-
sciously longed-for snow rendered conscious the until-then
unconscious memory of that healthy smell. Six years without

snow was apparently a long time for me, a child of temperate climates.

My partners and their wives were delighted with all the fine merchandise I brought for the new store. A good location was found, the decoration progressed well, the publicity set in gear, the opening day was announced and Father Daniel was asked to bless the new enterprise. The opening was a big success, with huge bouquets of flowers and the cream of Lisbon society signing the guest book. Customers started to come and my job became more demanding every day. Soon I had to face reality; we had to move to Lisbon.

The day before moving, we were sitting at lunch when Arlinda brought in the mail. The letter on top had a Hungarian stamp and the envelope bore Mother's handwriting. They were alive! We were not alone in the world.

7   Lisbon
1947-1948

We moved to a ground-floor apartment on Avenida Ressano Garcia. I chose it because there was a French-speaking kindergarten in the street. Tip spoke Hungarian to me and Portuguese to Arlinda, now he had French to pick up. He did not like his kindergarten, but it was not because of the new language as he mastered French very quickly. He disliked being closed in. He was accustomed to be outdoors, to roam, to think freely. The city and the classroom were strange and depressing to him. We discovered the *Estufa Fria*, a half-covered half-open garden where all sorts of tropical trees and flowers grew. We made it a substitute for our own garden. It was full of plants we had never seen before and the smell was new, so was the light coming in through slats, giving an atmosphere of a jungle. Arlinda and Tip went there often after his school.

I passed most of the day at the store, with customers. I hardly ever saw my embroiderers any more. The atelier remained in Carcavelos, Doña Ilda and Señhor Alberto would come in to bring the ready work, to take the new orders and buy the necessary materials. I started the atelier because I loved to create beauty together, and to see people happy working with each other and me. The financial results were welcome but they were never my sole concern. Now I had to change my attitude and I did not like the change from the friendliness of the atelier to the high-handed, impersonal commanding my new role demanded. I had to learn to command, while I prefer to consult and do things together. The mornings were rushed. I did not look forward to each day, so I walked up the street tired, as if I had a load on my shoulders or I was 70 years old.

The happiest days of the week were Fridays, because Father Daniel came for dinner. His visits were like an anchor on a strange sea. We could talk about everything that was of interest to us. Tip could tell him about the new songs he learned, show him the designs he made. I could talk about the happy moment of discovering that a sentence from my religious instruction gained a real meaning for me. It happened right there, on the busy avenue before our house. Tip, Gypsy and I went to the store across the street to buy some fish. The women in the store were smiling and said an endearing "Adios" when we left. Crossing the street, I felt a warm glow as Tip hopped along holding onto my hand, and Gypsy wagged his tail.

Suddenly I remembered, "Love your neighbour as thyself", and I realized that I felt happy because those women liked us, and we liked them, and we loved each other. The meaning of that sentence changed from a commandment of a powerful God, into advice from a loving Father. I told Father Daniel that I entered all the churches I passed when I had time to stop. I went in to pray and to cry, to pray for peace in the world and peace within myself and for God to grant me wisdom. Father Daniel told me he thought that I was praying for the highest gifts one can ever pray for.

I could talk with him freely about the ache I felt because I had separated my son from his father. Father Daniel knew Tamás and liked him but saw that he was not a father, as his life had not prepared him for that. He loved to play with Tip, just as he liked to have me for a wife, but only when it did not interfere with what was important to him, and that was his special kind of political activity. When I shared my fears about separating the child from his father, Father Daniel explained the other side of the question, the need Tip had for a harmonious, organized family life. He actually helped me to start a divorce. I did not have money to hire a lawyer, so he gave me the amount needed for a first consultation. That was all I ever had to pay to the lawyer who took care of the divorce. Besides his law practice, Antonio Bastos Guerra was a fine humorist. He and Andrée, his French wife, became dear friends to us. When I left Lisbon, I gave them a Hungarian cushion and a Japanese samurai in a black lacquered box. I received that samurai – as well as the painting of the lonely bird – as parting gift from the Inoue family when they returned to Japan.

Christmas 1947 will remain a low point for me. In the years of ease I used to invite lots of people who were alone for the holidays. Now I found myself alone for Christmas. There was a rush at the store before the holidays. I had no time to plan ahead and nobody thought of inviting me. After Tip and Arlinda went to bed, I sat alone, lonely. For a while I felt bitter; I who took care of inviting those who might feel lonely, and nobody thinks of me today. Then I admitted to myself that I had not invited others so much for their sake but for mine, because I enjoyed being good. Nobody owed me anything. I decided to be good that Christmas too. I filled a couple of bags with candies and set out towards the churches. People were gathering for Midnight Mass. As children passed by, I asked them if they would like candies and gave them some, with a "Happy Christmas" or rather, "Feliz Natal". I gave out all the candies and got many a smile and surprised *obrigada*, which means "Thank you" in Portuguese. But what I remember most are the two children who refused the candies.

The first one was a boy walking his drunken father home. He looked at me with incredibly sad eyes when I asked him if he would like to have some *doce*. He kept on walking, holding up his weaving father. The other one was also a boy. He was walking with his mother, both carrying bags of coal on their backs. When the mother heard me talk to the little boy, she tugged on his arm and said something in a rough voice. The thin little boy looked back at me timidly, I could see that he longed to have those candies, but the mother was pulling him and his poor little bag of coal. Only Gypsy woke up when I got home. Tip was sleeping peacefully and I was grateful that I had a comfortable home for him.

Soon after Christmas Tip came down with pneumonia, and my work at the store became unbearable. I will never know if it was my dislike for the situation, or that they wanted to replace me with a cheaper directrice, that caused the rupture between my partners and me. The fact is that they did not ask me to reconsider when I resigned and that the woman who succeeded me made 1.500 escudos a month, while my salary had been 5.000 escudos. I had no contract and left embroideries, embroiderers, everything behind. I was never a good business woman.

As soon as Tip was well enough, we left for Sezimbra, a fishing village in the south, to make him all better. There we passed our days on the beach, making friends with the vacationing people and with the fishermen. Around two in the morning we could hear a foreman call out the names of the teams that were heading out for sardines that day. It sounded quite like a cock waking up people. I went once for a morning of fishing for sardines. The men pulled out a huge net with a fleet of small boats. When there was enough fish in the net, they converged into a circle and started lifting up the net, with movements dictated by their rhythmic cries. The closer the boats got to each other, the more the fish jumped up from the water, only to fall back into the net, which became alive with all the frantic fish struggling to escape. At night the village was full of the smell of "sardinhas assadas", or roasting fresh sardines.

One windy morning I went out with the whale hunters. The sea was so rough that the harpoonist did not let go any shots, and the boat was called back at noon. Before they agreed to take me, I had trouble convincing them that I was not likely to be sea-sick. They were rather distrusting until they saw me sitting, hanging on to a pole with my legs crossed, taking photos of the whales coming up for air. At the sight of a big black whale the men started swearing, "The hunchback!" She had been shot once but got away with the harpoon stuck into her back. Now she came around to tease the whale hunters. She would come up only in bad weather and only twice, never for the third time which was when they would let the harpoon go. This time she appeared first on one side then on the other side of the boat, very close to us, as if she came to say, "You had me once. Try it, you will never get me again!"

When I went out with the fishermen, Arlinda came to the beach with Tip. She did not go into the water, normally she would wait for us at home, with our dinner ready. After the outing with the whale hunters and the meeting with the hunchback, we stopped at a restaurant which carried a sign saying, "I expect you on your way back", or "Na volta ca te espero." The tables were laid under climbing vines of Bella Portuguesa, the most beautiful climbing roses I ever saw. The cook was a fisherman's wife. She served us the freshest *pescada cosida.*

Besides feeding her customers, she also fed her chickens and the way she called them impressed us no end. We heard her shout, "0 Señhor Abade!", which means " Mr. Abbot, come here!" Whereupon a cock came running, the flock of hens running behind him. When we got home, Tip looked at our terracotta cock, standing on the mantel, a piece of typical Portuguese handicraft, and exclaimed, "Mama! Look! Señhor Abade!" Señhor Abade is still with us, a big antique cock from Caldas de Rainha.

Relaxing by the sea was good for us but money was running out. Once or twice a week I went to Lisbon to look for a job but nothing turned up. One afternoon I had tea with a Hungarian lady double my age. She knew my problems and decided to be of help. She told me that it was quite common in a business like the one I had been in, to have it started by a woman of style to give it contacts and publicity, only to replace her with somebody less expensive. She saw it coming and felt that I was a fool not to protect myself.

"But, Angéla, you don't have to struggle like that. At your age, with your looks!" She jingled the heavy golden bracelet on her wrist, "You see? If one is clever..." I laughed at her kind advice, thanked her for her concern, and, after a few more discouraging trips, one day I decided to try to follow her advice. I checked through the men who seemed to have a crush on me and chose the two richest ones and called on them. I met with complete success.

The first one, a divorced man, smiled as he listened to my predicament and said, "You know, I would love to find you in my villa in Estoril when I have the chance to take time off." He offered me one of his villas, with what it needs to keep it going. He was a very fine person and I was touched, thanked him and told him that I was going to think about it. The second was less romantic. He offered a flat amount, well beyond bare necessities, and specified that he would count on seeing me once a month and that otherwise my time and actions would be free of any interference from him. I told him that I would think it over and let him know.

As I crossed the square with the flower market, called Rossio, I met a young member of the Foreign Office. He was delighted to see me, he had wanted to speak to me, and would I care to have a cocktail? Somewhat sheepishly but quite proud of himself, he told me that he was now in a position where he could afford some luxuries, and would I accept to go to the opera, or to a good restaurant once in a while with him? I should not think of anything wrong. He did not want it to mean anything, but he would really appreciate taking me out at times. I understood that he would like people to think that he could afford a mistress like me. I told him that I would let him know.

I walked out of that cocktail lounge and started strolling up Avenida de Liberdade, the avenue of freedom, the broad, main artery of Lisbon, with the white and black marble mosaic sidewalks under the palm trees. I felt light and I felt free. I could never do it, now I knew! I had thought to use my body and my youth to earn a living, and now I knew that I could never do it. I was delighted to find out. I walked with a light head and heart on the avenue of liberty.

For some time somebody walked next to me. I turned to see who it was and recognized a young man who had worked on the publicity of the store.

"I was wondering if it was you, Madame Tamás, or somebody who looks like you. You seem so young and so happy." I laughed and said that I was actually very happy, although I was out of a job, with a son to take care of and no money.

"But you have friends," he said.

"Sure, but who is the friend who will come and hand me 2,000 escudos I need to put down on a home tomorrow?" I said still laughing.

"I would be honoured if you allowed me to lend it to you," he answered. I became serious.

"How do you know that I would pay it back?"

"I am sure that you would."

"And if I just up and disappeared?"

"Then I would lose a friend," he answered, and he lent me 2,000 escudos.

I only had the name and an address for that young man. A short time later I wrote to him, the letter came back, "Address Unknown". I left Portugal soon afterwards and tried to locate him through friends, without success. I hope that one day I can pay back that loan, and that in the meantime he knows that I have the intention. I would not like him to think that he had lost me as a friend.

As for the three men who made me the offers: the first one became more of a friend when I told him how I felt, the second one who only wanted sex never showed his disappointment and kept on inviting me to the parties at his hunting castle on top of a mountain, where he liked me to ride his finely trained horses; the third one, who wanted me to enhance his prestige, never could look straight into my eyes again.

The small house for which I needed the 2,000 escudos, to which we returned from Sezimbra, was called Chalet Oasis. It was behind a big apartment building, way back in a garden, in the Rua do Arco or the Road to the Arc. While it was being prepared, we stayed a few days in Cascais, with Magda and Elemér Ujpétery. Elemér was the Hungarian chargé d'affaires who served at the time of the take-over by the new regime. They had two sons, both a bit older than Tip.

It was in their house that I woke up on the morning of April 6, 1948, hearing, "Dreams, Nightmares and Dreams Again." It came in a Voice and I *knew* that this was the title of a book I was supposed to write. I started to write as soon as we got to Chalet Oasis.

Obeying that command led me to the Bahá'í Faith. Anyuka, the fine painter, the loving but unhappy mother, taught me to believe in God. Imu, my grandmother, the herbalist, the "white witch", Theosophist, taught me to believe in nature to cure bodily ills. They both loved me in this world and still love me from the world beyond. I feel that they have held my hand, guided and helped me when I was nearly snowed under by my ignorance. Without their help, I don't think I could have made it.

Imu died on April 9, 1948, three days after I had THAT DREAM. She went away on my birthday, right after I responded positively to that command.

I took the command to mean that I should write a book in three parts, the first about the dreams of innocence, the second about the nightmares of cruel, insensitive, stupid reality, and the final part to say that the initial dreams can be turned into mature, sensible God-guided reality.

I had just finished the first part, when my friend, Hilda Summers knocked on the door.

"You have been locked up long enough (It was in fact three weeks). Get dressed, you need some culture. There is a Shakespeare afternoon at the British Institute."

We went and saw members of the British embassy, normally so formal and serious, put on a hilarious show of excerpts from Shakespeare. In the interval Hilda met a friend of hers, Lucinda, who was with a stranger. She introduced me to her, a woman with an unmistakable American accent.

"You are an American, aren't you?" I told her that I was writing something in English and would need somebody to correct it. The title came in English, therefore I wrote it in English, although my written English was not good. She offered to help. I was a bit surprised at the prompt offer.

"It is rather personal. We should get to know each other."

"Fine with me. Where shall we meet? When?" We set a date for dinner at my house the following Thursday.

Over dinner I told Val, (Mrs. Hayden Nichols, born Valeria Lamb) that I was writing about the dreams and hopes of childhood, when one believes that what the grown-ups say is true, that justice prevails, goodness is rewarded and evil is punished. Then come the nightmares, seeing that the world around us is not like that at all... Still, we have to trust and carry on, knowing that it makes life worth living to work for those dreams to become reality.

"I came to Portugal to meet people who think like you," Val said. She told me that she was a Bahá'í and that meant that she believes that God has sent a new Messenger,

Bahá'u'lláh, the Glory of God. He came to fulfill the hopes, the dreams, to bring peace, to unite the world.

"Another religion? Don't we have enough?"

"It is to bring a world civilization."

"Religions have done the most uncivilized things!"

"God has now sent Bahá'u'lláh, with a new Message."

"To take Christ's place?" Thus we carried on till after midnight.

When she left, I accompanied her to the gate and walked back to the house in the fragrant late-April moonlight. I looked up to the moon, leaned against the house, and said to myself with a big sigh of relief, "If what she says is true, that is what I have been praying for."

Years later, in 1969, I visited Val, my dear spiritual mother, then pioneer to the Mayas of Yucatan. When I told her about that sigh of mine, she laughed.

"Do you know what I was thinking when I left you at your gate? That I should never try to give the Message when I am tired."

God bless her for not allowing the tiredness caused by a first, distraught reception! She took my finished pages to be corrected and invited me to an informal discussion, to continue our exchange. It was my first *fireside*. To begin with, she and the friend with whom she shared her apartment and her conviction, Louise Baker (Dorothy Baker's daughter), served a delightful supper on a low table. In the middle was one big bowl of salad. Until then I only had the kind of salad people used to serve in Europe, such as lettuce, or beets, or tomatoes. This was a colourful bowl of mixed greens, yellows and reds. We sat around the table on cushions and I felt at home with their friendly informality right away. This did not stop me from getting into a heated argument. I was not alone to argue. There was an American boy, Al, who had a dark green sock on one foot and a light green on the other.

"These Americans! They have to show off that they have two pairs of socks," I joked. He retorted by asking me to spell that barbarian name of mine.

Val and Louise were talking about the Message they brought to Portugal, one of the 10 European countries to which pioneers came during the second Seven Year Plan. It was all new to me and I listened and argued. They gave me reading material to consider until next Wednesday, when they expected me to return for another evening with them. To tell the truth, I was not overly impressed by the literature. It sounded like religious propaganda, people who believe that they have the truth; I had heard that before. I liked Val and Louise and the Message did sound like what I was hoping for, but it did not seem likely to become reality until they gave me Emeric Sala's book, *This Earth One Country.*

Emeric Sala was a Hungarian, like me. He lost his native Transylvania, just as I lost my Tátra Mountains, with the Treaty of Trianon. He saw in the Bahá'í teachings the solution to the social, economical and political problems of the world. I was one-third into his book when I decided that I wanted to be a Bahá'í.

There were many important decisions I had made; none was as important as this. Before making it, I was careful to ask all the questions I wanted to have answered about the Bahá'í teachings, because I was aware of the danger of falling into the trap of my idealism and need for solution to injustice and war. I saw too many people accept ideologies only to become disillusioned. It took three months and many arguments before I felt that this was a real answer from the real God, and that I wanted to work for it.

8 North America 1948

I was not aware of looking for a second husband or the danger of making a mistake with a second marriage. I was less intelligent than the whale who got away once and learned her lesson. After years of living in a sophisticated, disappointing high society, this young American who was at the first evening where I met the answers I was praying for, seemed all purity and nobility, a knight in shining armour. It took me all of two weeks to decide to marry him. I jumped into the sea without knowing how deep it was or how rough, and without even asking whether I was a good enough swimmer.

"He needs me" was my main thought about Al. His knee hurt; I touched it and his pain went away. He did not feel loved; I shall love him. He wanted to be a father, but worried whether he could be a father at all. I shall make him Tip's father and give him other children. He was 21, he had not yet finished his studies and had not worked other than at small summer jobs. This only made me see how much he needed me. His family did not see things the same way. They ordered him to take the first plane home when he wrote about wanting to marry this 28-year-old European divorcée with a five-year-old son. We passed a few days planning our future before he flew home. We were sure of ourselves and knew that the doors would open to happiness and success. We planned to start an atelier of embroideries, with Al in charge of administration, and me, of design, execution and education. He left for the States. I started selling things and getting the necessary papers.

My family took the news of my divorce from Bandi Tamás and my intention to marry an unknown American remarkably well. Apu's only worry was that I might have met Al while I was still married and that this might have been the reason for leaving Tamás. That would have upset him, and I did not get angry. On the contrary, I quite liked it that my father was anxious to know that I was an honest woman. The news from home was not rosy. The family had to abandon Kecskemét, our house was in ruin. Apu had a stroke and was not recovering well. Ákos was a prisoner-of-war in Russia. Attila was working on last ditch defence for the Germans and was taken prisoner by the advancing Russians. The convoy taking him to Russia happened to go through Cegléd, where they now lived. People noticed Attila in the school yard where they were kept, and alerted the family. Apu took his cane and painfully walked over to the school and implored the doctor in charge of the infirmary to allow the 17-year-old boy to leave the convoy. He gave the doctor a gallon of apricot brandy and Attila's name was added to those who were too sick to be good for the labour camp, so he was freed. Even though Mother had her hands full with her two girls and a sick husband, still, she wrote occasionally to keep in touch. My Hungarian passport had expired, so I asked the Portuguese authorities to give me a travelling document. The head of the Policia Internacionale, in charge of such things, very cordially said that I could have a paper called "titre-de-voyage" and that they would be happy to have me back any time, because I had contributed to the art and economy of the country.

Proud of that document and praise, I went to the Canadian Consulate. It was not possible for a stateless person from Europe to go to the United States to marry an American. There were quotas and long lists of people waiting. I could only get a visitor's visa if I went to either Mexico or Canada. I knew the Canadian consul and his charming French wife and son, so I thought of trying to go to Canada. Louise Baker had a good friend, Doris McKay, an art teacher on Prince Edward Island, who thought that the wives of the fishermen might be interested to work on embroideries. Doris and another friend of Louise's, Lloyd Gardner of Oshawa, sent me an affidavit of support each, so that I could go to Canada. This they did, before I declared myself a Bahá'í!

I sat in the waiting room of the Canadian Consulate. There was a wall-sized map of Canada, the first big map of Canada I had ever seen in my life. While waiting, I admired the immensity of that unknown country.

Permission to receive a business visa to Canada gracefully granted, I sold most of our things, bought our tickets, packed what we had kept of our belongings, and we boarded the plane for Boston. Arlinda was at the airport, with tears flowing. Gypsy was there, with his new owner, wagging his tail as if to say good-bye. The last thing I did was to mail a letter to Tamás with Al's address in the States where he could always get news of Tip. I was too afraid of what he might do if he knew that we were leaving to let him know any earlier.

Tip had never been in an aeroplane and he was very silent at first. He was glad to go to North America, to see real squirrels. His favourite picture was Albrecht Duerer's drawing of a Squirrel. Now he wanted to see the live ones.

Al was waiting at the airport in Boston. By now his family gave in to his desire to marry me and they received me with all the warmth they could muster. I was not very successful at fitting in. The first thing I did was to scratch a brother-in-law's brand new Cadillac with the fender of my future mother-in-law's car. The whole family was sitting on the lawn in the August sunshine when we left for a ride, with me at the wheel. The scratch happened as I was backing out of the garage. There was an icy silence, people held their breaths in horror and Al's mother motioned for him to take over the wheel. I did not hear the meeting of the cars, it's only the faces that I remember and the silence. When we were out of sight, I wanted to take the wheel, but Al did not let me. I could not convince him that the best thing would be to let me drive again. I was thinking of the time Tip fell off a horse and wanted to get back on it. I felt awful about Al not sensing my need to be trusted with that wheel. It made me feel that the paint on the Cadillac had more value than my feelings. But I was not accustomed to voicing my feelings.

Our wedding was held in the Lutheran church. Al's Catholic family was very gracious. They complimented the organ rendition of Beethoven's *The Heavens Laud the Glory of the Eternal*, played at my request. Al's mother fixed a piece of the most exquisite old lace from Bruges on my head and said some traditional verses used at weddings in America. While they were as kind as they could be, I still felt very stupid most of the time. I could be fluent enough in English to send reports of the English press to Hungary, but sitting at a dinner table with an American family, not often talking to foreigners, is a very different situation. I understood only about half of what was said but did not want to keep asking to "please repeat". Most of the time I smiled like an idiot and felt like one.

After the wedding we headed for Canada. On the way, we stopped at the Green Acre Bahá'í School and had a Bahá'í wedding. Two Bahá'ís, Mildred Mottahedeh and Bert Gottlieb officiated. Bert became our friend and came to visit us in Canada. He brought books to start a Bahá'í library and gave me two special gifts: a photo of 'Abdu'l-Bahá and a ring. He told me that the stone of that ring was a gift from 'Abdu'l-Bahá to the first American Bahá'í woman, Lua Getsinger. She received it before the turn of the century when she was in the

84

Holy Land. She had it set in gold by a jeweller in Cairo, where she died and is buried. I was too new a Bahá'í to realize then how precious was that gift.

By the time we settled in Canada, the plans about embroidery were put aside as impractical. Life was a serious matter. One had to face it with a reasonable outlook. Embroideries might have some value as decoration, but for earning a living one had to find work. I found a job first, as a knitting instructor at Eaton's in Montréal. They hired me because I was bilingual and knew how to teach handicrafts. I had never followed a knitting pattern before. I always made my own designs, but I knew how to read. So when my first customer arrived with her knitting book asking how she should execute her pattern, we deciphered together the meaning of the instructions. That job was a good introduction to Canada; I met French-Canadians and Anglophones, very elegant ladies from Westmount and a woman who was the first illiterate adult I ever met. She was a beautiful knitter. Two veterans who learned knitting while recuperating from their wounds were the first men I saw knitting. First they came together. Then when they gained confidence, one came alone, asking me not to tell the other that he needed help. They were in competition with their Argyle socks.

At first we lived in a tourist home in Montréal. Tip's fifth birthday was celebrated there. That day will always be a dark page in the book of my memories. We were walking on Mountain Street, Tip must have seen somebody eating ice cream and he said, "I want an ice cream." I asked how he would say it nicely. Al interrupted, "Those European niceties! Come Tip, we will have ice cream." I stood frozen, looking after my son going off with his new father, leaving me alone.

I muttered, "The best present one can give a child is respect for his mother", but neither of them heard me. I didn't know how to stop them, how to assert myself.

From a competent lady I became overnight an outmoded nuisance. It did not help that I was pregnant with Al's first child and that I had no idea about housekeeping. When I noticed a spot on the floor, I would expect it to disappear. When it did not, I got annoyed, and only then did I realize that there was nobody else to clean it up but me. We lived on Trans Island Avenue and there was a fire station nearby. Tip often heard the fire engines rushing on the street. He wondered how it would be when they came to our place, so one morning I woke to the smell of smoke and jumped to put out the burning cardboard box. Later he told me that when he grew up he would paint a picture of the silence after an ambulance. He did not want to speak any other language now but English. This boy of mine who used to walk on the seashore singing songs in three languages, now wanted to be a boy like the others along the street. There was nothing I could do but to pray that he would not regret it too much when he realized what he had lost.

Soon after we arrived in Montréal, we met Rosemary and Emeric Sala, the same Emeric whose book made me see that I was a Bahá'í, and his wife Rosemary, the kindest, finest friend. They took us to the Laurentian Bahá'í School at Beaulac. That fall in the Laurentians, my first Canadian fall! The maples gave us a full show. The Swiss overseer of the Beaulac Summer School, Bill Suter and his dog, Quinty, promptly took Tip into their warm hearts.

That lovely fall visit to Beaulac started a remarkable string of visits to the Laurentian Bahá'í School. There were summer and winter sessions with teachers like Stanwood Cobb, Dr. Furútan, Geneviève Coy, Mehdi Firoozi, Emeric and Rosemary Sala, just to name a few. Bill and Priscilla Waugh gave a terrific contribution demonstrating the principle of the equality of men and women, of how husband and wife can work together in the kitchen, mostly regarded as "women's territory", without ever losing their good humour!

With friends like Nora and Brad Henderson, Virginia Young, Adeline and Karl, Walter and Ilse Lohse, and many others, searching, eager, burning hearts, we studied the letters from Shoghi Effendi, the history of the Faith, the Writings of Bahá'u'lláh and the Tablets of 'Abdu'l-Bahá. The religions of the past became stepping stones to the future, meaningful in the great drama of human history.

These sessions gave me a grounding in the study of the Faith which served as a greenhouse for all the years to follow. I gained an assurance that, whatever pain I had suffered, and will still suffer, will water the plants I cherish in my heart. I am deeply grateful to God to have allowed me to be present at those memorable lectures, so soon after arriving in North America. It was a blessed beginning of a period of my life that brought many trials and tribulations. Here I gathered the knowledge needed to face life as it was opening then for me. This helped me through everything.

9   Montréal – Verdun
1949-1955

When Sandy arrived, Tip stayed with the Salas while I was in hospital. He loved it and Rosemary did too.

On one of their walks they saw a little boy pulling a wagon like the one he had in Portugal. Rosemary saw the longing look and remarked "that little boy has a nice wagon but maybe he does not have a little brother." Whereupon Tip came out with one of his famous statements: "People are more important than things."

When Sandy was born, I did not have a friend to hold my hand, no midwife to care for us, no nurse for the baby. The doctor did not tell me not to lift my head after the spinal anaesthesia. I had a horrible headache for days because I lifted my head to look at my newborn son. The fashion was not for breast-feeding then, and I had to fight with the nurses to stop giving him the bottle. When I went home, there was no Arlinda to prepare our meals and clean the house around us. When the *Victorian Order of Nurses* (V.O.N.) nurse came to call, she found me crying. She asked what I was crying about. All I could say was: "My back hurts when I shake out the carpets."

The visit of the nurse from the *Victorian Order of Nurses* resulted in the first appointment with a marriage counsellor. She listened patiently to my story about my background and what I found hard in my new life, then she wanted to see Al. He went to see her willingly. We both found her nice, she also liked us and recommended that we apply for a *DP* to be assigned to us. *DPs,* or "Displaced Persons", were those newly arrived refugees from Europe who had to work a year in a household to be allowed to settle in Canada. We applied for and got a fine young lady from Czechoslovakia as mother's helper. A young baroness from Prague, to try to help me cope with a difficult situation! I had a chance to see how kind one of those people whom I used to call thieves for stealing my country can be! I think that Issi's few months with us remain in her memory as somewhat of a nightmare too. She was no more prepared for housework than I was. When her parents bought a house and arranged for her to go to join them, I was happy for her. How I wish that I had learned to cope with a household and care for children before I started having children in the New World!

Al had been a student in third-year chemistry at the *Massachusetts Institute of Technology* when he became disenchanted with life as he knew it and wanted to see what the other side of the world found worth living for. He finished the third year and went to Europe. There he stayed first in France, learning the finest French in Tours. Then he went to Salamanca and picked up the finest possible Spanish. When we met, he was in Portugal for barely a month but already spoke Portuguese with a good accent. This might have helped me to fall in love with him. But now it was necessary to finish his education. *Sir George Williams College* in Montréal offered evening classes and he took up the challenge. He had a job that paid little and we had trouble meeting our bills. How we hoped that one day we might have 300 dollars a month! For his graduation from Sir George, I wore a yellow polka-dotted dress, the first dress I ever made myself. It was a maternity dress, because I was expecting Katherin.

Al declared himself a Bahá'í on my first birthday in Canada, made friends at Sir George and invited them to our firesides. One of the participants, a student of international law, was from Kenya. I still have his letters written after he left, because he was the first person I met on this side of the ocean with whom I could really talk about what was the most burning issue for me, the need to work on the betterment of human society. The son of a hereditary chief, he had a high concept of duty towards his people. He studied in North America in order to serve his people and not to become rich. I felt closer to that man from a far-away country I had never visited and maybe never will, a man whose colour was as black as a skin can be, than to some of the childhood friends who went to school with me. Without yet knowing much about the Faith, I knew that it was the right choice to become a Bahá'í. We moved to Verdun, the first Bahá'ís to settle there. In our Wednesday evenings we discussed such questions as the need to eliminate extremes of riches and poverty, for the workers to share in their company's profits, for the riches of the world to be distributed equitably among small and big nations, for a world government to decide what is just for all, and a world police force to safeguard peace. We placed ads with quotations in the local paper, giving our telephone number for further information. Among the people who phoned were those who wanted to invite us to their meetings. They belonged to the Communist Party, outlawed in Duplessis' Québec. I knew that there might be danger in associating with them, so I called the *Royal Canadian Mounted Police* to ask whether it was safe to respond to the invitation. A handsome officer came to see me, asked all sorts of questions, while my Sandy was walking around the kitchen table with his beloved "tootiger", that is to say screwdriver, and Kathy stood in the corner of her crib, watching us with her big brown eyes, one of them a two-tone-brown eye!

The officer from the R.C.M.P. asked me to join the group that invited us and to report on their activities. I said that I could not possibly become a member in any political movement, and that I would not want to join with the intent of spying on them. As far as letting the R.C.M.P. know if ever I saw anything that might be dangerous to Canada, I would of course not hesitate to alert them. Upon that he encouraged me to get in touch with the callers. This was in the spring of 1952. In May there was a big Peace Conference in Toronto, with Dr. James Endicott as the most prominent participant. I was one of the speakers at that conference because my new friends in Verdun, knowing my interest in world peace, asked me to go with them and to present my views. I called my friend at the R.C.M.P. and asked whether it was safe to go. He offered to pay my expenses, which I declined. I went because I was interested. I wanted to hear what they had to say and say what I wanted to communicate.

We had very little money, but Al let me go because the friends from Verdun drove me and I was going to stay in the home of Audrey and John Robarts, in Forest Hill Village. Those three days in the Robarts home was a real vacation for me. Looking out from their kitchen window, I saw the first Japanese quince since I left Kecskemét! It was in bloom.

John and Audrey sat in the gallery watching and praying when I had the distinction of being the only speaker whose talk was given in only one language. When I finished my seven-minute contribution in English, I asked if they wanted me to repeat it in French myself. The secretary whispered quickly, "There is no time for it."

It was like the bad atmospheric conditions when Berlin did not want my news to reach Budapest. If there is anybody who knows how it feels to be marginal, it's me. What I said was my deepest conviction, my plea for peace. It was not in the prevailing tone. I told them that peace could not be reached by fighting. One could only work for it. We could build it by looking into history, studying what made warring peoples become friends and work together. I advised them to learn about the great teacher of the nineteenth century, Bahá'u'lláh. My plea was drowned in belligerent songs. My

Communist friends were apologetic on the drive home. A few days later they called to ask if I cared to invite Dr. Endicott and a few of his clergymen friends for tea. Dr. Endicott was a Protestant missionary to China. They came for tea and Dr. Endicott told about how horribly Americans treated the Chinese people. I could not stay silent.

"War is to be blamed for those horrors, not particular nations. Talking like you do creates hatred and results in war." He pushed my objections aside and continued about the realities they should be aware of. I stopped him again by reciting a well-known passage from the New Testament about loving our enemies. I never knew that I could recite that passage by heart!

As if I had not said anything, he started to show photos of American soldiers holding a cut-off Chinese head, and I could not stand it any longer: "That act was an act of hatred, taking the photo was done out of hatred, and your showing it creates hatred. Do not tell me that you work for peace!" I went outside. Poor Dr. Endicott did not know that my first job with Bandi Tamás was adding paint to photos of victims of atrocities committed by members of the Romanian Iron Guard. The purpose was to show the world how barbaric Romanians were. I spotted what was a heightening effect on those photos. The crucifix on the bare chest of a soldier holding the head! That was a master's touch in view of the specific public of the day.

Standing in the door, trying to cool down, I noticed the Royal Canadian Mounted Police man watching our house from the other side of the street. He was keeping an eye lest the Québec police tried to break up the meeting. The comic relief of that situation calmed me down and I could say a well-mannered good-bye to my quickly departing guests.

I could not say now if it was this or some other similar event that filled the bucket for Al. He started to be unhappy with my attempts to save the world. I did everything in order to create a better world for our children, but he felt that I was

93

neglecting them to save the world. This of course could not go on, so I decided to become involved with something that was immediately helpful for the children. I started discussion groups on child-psychology for the parent-teacher association of Riverview School where Tip was a student. This was the first such attempt in the province of Québec. There were discussion groups led by trained leaders, but we did it among ourselves as parents, using an outline from the Department of Extension of the University of British Columbia. Audrey Robarts "just happened" to visit when I was asked to be president of parent education. She was involved in the same activity in her community, advised me to write to U.B.C. and get the fine outline. We met every second week to discuss what the "experts" said and then add our questions and opinions from our own experiences. Most of the women who formed the group had never been in a library before. Now everybody had to take turns to find the books the outline referred to and to report on them. I made sure that even the most timid of us had a chance to rub shoulders with the world of those who were supposed to know.

The success was instantaneous, and a second group was formed. Then a third one wanted to start. I could not give another evening to it, so I asked whether anybody would care to volunteer as "traffic officer" of the new group. The secretary of the first group, Helen McGuire, offered to start the third group, the same Helen, who, when I asked her a few months earlier to be secretary of the first group, answered that she had never done anything like that and would not know how to do it! By now we all knew that to work together, helping each other, did not require a doctorate.

For me, the most important result of these discussions was what happened when we got to the discussion of sex education. The girls felt that I should tackle that one as they all felt shy about it. Of course Angéla will be up to it. Sure I will do it, I said. I prefaced the presentation by giving two examples of people who had trouble in their grown-up lives because they did not receive proper sex education when they were chil-
94

dren. A man who was told that masturbation causes sterility became a homosexual. And I told the sad story of a woman. When she saw the first boy's genitals, she asked her father about it. The father shook her and shouted, "What did he do to you?" This frightened the little girl so much that she never asked such questions, avoided the conversations of her friends when they touched on that subject and grew up in ignorance. Had there been a relaxed informative attitude about sex, she would have been spared a great deal of suffering. Then I presented the readings and led the discussion. We had our customary tea and went home.

Next week the same subject was given in the second group, and I started the evening the same way. As I ended the story of the ignorant girl, I started feeling sick. My whole body was trembling. I had only time to ask somebody to take over and to reach the bathroom. I became violently sick, throwing up, throwing up. I had just realized that I was telling my own story!

Had anyone asked whether it was my own story I was using as example, I would have likely said "yes, it was." On an intellectual level I was aware of what I was doing: I was telling something I really knew about. But I needed to tell about it a second time to have it penetrate my guts, to see and FEEL the horror I went through. And it took my need to help others avoid causing such suffering to their children, to start getting it out of my system.

I started my earthly life as a dispossessed child through historical events, none caused by myself or my parents. Entering adulthood, I was totally ignorant about what it meant to be a woman. That ignorance gave me an innocence that made me vulnerable to become a victim of abuse, but at the same time surrounded me like a protective coat. No stupid choice, no unwise action was able to take away that protection. I can only thank God for it and my mother, who took care of me from the other side of the Gate. Her love led me to Bahá'u'lláh, and enabled me to recognize Him.

I know, I really know why I want to build a better world!

When, in 1953, Shoghi Effendi, the Guardian of the Bahá'í Faith called pioneers to go to virgin territories, in the Ten Year Crusade, Al and I, volunteered for the Marquesas Islands. Our offer was accepted. My husband, on the contrary, found this to be too much, the famous last straw.

"This is your crazy idea. If you want to bring up our children as monkeys, climbing on palm trees, I will not stand in your way." And he left me. By this time we had three children, my son from the previous marriage, our son Sandy and daughter Katherin.

I wrote to the secretary of the committee in charge, asking whether a mother with three children would also do. She answered that it would be wiser to wait for another opportunity to pioneer. I decided to unite the family before uniting the world. I called my husband back, and, instead of becoming a Knight of Bahá'u'lláh for opening the Marquesas, I became an inactive Bahá'í. There was no question of spreading the Message, in words, while my husband felt that I was neglecting my duties as wife and mother.

My spiritual mother, Val's example was clearly before me. When her husband Hayden Nichols, who was not a Bahá'í, asked her to return to the States from her pioneer post in Portugal, Val wrote to Shoghi Effendi for guidance. It came: "Your first duty is to your husband." Val joined her husband in the States. In a few months, he moved to Portugal with her. They went together to the Yucatan. Hayden became a Bahá'í many years later, as a very old man, to the joy of his faithful wife. Val's example of obedience to the Guardian's instructions was a sure sign for me. To affirm that the decision to follow my duty to my husband was the right one, God gave me a sign. My daughter, Sara, who was conceived and born after I became "inactive" as a Bahá'í, was my first child to become a Bahá'í.

My marriage was not to become a real marriage, ever. We had to break away from each other to find the road we could comfortably travel. When he left me, he also left the Faith. As the Ten Year Crusade ended and The *Universal House of Justice* was elected for the first time, I took off my wedding ring and put on the Bahá'í ring Bert Gottlieb gave me. I remembered only vaguely that he told me how special that ring was and, now, I wanted to find out the history behind it. I wrote to him to ask how he came to have it, and why he gave it to me. A letter came from his community, West-Englewood, saying that Bert had passed away and nobody knew about the ring. This was when the ring of the first American Bahá'í woman, Lua Getsinger, became the most important object I have ever owned. Any time I feel down, at the end of my courage, I just look at her ring to hear her say, "I could not go on, I died too early. Don't you lose your courage!"

During 10 years we tried a few different sets of marriage counsellors. My back was often sore, the doctors prescribed tranquilizers. I would walk around the house, praying, "Make my heart overflow with love for Thy loved ones!" I could go no farther than to circle the house. I was not able to go away from the problems, to gain perspective. I had decided to make Al happy, and was sure of succeeding, with a bit more trying. By the time our second little girl, Sara, arrived, I gave up trying to get answers from counsellors and tried to fit my world into his and concentrate on building a materially comfortable life. If at moments things became unbearable, I went to the doctor and most of the time, a new kind of tranquilizer was prescribed.

News from my family in Hungary was not joyous. My father's condition became worse with each letter. The photo I received a short time before Sara was born showed the family with Apu sitting in front, with his cane, looking as if he were 92, when he was only 62. The last letter he wrote was his answer to Sara's arrival. He ended it saying that he sees now that the conversation he was hoping to have between the two of us would never happen. When I first read it, I took it as I always took his letters, by stealing myself against the hurt. His letters always reproached me for something. A few days later came the news that Apu was taken to the main insane asylum in Budapest. Diagnosis was *paralysis progressiva*. For the first time, it occurred to me that it might be not all my fault that he was never satisfied with me. He died four months later and his last words that I know of were, "I am going to Aranka. Maybe I should have allowed Angéla to marry George."

10 Montréal – Boucherville
1956-1963

I went to see a psychiatrist because I was afraid that I also might end up in an insane asylum. He suggested psycho-analysis. It would have been awfully expensive, besides I didn't have confidence in him. He did not take my faith seriously, considering it a crutch from which psychoanalysis should cure me. Instead of that cure, I convinced Al to take a vacation, the first one since we came to Canada.

We rented a small cabin for a week on a lake near Montréal. Although it was a great strain on our finances, the week was really useful. It gave us a chance to step out of our poverty and to talk a little when the children fell asleep after a good day of water and sunshine. One night we took a boat and went out on the lake. When I proposed the boat ride, I had hoped to re-create the mood of our first conversations, the good ones we used to have after the firesides at Val and Louise's when he walked me home on the fragrant Lisbon streets. Now I met a blank wall when I tried to speak about the goodness God had shown to us. Al made my remarks sound really silly, and when I tried again, it turned into an argument. The next time we had a chance to talk, I started by talking of buying a house. First, Al thought that we could not afford it, but we went through our finances again and the prospect became less impossible, until one day we started looking for a home of our own.

We found it in a new development called Beaurivage Gardens, in Boucherville. While it was being built, we moved to an old house in the village. There we prepared ourselves for the role of new home-owners. Until then Al believed that books alone were important; now the prospect of having a house made him try his hand at something less intellectual. I surprised him with a set of power tools for Christmas and he started building a workbench right away. For next Mother's Day, he let me take his car to pass a day in town. I went to the *Montréal Museum of Fine Arts* to look at an exhibit of Paul-Emile Borduas' paintings and strolled along Sherbrooke Street. In the window of a store I spotted a set of woven lampshades. They were lovely, and expensive. As I looked at them longingly, I remembered the weeping willow in the garden of the old house we were renting. It had long, thin branches touching the ground! I hurried home and made of them our first lampshade.

The farmland on which our split-level was built had no trees. The ground was full of building rubbish when we moved in. At times I worked well after midnight, and soon there was a garden around our house. When winter came, Al made a skating rink on the empty lot next to the house. Sara could hardly walk up and down the stairs, but she managed well on her skates. Kathy and Sandy were by now experts. Tip, born in a land without snow, became an avid fan of all winter sports, skiing taking first place for him.

Al fretted a lot over finances, so I soon decided to take a job. I hired a maid and went to work in Morgan's *Ladies Better Dresses*. Sandy and Kathy were already in school but Sara was only three and I worried about how lonely she might feel when I was at work. To prepare her, we went to the garden and chose a smooth rock and named it *The Lonely Stone.* Sara was to sit on that stone any time she felt lonely. She sat on it three times, then she got accustomed to Rose, who was a loving, kind person.

It was great to meet people. I specially liked to serve old ladies. One of my customers was selling the furniture of her big home because she was moving to a smaller place. I went to see her lovely old home and bought a beautiful mahogany table for 50 dollars and she gave me an old Persian carpet and a cute little rocking chair. I was proud of them until Al looked at what I brought home and declared that I was out of my mind to give money for such junk. The table was too big to be put into the crawl-space. It had to be placed into a corner of our bedroom and became my first writing desk. The carpet and the rocker just joined the boxes of my embroideries, which were by now relegated to the basement.

One nice day a friendly customer, a member of the Molson family, suggested that I apply for work with the *Canadian Handicrafts Guild.* They needed a co-ordinator and I was hired. I enjoyed working with old and new Canadiana and with the volunteer ladies, specially with Alice Lighthall who was enthusiastic and kind and introduced me to Eskimo carvings, to French-Canadian and Indian art from the Atlantic to the Pacific coast of Canada. We prepared the first catalogue and the first exhibition of the Permanent Collection which was the result of the Guild's efforts since 1902. The exhibition was on Ste-Helene's Island and it was a success. But the pay was not good, and Al was fretting on the 15th and 30th of every month. I wanted to make him happy, so I asked for a raise. When it was refused, I left the Guild. Many years later I was shopping at the Peel Street store. The bill was made out and I gave my name. The lady serving asked, "Was it you who organized our filing system?" It was good to know that my work left lasting results. I learned a great deal about Canada's treasures while working there.

Then came *McGill University*. I started by filling in for a young lady who was in charge of the housing arrangements for a congress of geneticists. A few days before the congress started, she left to have her baby. Taking the job was greeted with relief. I had never made housing arrangements before but I am a good organizer and I like a challenge. Geneticists from all over the world came, including the Soviet Union. My sister Emese was then studying at the *University of Moscow* and I mentioned this to the nicest Russian professor. He offered to take something to her. It was the last day of the congress and they were leaving. I did not have time to get anything, so I emptied my little purse, put Emese's name into it and gave it to the kind professor. It took him weeks to track her down. The *University of Moscow* is a huge place. He left messages everywhere until Emese finally got in touch with him, and received the tiny old purse.

Next I applied for a position as secretary to Donald Olding Hebb, the psychologist, who had just published his cell-assembly theory, and was the first non-American president of the *American Psychological Association*. He hired me on condition that I learn to type. I learned and it became a very useful skill. This was 1958, a fascinating time at the Donner Building of *McGill University*. It was the era of the sensory deprivation studies, to find out how brainwashing could be done, research with people on whom Penfield did frontal lobotomy operations, cats with electrodes to measure their intelligence, rats in tranquilizer studies, and conditioning of cockroaches. Hebb experimented with dogs and found that the stupid ones could be trained for exhibitions while the bright ones were too interested in what went on and would not stay put.

I bought my first car so that both Al and I were free to come and go. It was a bottle-green Volkswagen with an open roof and we called it "Simon". The children loved Simon, adored to stand up and stick out their heads in the wind. They fought for the place behind the back seat, which they baptized "the junkyard". We passed our vacations on Cape

Cod and they would have ridden the whole way down with their heads in the wind or sleeping curled up in the junkyard.

At times it frustrated me to see all the separate studies in psychological research, as if there were no connection among them. Of course I talked about my work at home. One day a funny little lady came to see "Mister Professor Hebb". She spoke English with an atrocious Russian accent and when she spoke French, that also sounded Russian. Her name was Dr. Maria Alexandrovna Sergeyeva. She worked as histologist at the *University of Montréal.* She wanted to talk to Hebb about the morphology of the pancreas. At one moment she sounded like a very humble person and in the next she affirmed with assurance that she had found the cure for schizophrenia and mental illness in general. She talked about the second hormonal element of the pancreas which produced – in species starting with the dog – a hormone which regulates the oxygen metabolism, influencing the development of the higher nervous system. She called this hormonal element "vagotonin". She had a friend, Ala Koroleff, who was a Bahá'í. When Ala heard that I worked with Hebb, she asked me to help Sergeyeva. I wanted to help her because I was excited by what she said and hoped that people would look into what she claimed to have found.

"Even if there was only a one percent chance of her being right, it would be important to check it out," I declared at the dinner table. "But somebody has to help her because she does not know how to present her findings."

"Why don't you help her?" asked my Sara.

"Because I am not qualified."

"Why don't you get qualified?" she asked with the clear logic of her eight years.

Several days later, after a specially frustrating day at work, her question popped up in my mind on the drive home. "Why don't you get qualified?" Why don't I? Al thought it a good idea too.

"You used to be good at school." He always had respect for science. I applied to *Sir George Williams College* and got accepted in arts instead of science where I wanted to go. I had no transcripts and I failed the mathematics part of the "mature matric" badly. I never liked mathematics and promptly decided to forget biochemistry and help Sergeyeva by building a better society where everyone would get equal attention, not just the polished academic types.

Maria Sergeyeva is one of those people I look forward to meeting again when I get to the other side of the Gate. She came from a modest Russian family, gained her doctorate in 1925 under the Soviet program. By 1930, having repaid the five years service she owed to the State, she emigrated to Canada. Her heart and mind were highly refined, but she was incompatible with the social dictates of academic circles. She was employed in unglamourous positions, not to become an important contributor to the scientific society of the day. She did play an important part in my life; she inspired my decision to return to school with the aim of gaining a degree. I assumed that a degree would help with the acceptance of Bahá'í ideas in academic circles.

At *Sir George Williams College*, I chose courses such as an overview of French grammar and English composition. Al wanted to be helpful and told me to use the course to learn English composition and not for saving the world.

"Just practise it, like fencing." I tried to follow his advice and failed the first exam. Then I failed the second.

For the third exam, we had to choose from several topics, among them was "Education". I chose that one and started out by practising. I listed all the benefits of education, like progress, better health, etc. Then I slipped in, "Education on the world scale will bring better understanding among peoples and will result in world peace." Our instructor – God bless her wherever she may be! – put a big red circle around that sentence and marked in the margin, "This is your main thought, why don't you elaborate?" She gave me a passing

104

mark. My marks improved as I expressed more and more of my interests.

Al and I were certainly at the opposite ends of the spectrum. He worried about money, I wanted to make everybody happy, most of all, him. He believed in Bertrand Russell and I wanted him to believe in God, to trust, to become confident about tomorrow.

There was a red rose bush in our front yard, which did not bring any flowers in the first year. He wanted to throw it out. I pleaded. The rose was spared and gave us the most beautiful crop of roses the following year. I thought he would remember and see that patience brings results. But he had forgotten last year and was worrying about that day's problems.

One day we were on our way to visit his parents, when things became unbearable for me. I tried to sit quietly next to him on the front seat. He drove too fast for my comfort. I was not brought up like he was, in a country with many cars. Sitting in a fast-going car with a baby in my arms, I had what people call a back-seat driver's psychosis. This time I felt the fear in my throat and stomach. I tried to control it, but he said one too many harsh words. I asked him to stop the car and let me out. It was a warm summer day. I wore a skirt and a blouse. In my pocket I had only two quarters. No papers, no pocketbook, and on the highway somewhere in New England. I started walking and rain began falling. I kept walking in the rain and it felt good. The more it rained and the more I walked, the better I felt – free and clean. I had done all sorts of things to please Al that went against my grain. I never thought of how I liked doing things; my aim was to please him. This could not go on forever. As I walked in that rain, freed from a stressful situation, a car stopped and offered a ride. It took three rides to reach the house of my parents-in-law. I got there before Al and the children. I tried to tell my mother-in-law what had happened, trying to make it humorous. She cut me short: "We don't discuss things like that."

105

What was even more significant, Al and I did not discuss it either. We did not know how to communicate, and by that time we did not even try.

We played tennis at times with the children. One morning Al challenged me to a game. When the score was 4 to 0 to his advantage, I finally noticed that he was out to beat me. He was not simply playing, winning was somehow going to "prove" something. I gathered myself and said to myself, "No, sir!" and put my best into the game. Soon we were at 4:4, then 5:5, 6:6 and when we reached 10:10, Al threw his racket to the ground.

"I shall never play with you again."

I think that the fatal blow to our marriage was the joyful news I brought home one day. Dr. Wallace Lambert, a social psychologist, then at *McGill*, was working on the effect of bilingualism on attitudes. When he heard that I was continuing my studies, he asked how I would like to do my master's with him working on peace research. I flew home that evening, burst into the house.

"Al! Wally Lambert wants me to do peace research with him!" A silence greeted my joy.

"What are we going to have for supper?" he asked.

By that time we had no maid. We let her go as fast as the salary could be saved. Our finances were getting into a fair shape but my back was not. I worked a full day at *McGill*, went to school at night and took care of the house. I tried to ignore the pain, but it was getting very bad. One Sunday morning I was ironing Al's shirts in the basement when the pain grew so intense that I doubled over the ironing board and stopped working. Al was not home. When he arrived, I asked him to take me to the hospital. On the way to the Neurological Institute, where they operated on my back, he asked how he should take care of the children should I die. I said that I would like him to marry a nice person to be a good mother to them. I had no idea that he had already chosen her.

106

11 Boucherville
1963-1964

The surgeon took out of my spine a herniated disc. He called it "a dried-out stick". On the evening of the operation I got up and could stand for the first time in months without pain flooding my legs. Soon I was well enough to go out to shop. Sandy, my faithful helper, walked with me for protection. As I walked, carefully watching my steps, I held a conversation with myself about that morning.

We were in the kitchen having breakfast, the children and I, in a calm, nice atmosphere around the table. When Al came down, he noticed that the air turned tense.

"You see that you are happier without me? I have to leave."

"Oh Al, you know that we all love you!" I said as I did so often.

Now, on my walk, I was ruminating about marriage and found myself saying to myself, "The success of a marriage is a question of faith. If both have faith in it and work on it, it will succeed. If only one believes in it, no matter how strong that belief may be, he can break his back, he will not succeed." I stopped, staring at the crack in the sidewalk. It dawned on me that I had just broken my back. It was probably my son walking with me that gave me the strength to finally allow my brain to accept the fact that Al wanted to leave me. When we got home, I called him at work and asked if he really meant it. When he said, "yes", I asked if he had made enquiries about the possibility of divorce. No, he had not. Would he like me to enquire? Yes, he would. He came home, packed and left that evening. One of the things he took was his tennis racket. He specially came back for it.

When a good friend heard that our marriage had ended, he said, "I am going to ask you something I wanted to ask 15 years ago, when I first met you. What made you marry Al?" I could only say that I thought that it was meant to be.

We were, of course, not prepared for his departure. I was far from well, but there was nothing else to do but cope.

Tip tried to fill in the role of a father as he imagined it should be done. He started fretting about everything. I had a talk with him and Tip decided to move to town. He had a good job as a salesman with *Algoma Steel.* Before leaving, he made two pieces of furniture he felt we needed. When he came to visit, he stopped trying to play father and became a good big brother and a helpful son.

We brought up the old Persian carpet from the basement, spread it before the television and the children had their lunches on it, watching Johnny Jelly Beans. They were never too keen on television and I did not encourage it either, but those funny programs acted as a soothing balm and, breaking our routine, made things more like a holiday than a family tragedy. The piano, the canoe, and Ruby made the transition complete.

The piano entered our house a short time before my operation forced me to leave the job with D.O. Hebb. He heard me say during a coffee break that Kathy would like to take piano lessons and that I wished I could buy a piano for her.
108

He asked if I really wanted a piano and I said yes, "but I could not afford it."

"If you take care of transportation, you are welcome to mine." He was then moving to a smaller home, and was happy to see that the fine piano would be useful. Al thought that we did not have a place for it, but the rest of the family won out this time and the piano moved into our living room. A French piano teacher had just moved into the next street and Kathy started taking lessons. Sometimes when I went to get her at the end of her lessons, the teacher asked me to sing. We passed a few wonderful evenings that way. Singing always lifts my drooping soul.

We bought a canoe as soon as school was out, put it on top of Simon and headed for a lake on Mount St. Hilaire. Sandy was 14 years old, Kathy, twelve, and Sara, nine. They were all good swimmers and I could trust them with the canoe. I swam a bit but mostly relaxed watching them from my blanket laid out in the shade.

Then Ruby entered to complete our life as a new kind of a family. Ruby was an Irish setter, a baby Irish setter. Her mother, Sally, belonged to Celeste McCoullough, a psychologist from *Oberlin College*, Ohio, doing a year's research at *McGill*.

Celeste became a good friend of the family just as Al left us. My kids loved her and her beautiful dog. Ron Pritchard, from England, also working at *McGill*, had a purebred male Irish setter. Celeste wanted to let Sally have puppies, but she lived in an apartment in Montréal, not an ideal place even for Sally, a grown dog. I offered to bring up her puppies and we got Ruby out of the deal. It makes children happy if they can love seven tiny, but fast growing Irish setters.

I was of course brokenhearted. After trusting for 15 years that tomorrow everything would be happy around me, facing the end of a dream was painful. I felt like a failure and kept on thinking of how and where I could have done better. Instead of becoming angry with Al, I felt sorry for him, and angry with myself for letting him down. One Sunday afternoon Kathy was practising on the piano while I was listening from my room. The sounds came upstairs, softly, lovely, and a wave of great sadness flooded me.

"Poor Al, missing all this! How happy it would make him to listen to Kathy now!" Even after he left me for another woman, I still worried whether he was happy or not. I gave him a call and he came right away. But hearing Kathy play music was not what Al missed. The passionate way he acted made me call the girl to whose home he had moved, and I asked her whether she loved him.

"Yes, I do, and we will get married as soon as he is free." This relaxed me. If she loves him, she will be able to make him happier than I could. I told Al that hopefully I had given him enough experience to help him become a good husband for his second wife. I made sure that she knew when the divorce was declared. I sent the children to their wedding and wished them happiness.

As a woman, I was quite a misfit, but I always did well at school. Even then, and over 40 years old, I found learning easy. Sandy was a great help. He was often on the front lawn when I came home from school, waiting to see if I was well. We had a warm snack and a short chat before going to sleep. At the end of August a small knot was found in one of my breasts, resulting in the removal of the whole breast and surrounding tissues. It was probably an unnecessary operation as no cancerous cells were found in the mass that was removed. I did not consult anybody else when a doctor said that the simplest thing was to remove everything. I guess I wanted to suffer, to be punished for not being a "good" wife.

Sandy was away on a trip to Washington with Celeste. When they left, I was getting better and stronger each day. When they came back, he found me in the hospital with another operation. Until then Sandy felt that he could help me. He then realized that my troubles were too much for him. He stopped acting responsible for me, but he did give me the most beautiful compliment I ever remember receiving. He

110

told me that he and Tip were both happy that I was in such good spirits.

"We were wondering how this will affect you, after all, you are a woman. You know, Mom, I think that this might be good for you in the long run. It is going to keep the riff-raff away from you. If a man ever falls in love with you, he will love the real you and not a woman with beautiful breasts." To get that from my 14-year-old son!

The winter was busy with school and survival for all of us. Then the boys had an accident with Simon, our faithful Volkswagen. Their wounds were superficial, but there was a lot of blood, specially on Sandy's face. He was sitting on his bed when I arrived home from the office, his face covered with big stitches on bloody scars. I can still feel the sting of pity and admiration that filled my heart as I looked at him, my big, little boy. He looked so brave and so lost! He needed a father so badly. I tried to replace his father by being strong. How I wish now that instead of trying to replace his father, I had been a more loving mother! This way he "lost" both father and mother. Somehow we limped through the rest of the year.

Next summer Mother came to visit from Budapest. My brother Attila arrived in Canada in 1957 with his wife and little girl and they became quite well established. They arranged for Mother to come. She came with one suitcase but there were pictures painted by Anyuka in it. As I stood above her while she unpacked, my eyes beheld a green crystal vase, my favourite vase! My stepmother whom I thought of as a rather cold person, had found place in her heart during all these years of war and fleeing, with small children and sick husband, carrying all their belongings on a truck during one night, to save that fragile thing, because she knew that I loved it!

She had a cousin living in Québec City, whom she wanted to visit. I offered to drive her, saying that this would give me a chance to visit *Laval University.*

"I should really look into *Laval* before leaving Canada." I was considering leaving Canada for the United States, because I did not think that I could find a university here where I could continue my studies and earn a living at the same time. I wanted to study either social psychology or political science.

I drove Mother to Québec City. I phoned the department of political science at *Laval University.* The secretary, Vincent Lemieux was apologetic about the condition of their building, but invited me to call on him. The *Laval* campus was new, some of it was still in construction. The stairs in *Pavilion de Koninck* were not finished, only the steel frame was in place. To go up to the third floor, people usually took the elevators, but when I arrived the electricity was out, so I had to use the unfinished staircase.

Half way between two floors, where I had to turn, I suddenly realized that I was living one of my recurring nightmares. Like many, I had dreams that would come back again and again. In one of the worst ones I found myself in a high spot, going up on slopes or stairs, suddenly all support disappeared, leaving me afraid that I was going to fall. Now I was going up on stairs without railings, no support whatsoever! As I realized it, I took a deep breath, called God's name, turned and, looking ahead, walked up the rest of the way. I never had that nightmare again. I realized later that I had to walk stairs without railings all my life, going up, up on roads without knowing for sure that I shall not fall. There were no railings to hold on to. The roads I walked were not marked out by tradition or example. The world into which my parents were born disappeared before I was born. I was accustomed to not knowing for sure about tomorrow, because I never tasted a secure today. My security was not in the protection of railings, but in the help from Above. I always found the world under my feet, because I hung on to the security that comes from There.

Vincent Lemieux received me kindly and wanted to know what made me decide to go back to school at my age. I told him that I wanted people to pay more attention to what I had to say. I wanted to get a doctorate with a thesis about the *World Order of Bahá'u'lláh*. For the present, I wanted to study the partyless political systems of North America.

"What do you mean by partyless political systems?" I explained that I would like to study the way Indians and Eskimos organized their communities, because there must be something in their traditional ways that made them able to quickly grasp the Bahá'í message. He asked what that message was, and I told him about the Faith. I was not trying to show a good face to a prospective teacher as I was not thinking of Laval as a possible school for myself. I just answered his questions.

When I got up to take my leave, Lemieux walked me to the elevator, working by then, and said, "I hope that you will decide to come to Laval." I could not believe my ears. A serious scholar, wanting me to study at his university after hearing about all the dreams I had! He did not laugh. He wanted me to come to their school! I drove home on a cloud. God! If I could afford it!

When we entered the house, the phone was ringing. It was a woman and she called to say that she would like to buy the house. It had been up for sale for some time but nobody showed any interest. If this woman buys it, I can go to *Laval*, I thought, and sent an application to the department of political science of *Laval University*. By the time the answer arrived, I was so convinced of the rightness of that move that I decided to move to Québec even if *Laval* did not accept me. Laval did accept, but the woman backed out of buying the house. It did not frighten me. I knew that the Faith needed people in that region, and that I could take a job to earn our living.

Mother spent most of her visit with Attila, but she wanted to visit us in our new home before going back to Hungary. I discussed this idea with Baba néni, the wife of Mother's cousin. I was under enormous pressure and felt that I could not bear Mother to stay with us for another visit because we could not discuss problems I would so much have liked to talk over with her. Baba néni gave me a talking-to, she told me that I should think about Mother's happiness. There might be no other chance for me to be kind to her. She was sure that I was up to it. Of course, that was the right kind of talk, and the result showed it. Mother passed a few days with us. The children enjoyed her and vice versa.

When the time for departure arrived, I went to a florist to buy half-a-dozen roses. The florist had only five left, but they were nice, so I bought them. I settled Mother in the train, gave her the box with the roses, kissed her good-bye and left.

As I was about to leave the station, I looked at the clock and saw that there were 15 minutes before the train was to leave. I decided not to let her sit alone. I went back to be with her all the time we could pass together. As I came in through the back of the coach, she was sitting with her back to me. When I reached her, she was looking at the roses in her lap. She looked up with tears in her eyes and whispered, "You remembered that he used to give me five roses!"

I never told her that I had asked the florist for half-a-dozen.

12 Québec 1964-1966

By the time we moved to Québec, I knew that the woman would not buy the house so I would have to find a job. It was the first time that I became a teacher, a regular teacher in a school, teaching English in a commercial high school in Levis, across from Québec City, on the other side of the St-Lawrence River. The school was run by nuns and the directrice was Mother Ste-Solange, a tiny woman with great energy and a broad mind. What she did to earn my admiration was to ask me to give an hour a week of "general education" in each class where I taught English. During that hour the students could ask anything they wanted and I could answer their questions in any way I saw fit. There was no sign of anxiety or distrust about the way we used that hour. At times we used it to learn Hungarian dances. There must still be a few French-Canadian girls around who dance the *csárdás* as well as any born Hungarian. They asked about my religion and I answered honestly, without any bad consequences.

I have taught people embroidery and knitting and basket-weaving, but I have never been a professor in front of a class before.

Sandy said to me on the morning of the first day of my teaching career: "It might look frightening at first, but you will make out alright. I shall be thinking of you." My day went well, I felt at home in front of these classes of teenage girls, as if I had been a teacher all my life. Maybe it was the blood of generations of teachers in my veins, maybe it was the thought of an understanding son that made me feel like a happy fish, back in water.

Now, for the first time, we lived in a predominantly French-Canadian society, and we felt at home right away. There must be strings in the hearts of Hungarians and French-Canadians that vibrate in the same chord. The family of Mother's cousin was there too. They were really aunt and uncle and cousins to us, even if it was only through a distant relationship via my stepmother. It is the feeling that counts, and there was much warm feeling when Baba néni served us a dish of cabbage rolls in sweet tomato sauce.

One Sunday we ate lunch at their house. The previous evening I had attended a *Moral Rearmament* meeting with their daughter. She asked over lunch what I thought of the meeting. I said that I liked much of it, even if it was clear that this philosophy would not bring the hoped-for peace.

"What will bring it about? Bahá'u'lláh?" The mocking tone in which she asked it made my insides curl up into a knot. I had to dash out to the bathroom to have a quick cry. On the way home, along a deserted road, my tears were flowing and I cried out, "I am alone, alone as a Bahá'í!"

We were the northernmost Bahá'ís in the Province of Québec at that time. Bill and Priscilla Waugh and a few friends were in Beloeil and Barney Legault operated a radio station in the Arctic. Québec City only had a short visit from Mary Zabolotny (later Mrs. Kenneth McCulloch) some time before our arrival. When we arrived, on July 14, 1964, we were the first Bahá'í family to settle there.

After that cry of loneliness, I was changing when the doorbell rang. Sara went to answer and I heard a woman's voice say that they were Bahá'ís and they had come to stay. It was Gloria Wenk, from Bute, Montana, arriving with a jeep, three sons and four mattresses. TO STAY! Standing around the kitchen table, staring at each other in amazement, Gloria, Conal, Neal, Stephane, Sara and I, my tears again flowed. Little Stephane looked at me and asked what was wrong. I told him that there are times when I cry for joy. They moved into the apartment across from ours that very afternoon.

The children went to Québec High School and were happy with their teachers and schoolmates. Our house was open to their friends and I became a surrogate mother to some. It is at times easier to talk to somebody else's mother. Sandy was very good in math and helped some of his friends overcome their feelings of incompetence. The greatest joy for me as a mother and teacher was to find that my children could surpass me. Kathy followed in my footsteps as a good gymnast. She was in all the athletic games and came home with medals and ribbons. But she was happiest teaching swimming and as camp counsellor. Some girls who felt lost at camp gave her the name *goutte de rosée* ("dew-drop"), she was so good with them. Sara was also good in gym, but her speciality turned out to be drama. Her impersonation of the seductive girl in rags in *Li'l Abner* was quite convincing.

Ruby, by then a big Irish setter, was the only member of the family who was not happy with our move to Québec. She started out by running into a car, breaking her leg, then walking around with a big white cast for weeks, showing it off like a prima donna, making sad faces. She became addicted to garbage cans. That "aristocrat of all dogs", as Sergeyeva called Irish setters, was poking into everybody's garbage can looking for chicken bones. The police soon knew her well; they had to bring her to the same address again and again.

Tip came to visit often. He was now a successful salesman and a member of the *Canadian Ski Patrol*. One day he
came to consult about a letter he intended to hand in next
day. He felt that he could learn everything there was to learn
in his company and if he did, he might end up becoming
vice-president. Yet, he did not think that would be worth his
life. He resigned and became a full-time ski-patrol at the newly
opened *Mount Ste-Anne*.

There he had a never-to-be-forgotten experience. He
brought a man back from death by administering mouth-to-
mouth resuscitation. He saw him collapse and realized that it
was a heart attack. He started working on him right away, but
the heart stopped and Tip heard the doctor declare him dead.
He went on breathing, at double rate. After some time, that
seemed very long, he felt tiny pangs. Timid, uneven, then
they got stronger, and finally the heart was beating strong
enough for a friend to take over until the ambulance arrived.
Tip faded out from the effort.

The man said to Tip a few days later, "I hear you did
me a good turn." That was sweet, the award he got was sweet,
but for Tip nothing could surpass the glory of those first timid
pangs. When I asked how he knew that a person who died
with a heart attack could be brought back by mouth-to-mouth
resuscitation, he said that he did not know, he had never heard
about a case before.

"What made you keep on after the doctor declared
him dead?"

"I don't know, I just had to do it." When the skiing
season was over in Québec, he left for Aspen, Colorado, but
not for the fashionable slopes. He took a job at a picture frame
shop where there was a piano everybody who entered the store
was welcome to play. When that work ended, he crossed the
States with his old car, heading for the Pacific Coast. One day
we received a box from the Nevada Desert. It was closed tight
with black masking tape, and neatly filled with white tissue
paper to protect two cactus leaves. I wonder if anybody ever
118

thought of picking cactus leaves to send back to the family in Québec... From the Pacific Coast he headed north. The next letter came from Dawson, in the Yukon. He was washing dishes in a hotel and his love affair with the Yukon had begun.

At *Laval University*, I was the same age as most of my classmates' parents, but this made our contacts easier in a way. There were many things I wanted to know from them, and they wanted to ask me many questions. The professors were interesting. The atmosphere at *Laval* was pleasant, with students from abroad, some of the professors too. I felt that the centre of French education had shifted from Europe to Canada, from the crowded, traditional schools to the open, spacious, promising vistas of the yet unknown.

Dr. Gerard Bergeron, who became my thesis-advisor, asked what I would like to write my thesis on. I told him that I would like to write my doctoral thesis on the *World Order of Bahá'u'lláh*. For the master's, I had three ideas to choose from: first, a study of the partyless political systems of Canada, meaning the first nations' governing methods; second, a sketch of the central concept of political psychology, meaning mentality; third, I proposed to review Emeric Sala's book, *This Earth One Country*. He went through the material I gave him and called me to his office. He said that he was deviating from his habit of allowing his students to choose their topics, because he wanted me to write my master's thesis about the political proposals of Bahá'u'lláh.

"You are acquainted with that and we are not. That will be your best contribution." I went home and started shaking in my boots. When I told Gloria that I was overwhelmed by the responsibility of presenting the Faith, when I knew so little about it, she suggested that I write to the *National Spiritual Assembly of the Bahá'ís of Canada* for guidance. Greatly relieved, I wrote to the NSA that my advisor at *Laval University* wanted me to write a thesis under the title, *The Political Proposals of Bahá'u'lláh*. The answer came that *The Universal House of Justice* wanted me to change the title, to avoid possible mis-

119

interpretations, and that the *National Spiritual Assembly* had appointed one of its members to help me.

I changed the title to *A Proposed World Order; Bahá'í Teachings and Institutions,* and started working on the first draft. When I finished, I mailed the 55 pages to my Bahá'í advisor, asking him to correct all he saw fit, adding that I had to hand in my draft by June 15.

Gloria was not yet working. She chose the Writings for our Feasts. It was uncanny how exactly they fitted the questions asked at *Laval!* I only had to mark the references. Had I been a seasoned Bahá'í and a self-assured person, I would have been confident in knowing that Bahá'u'lláh does not give you a job without supplying the tools to do it. I was neither a seasoned Bahá'í nor an assured person, so as June 15 neared, I worried, wishing the opinion of my Bahá'í advisor would arrive. Instead, a call came from Montréal, from Emeric and Rosemary Sala.

The Salas had pioneered in Africa since 1953. The last time I saw them was in the summer of 1957, in the middle of my 10 years' inactivity and the middle of the Ten Year Crusade for people lucky enough to serve the Faith in one of its goals. They were passing a few days in Montréal and asked me to meet them at the Maxwell House, which later became the Shrine.

Walking back and forth on the terrace, Emeric asked a question, "What do you think is the problem in the Faith at the moment?" I knew that his question meant that he wanted to tell me something, so I asked what he thought was wrong.

"Personality cult," he said, and I agreed. What we meant by this was the love and adoration that was showered on the person of Shoghi Effendi, the Guardian, without following his directions. When a few months later the Guardian died, Emeric and I were of course moved, but neither of us was disturbed. We knew that Shoghi Effendi always did what had to be done for the Faith. The Faith of Bahá'u'lláh is in sure hands. We Bahá'ís are like children coming out of the dark ages, looking into the light with eyes that are not yet accustomed to its brilliance. The Covenant is our solid guide; we have to trust and serve it.

The Covenant is the pact between God and man. "If you want to be happy, follow My commandments." For us, as Bahá'ís, it translates into a clear pattern of authority. We always know where the immediate guidance comes from. Those who did not accept the guidance of 'Abdu'l-Bahá, who was appointed by Bahá'u'lláh to be the Centre of the Covenant at His passing, instead of forming a sect or branch of the Faith, as happened after the death of previous Messengers, became Covenant-breakers, eliminating themselves from among the believers. The Bahá'í Faith is sent to unite mankind, and is equipped to do so. 'Abdu'l-Bahá appointed Shoghi Effendi to be the Guardian of the Faith to whom all were to turn at the passing of the Master. For me the letters of Shoghi Effendi were the sure confirmation of the divine origin of the Faith I embraced. In exquisite, unique English, he acted as the general who sends his troops to conquer the planet. Not for the joy of conquest, but because this is what will bring unity, peace and security to a much-suffered mankind.

Emeric and Rosemary always appeared when I most needed human hands to hold. Now, in June 1965, they wanted me to go down to Montréal, to pass an afternoon with them. Sure, I would go, specially if Emeric could look through the draft I had to hand in at *Laval* in a few days! He corrected three spots and said that my thesis was the continuation of his book and that he liked it quite a bit. With that assurance, I typed up the draft and handed it in on June 15. When I came home from the university, a big envelope was waiting. My draft, with the opinion of the Bahá'í advisor that it could not be done that way.

Now I was really anxious to hear Professor Bergeron's opinion. It came and it was most encouraging. He was anxious to see more, because he found the proposals far ahead of anything then known in political science.

"Don't hold back! Je vous impose (I order you) not to hold back what can be of help to future political scientists," he said on May 20. "I see that you have to become two people: a believer and a political scientist. You have no right to hold back. This is a somewhat special thesis. Go ahead!"

He suggested that I bridge the gap with a review of the literature about the utopists. I did what he suggested, reviewed *Precursors of International Organization*, by Laszlo Ledermann, another Hungarian! Then he wanted a chapter added on the history of the Faith, on the Báb, Bahá'u'lláh, 'Abdu'l-Bahá and Shoghi Effendi. When that was done, he wanted a chapter with quotations from the Writings. Then he was satisfied.

On the 7th of November, Gerard Bergeron, devoted Catholic, author of *A Theory of the State*, wrote: "It does meet our standards! G.B."

This made me of course happy, but at the same time I was awfully embarrassed, because I didn't know what to do about the opinion of my Bahá'í advisor. For a time I did not write to him at all about the good news from *Laval*. Had I been a more mature Bahá'í, I would have thanked him for doing his best to help me. I would have apologized for having asked him to give his opinion without hearing the questions I was asked and had to answer. On the other hand, I would have thanked Bahá'u'lláh for not allowing the negative opinion to reach me before I handed in my draft!

At Laval, good things were coming my way. The *Rotary Foundation of Québec* recommended me to the *International Rotary Foundation* for a scholarship in international understanding, and I was awarded a year of post-doctoral studies at the university of SãoPaulo, Brazil. How strange that the *International Rotary Foundation*, with headquarters on Sheridan Road, Evanston, Illinois, across from the headquarters of the *National Spiritual Assembly of the Bahá'ís of the United States,* which is on the Wilmette side of Sheridan Road, should send me to Brazil to promote understanding among people!

Things happen to many of us that make us look up and say "Thank you!" We say thank you of course to God, but it does not mean that we expect God, personally, to speak to us or arrange things to our convenience. Bahá'ís use the term, "Supreme Concourse", signifying those who have gone on to the next world and help us, if our steps are moving this ever-advancing civilization closer to its God-intended goal. Many of us have experiences when we feel a guiding hand, or hear a voice directing us. It is the wisdom and power of love which are aware of us and want to help us, if we just listen. Even if we cannot see those who have left the world of space and time behind, they can pray for us, as we pray for them. I feel great awe and gratitude in such moments. One of these moments was in connection with the trip to Brazil.

I was working in the library of the university one day during the Christmas holidays and met one of my colleagues, looking for information on scholarships. I helped her locate those that would interest her and, out of curiosity, looked up others that might interest me. I made a few notes on a slip of paper. When I got home, I put the paper on my desk and forgot about it.

One morning the following spring, during the Fast, I think it was March 8, I woke up before daybreak, hearing a Voice say, "Get in touch with the *Rotary*!" It was still pitch-dark but I got out of bed, went to my desk and at once found the notes taken last December. Among the awards listed was one offered by the *International Rotary Foundation*. I could hardly wait for morning to call the *Rotary Club of Québec*.

Gustave Baudry, president of the *Rotary Foundation* said that it was a pity that I did not call earlier because the deadline for applications was March 15, so close that there was no hope I could make it. Besides, they usually gave scholarships to unmarried men, between the ages of 20-30. When I told him that I was then working on my thesis which deals with world order and world peace, he asked me to send a copy to him. He added, "After all, miracles do happen."

A miracle did happen this time. Monsieur Baudry, a devout Catholic, found my work "the most catholic thing he ever read." I ended up with an award for a year in the department of political science of the *University of São Paulo*, Brazil. I chose São Paulo from among the many places to which I could have gone because I speak Portuguese, and because of the similarity between São Paulo and Québec. They are both old parts of their respective continents, developed before the rest and they are both proud of being different. Winning that award was a source of pride to both *Laval University* and to the *Rotarians of Québec*. It was the first time anybody from *Laval* had won it, and the fact that I was a middle-aged woman, with children, a very unlikely candidate, made it all the more remarkable.

I found contact with the *Rotary Club* extremely interesting. This was the first time I had been in touch with a service club and I found it uplifting to exchange with them, solid business people, wanting to help the ideals to which I dedicated my life. The award was announced in November 1965, to take effect in early 1967, so we had time to prepare.

13 Hungary
Summer 1966

The first step in my preparation was a big one; a trip back to Hungary. When I left in 1941, I thought that I was to be away for three months. Now, 25 years later, I went home for a short visit of three weeks. Every day of those weeks was planned by Mother who got in touch with family and friends and was waiting with a schedule that left no time to ask what I should do next. My closest friends from school gathered to celebrate my homecoming. Cousins, uncles and aunts expected me for meals in Budapest and in Kecskemét.

I saw Mother last when she visited us just two years earlier. She had not changed much since then. But my sister Emese was not even in kindergarten when I last saw her. Now she was a university professor. Hajnalka, who was a toddler, was a librarian in the *Ministry of Education.* My brother Ákos was an impossible nuisance when I left. Now he took me by the arm to go for a walk. We walked along streets that had not changed as much as I had expected, only that there were bullet holes on houses and some houses were not there at all.

Ákos had a special purpose in taking me for a walk. He did not beat around the bush. There was something he wanted to clarify.

"You know, Angéla, as well as I do, that our father was positive toward me and negative toward you. Do you agree?" I did and he continued.

"What I want to know is this: is the result of his negativity positive or negative for you?"

I had to think about it for a while, then I answered, "Positive."

"And for me it is negative." And we walked on, feeling at peace with each other. When he was 12, he kicked me in the nose and I got bawled out for having made him angry. That was a still burning memory of being treated unjustly. He must have felt badly about it too, and he now made his peace with me. We had grown up. It was good to be walking with my brother. It was comforting to see that my memories were not just imagined, like a dream or a wishful thinking. I really have roots. This was important to feel before I went off to South America, a new continent for me.

I went to visit my beloved Gizi néni. She was father's sister, the aunt who shared the cattle car with us and nursed me when my mother had little milk. Now she was a retired professor in Kőszeg, a lovely old town near the Austrian border. We walked in the garden of the Lyceum where I last visited her nearly 30 years earlier. She was known as a lover of birds, especially wounded birds. People would bring her birds with broken legs or wings and she would nurse them until they were well, then let them go. Some birds did not want to leave her. Now she was nearly blind but she noticed a bag of discarded potatoes in a garbage can by a door. She stopped, looked at the pale shoots growing out of the eyes of those withered old potatoes.

"They would so much like to be in the earth!" she said, with her compassion for all living things. As we entered the gate of the Lyceum, I noticed the cord of the bell hanging as it did those many years ago. That cord! I could not stop myself, I had to give it a tug. The ringing of the bell went through the old buildings as it did when I was a child. I guess neither of us changed much with age.

I went to find the place in Kecskemét where our house used to stand. In the bus, I asked people directions. The area looked totally different. The bus, of course, was new too. A woman said she was going that way and would show it to me. We got off, and had walked for a while when she turned to me.

"Are you Angéla?" I asked her name. It was unknown to me. She explained that they moved from Transylvania ten years ago. So, she had never met me, only through what she heard from her neighbours. We reached her house, she pointed toward the spot I was looking for, where our house used to stand, and asked me to wait a minute. She came back with a bouquet of flowers from her garden.

"Would you like them for the cemetery?" It seems that I had become somewhat of a legend around there. The house was of course gone. I did not expect it to be there either. In fact, I did not expect to find anything besides memories, but I did find a lot more.

I found the Emperor pear tree, the one in the branches of which I used to read. I thought that the tree was very old when I was a child! I found it full of beautiful big pears, as if it were saying, "I am glad you finally came! Why did you take so long?"

I found the street corner where the policeman stopped me one day as I was going to school. He reached into his pocket and took out a brooch I inherited from Anyuka.

"I am quite sure that this is yours. It was found on the sidewalk here." I hadn't even noticed that I had dropped it.

I went to the cemetery, to visit my mother's grave and put the unknown woman's flowers on it. I found it double size and a second white marble tombstone with my father's name. The bench was not there anymore, so I just stood there for a while.

127

14   São Paulo, Brazil
1967

Before departure for São Paulo two important things happened to us in Québec. The first one was Sandy's leaving for Europe, the other was a seminar in world religions at the department of theology of *Laval University.*

Sandy finished high school and was not set in his mind on a course of study. I believe in travel to give direction for one's thinking, so I encouraged him to take time for a trip to Europe. Tip was by then working in a new asbestos mine at Clinton Creek, Yukon. Sandy went up to Clinton Creek and in 10 weeks earned all the money he needed. He bought his plane tickets and a Eurailpass to travel all over Europe, and I drove my bear cub to the airport. Calling him "my bear cub" was showing how I felt about letting him go out into the big wide world all by himself, at 17. In Walt Disney's charming little film about "Nature's Half Acre", a mother bear decides that her two-year-old cubs should be ready to start fending for themselves and she leaves them. The cubs are frightened and confused. They want to go after their mother but she chases them up a tree and goes away leaving them alone. I wanted Sandy to see the world, but I felt anxious about how he would make out. Was he ready for it? I wanted to be a strong mother, but it felt awful to let him go. I gave him a small book, a collection of photos of Rodin's statues, and kissed him good-bye.

The seminar at *Laval* was an extraordinary experience. A group of priests and teachers who taught religion in schools around Québec wanted to study the great religions of the world. I was hired by Dr. René Barbin, a Jesuit, director of the *Institut de Cathechese* of the Department of Theology, to be their leader. We studied all the major world religions and finished the semester with an authentic religious experience using the Qur'án, the holy book of Islam.

I marked out a prayer, the Moslem equivalent to the Lord's Prayer, and enough passages for about 20 minutes. The group kept on reading even after they reached the end of the marked passages. They went on and on, for quite some time. When they had their fill, they sat, thinking for a while in silence, then they got up and walked around the grounds in front of the Institute, meditating. The way they entered into the spirit of that "strange religion" surpassed my expectation. For Christmas they gave me a three-tiered gift, symbolizing the trinity aspect found in all major religions. There was a beautiful oriental teapot, because of the tea ceremonies of the East, a pottery pendant with the goddess Minerva in all her armament, with her snake, the symbol of wisdom and not of sin! On top, there was a card on which each student wrote a sentence from sacred texts, with the same meaning as the Christian Gospel's "Love thy neighbour as thyself". The card showed the Québec harbour in winter with boats locked in, surrounded by ice. My students explained that they chose that card because the boats were waiting for spring, the ice to melt, and to let them take those messages of love all over the world.

One of the students, a Redemptorist father, a missionary to Japan, gave me a small Japanese ceramic pigeon which was really a whistle, and told me to blow it in time of need. He also gave me the address of a friend in São Paulo, with a letter of introduction. He came to the airport to see us off, to take photos of our departure and to lend his shoulder to Tip to cry on, when our plane disappeared in the sky.

Angéla – February 4, 1967
Québec Airport on the way to São Paulo.
"Mom's on her way" wrote Tip on it.

Tip came back to Québec to take over our furniture and household things. He rented an apartment where I had tea with him before driving to the airport. I was exhausted as one usually is before a trip. Tip handed me a cup of tea, I looked around and found his living room lovely.

"It is nice to be surrounded by beauty that was not created by me." He responded, without a second of hesitation, "It was created by you, mother."

He sobbed like a child when he saw our plane take off. There we were in that parting plane, Kathy 15, Sara 12 and I, 47. Sandy was somewhere in Europe. It was February 4,1967, and our family was now strewn over three continents.

The girls had never seen real poverty before and I had never met the effects of colonialism. Brazil was a terrible shock to us. From the luxurious airport we were driven through a devastatingly poor district to reach our hotel where liveried footmen enquired what we would be pleased to consume before going to sleep. I fell asleep fast, but the girls told me later that they were awake for some time, discussing whether they should try to go back to Canada right away or jump out the window and die. They had just met the other half of the world and they were appalled.

Next morning I met a part of my inner world I was not aware of. I woke up from a dream in which I was speaking Portuguese! It meant that my subconscious mind is conscious of where I am and that I am a multilingual person. This explained why I had not forgotten languages even when I did not use them for years.

The first person in São Paulo with whom we got in touch, besides the Rotarians waiting for us at the airport and taking us to the hotel, was Frère Alfredo Lamy, the friend whose address my Redemptorist student gave me. Frère Alfredo made all the difference to the girls. In him they found a friend. He became like a father to them. They could visit him in his office in *Escola Cor Jesu* (Sacred Heart School) and through him they met nice Brazilian girls. He helped us find an apartment and to furnish it. When I ran out of money, he asked me to teach a course in his school.

Kathy entered a school run by American nuns for children of rich Brazilian families. She was horrified by the snobbish teachers and students. Sara went to the school of the Rotary Club of São Paulo. She did not speak Portuguese yet, and the curriculum had many more classical subjects than her studies in Québec. She felt like a fish out of water. Normally she liked demanding situations, she thrived on changing from French kindergarten to English first grade, but the school in São Paulo was too confusing for her. She did not make friends in school, preferring the less pretentious people she met at Frère Alfredo's place.

132

Kathy's athletic talents were quickly noticed and she was asked to be a member of an elegant club and to train for the Olympic Games the following year, in Mexico. For a few weeks the excitement of the training made her forget her sorrow over the social inequities, but that ended with the first competition. She was livid when she arrived home, saying that a Japanese girl whom she considered an excellent athlete was eliminated in favour of a less capable but richer girl. At the next training session she fell off the uneven parallel bars and broke her leg. She stopped being a member of the Olympic team and became an assistant to the trainer. This way she could help and encourage others, even with the cast on her leg. I have wondered about that broken leg. Was it not a way to get out of a situation she did not want to face and did not know how to handle otherwise?

After Kathy broke her leg and Sara became really unhappy, we held a family council and decided that they had better go back to Québec and finish the school year there.

Just before they left, we got a postcard from Sandy. From Munich he wrote, "I guess home is in Brazil now." This tore into my heart. Poor lonely Sandy! He needed a home badly and so did we.

Kathy and Sara returned to Québec, moved in with Tip and finished their school year, while I tried to do justice to my duties as a Rotary scholar who was supposed to and wanted to help promote international understanding.

The academic year started its second semester as we arrived in São Paulo. It started with noisy demonstrations. The students were asking for a more just and equitable distribution of resources for education. They were protesting against the injustices that caused illiteracy among the poor. There were big signs with slogans everywhere. The atmosphere was not good.

We had a professor who was lecturing on the anatomy of revolutions. He was editor of the biggest conservative newspaper of Brazil, was known as the ghost-writer for the generals who were in power. As a professor of political science, he

133

taught a fiery Communism. He had three different hats and wore the one that fitted the moment.

One afternoon he was lecturing on the conditions that lead to the explosion of public discontent. He drew a diagram about the pressure mounting and the repression controlling it, to a point, but was unable to contain it beyond that level. He stopped. Then, with his back to us, said, slowly: "You must have heard that Ignatius of Loyola used to say, 'Give me a school and I give you Catholics for life.' And you know that Lenin said that one needs only a newspaper to start a world revolution." He waited for a few seconds, gave us time to remember that he had both a school and a newspaper, then he turned around and broke out laughing. With his black beard and cynical laughter, he reminded me of Mephisto. The young professor of political science sitting next to me whispered, "I could kill him!"

We were friends from the first day we met. His name was not Julio, but I shall call him so. He was a Communist. His uncle had a very high position in government. I told him that I heard people say that his uncle was an honest politician.

"Yes, that is a family illness with us. It means that people behind him can be even more corrupt." He asked me to give a lecture to his students. When they heard me speak English with him, they asked if I was an American. I said, no, I was a Canadian. Their faces brightened and I heard, "Ohhh, then you are civilized."

Julio warned me not to mention that I was a Rotary scholar, because rich Rotarians were exploiting the poor and his students would not take things seriously from me if they knew. I told him how I look at the lack of justice in the world. I spoke to him about Bahá'u'lláh. At first he brushed my words aside as unfounded idealism, but when I told him some more, he asked for a book. I gave him Esslemont's *Bahá'u'lláh and the New Era*. He read it and when he brought it back, he held it up in one hand, holding Marx's *Manifesto* in his other hand.

134

"Look, the date on this one is 1848 (that was the *Manifesto*), and this began in 1844. This one has already conquered one-third of the world. Who knows of this one?!" I told him to keep the book and to compare the two and their effect on the world as time goes by.

I was very fond of Julio. He was honest and he did care, even if he was bitter, very bitter. I liked his wife and his son, and would have liked to see them happy. His wife worried every night while Julio was away at meetings; she wondered whether he would be back. When I tried to make him see that a revolution would not take care of the problems, Julio would say to me,

"If you ever saw the favelas, you would not try to convince me of the likelihood of a peaceful solution." He wanted to show me the slums around São Paulo, to make me see that he was right. I did not want to go to the favelas. I did not need to see them, I was aware of their needs. The terrible lack of social justice was a big part of the driving force behind me, but Julio thought that I was avoiding reality.

The functions I attended with the local *Rotary Club* were charming, with fine food and beautiful speeches. I felt as if I were part of two separate worlds, each real and unreal at the same time. I was in Brazil to promote understanding, but I encountered misunderstanding and hatred with every new meeting. I felt the need to discuss my quandary with the president of the Brazilian *Rotary Foundation*. He listened with interest and became enthusiastic when I told him that the students would not listen to what I had to say if they knew that I was a Rotary scholar.

"You should tell that to all the Rotary Clubs you are able to visit. They will listen to you. We have to organize a round of lectures for you to make our people aware of this! That is how you are going to help us most." I was glad to hear that and looked forward to it.

In the meantime my money was running low. Frère Alfredo wanted me to give a course on world religions to teach-

135

ers of religion in the Catholic schools of São Paulo and surrounding villages. He suggested that I entitle the course, *The
Scientific Basis For Choosing One's Religion.*

"But Frère Alfredo, then I will have to tell them why
today everybody should become a Bahá'í."

"If that is what you believe, then that is what you should
say," he answered.

"But Frère Alfredo, that would be the end of your institutions!"

"If our institutions should go, then they should go."
He reached into a drawer and pulled out two pamphlets published by the Jehovah's Witnesses.

"God is working everywhere, even in the most destruc-
tive things." We agreed on that, and I prepared a course to
which I gave the title *The ABC of Religion.* This was meant for
one semester and covered religious teachings from Abraham
to Muhammad. For the second semester, I promised to teach
about the Báb and Bahá'u'lláh.

My 36 students loved what they learned. The world
gained new colours for them. Their excitement became really high when we reached Islam. Until then they knew Muhammad as the barbarian who had cut off the heads of Christians to have them as slaves in another world. Now they met
him through his own words, as one who continued the work
of Jesus, a descendant of the same family, the family of
Abraham. They now met Muhammad, the civilizer of the Arab
tribes, who said that "the ink of the scholar is holier than the
blood of the martyr", whose teachings gave birth to the first
universities. But they started to look for me after the class, to
talk about doubts they had about their own religion. This is
what I thought would happen when I cautioned Frère Alfredo
before the course began, but he did not understand what I
was talking about. He did not see why I was upset, but I could
not go on with that second semester and be paid by the *Association of the Teaching Brothers of Latin America*! I knew that I
would have to do something drastic to find a way out. I went

for a walk in the evening breeze blowing among the trees of Avenida Paulista.

As I walked, thinking, I happened to look up to the moon and noticed that something was funny about the old lady. She did not look right the way she was hanging on to the sky, as if she were upside down. Then I realized something that I should have been aware of; I was looking at the moon from the other side of the world! She looks like a tilted hat from one side, and like a tilted bowl when you see her from the other side of the Equator. From Canada we go south when we want to avoid the cold, from São Paulo I went south to see the only snow I saw while in Brazil. Upside down world, I said to myself, I will have to figure out what to do about it.

Next day the Chinese chauffeur of the Rotary president brought an invitation "to an informal dinner". I had started to wonder what had happened to the idea of a useful speaking tour. I thought this evening was meant to plan for the tour. I went dressed in a summer dress, which could be taken for a cocktail dress. This turned out to be the right thing to wear because the occasion was anything but informal. The floral decorations could have nourished a family for a year, white-gloved servants carried trays of fine food and drinks, soft Hungarian music was playing in the background to delight me, the "professora de Canada" of Hungarian origin. Everybody was most kind and appreciative and I thanked my hosts for the evening which they planned to please me. I went home and cried. What hurt most was that they wanted to make me happy.

When I discussed my quandary with the president, he spoke about the hundreds of abandoned children who roam the city, and he was obviously and sincerely appalled at those conditions. But he did not realize that the reception they gave to please me was the fatal blow to my sense of mission. He belonged to the privileged class and did not see the people sleeping on rags under the doorway as human beings, as people. They were an abstract thing to him, known but not

137

felt. I recalled a book I had read, Jorge Semprun's *The Long Voyage*. He talks about a German family living next to the camp of Auschwitz. Their living room window was facing the camp and from it they had a perfect view of the gas chambers and the chimney of the crematorium. How were they able to live, to work, to go to church on Sunday, to have a good meal and relax?

Semprun went to visit that farm after being freed by the Allied victory. He stood at that window. "How could they enjoy their Sunday meal?!" he thought when he heard the farmer's wife say, "It is a comfortable room, isn't it?" He turned around and gazed at her in disbelief.

She realized what he was thinking and said, as if to defend herself, "I lost three sons in the war," as if the bodies of her sons would protect her from the verdict of insensitivity. She could do nothing about the situation. Therefore she had to ignore it. She had to block it out in order to be able to survive. This is what my gracious hosts were doing with the glaring problems surrounding them. Their blinds had to be pulled down, to block out what was unbearable.

When Brazil was freed from Portugal, there was a class of their own people who had become rich while most of the country lived in utmost, degrading poverty. It created material misery for the colonized and spiritual atrophy for the colonizers. There was no hope for a real change unless the rich became aware of their ability, and were willing to start changing things. Revolutions cannot bring lasting remedy. There has to be a spiritual revolution which changes the values of the rich and poor alike. The rich have to start it because they have the means to do it. This is when I realized that I had to go back to Canada. Not just because my daughters were already there, not only because I could not bear to look at a hopeless situation which was bound to become worse, but because I felt that the solution could not be found in Brazil. It had to be found in a country like Canada, where there IS a chance for finding it. This is why I became a Bahá'í. I didn't become a Bahá'í to serve the interests of any religion but to help mankind into a better world. I packed and took the plane to Canada.

Both Frère Alfredo and Julio offered to drive me to the airport. I accepted Julio's offer and asked him to come a bit earlier than necessary. When we reached the road that led to the favelas, I asked him to take me there. He stopped the car.

"I know why you did not want to visit the favelas; you don't need to see them. Besides, they do not need to see you looking at them either."

He drove me to the airport and we had a wonderfully warm, long conversation. I promised to pray for him and for his family and for his people and for the day to come soon when there would be no more favelas in Brazil, or anywhere in the world.

São Paulo brought us a great deal of suffering, but it also brought new insights of the road mankind was now traveling. Friendship with the desperately Communist Julio made me see how Bahá'u'lláh's influence touched those who saw the plight of man and wanted to relieve it. With his long antenna, but without the infallible guidance of God's plan, Marx captured the main need, justice! Because he was not the mouthpiece of God, he attacked injustice, instead of building the just world. There is much to attack, but the solutions human beings devise may cause even more injustice. Still, what they do achieve may turn into a step towards the real, God-planned goal.

While in São Paulo, I went to Porto Alegre, not to see snow in Brazil, but because the Bahá'ís of Porto Alegre invited me to visit with them. They arranged two talks for me at the *Universidade Apostolica Catolica of Porto Alegre.* I spoke on the *Psychology of Religion* and the *Sociology of Religion.*

In the first one, I talked of how religion is indispensable for an integrated personality, for individuals and for communities, be it a family, a nation or the world. Religion ties

139

together, makes disparate parts whole. It also renews the ties between people and our loving God, who promised to guide us. On the sociology of religion, I talked of the string of revealed religions which form the history of mankind. All the Dispensations, like the Mosaic, followed by the Christian, then by the Muhammadan Dispensation, and now the Bahá'í Dispensation, build the ever-advancing civilization of humanity.

As a result of those talks, the *Spiritual Assembly of the Bahá'ís of Porto Alegre* was asked to supply a teacher for a course on the Faith at that university. It comforted me that my toil and tears were not in vain.

15　Chaudière Bassin
1968-1971

Four people waited at the airport in New York: Tip, Kathy, Sara and a handsome tall girl, standing very straight by Tip. He introduced her to me as Susie, the girl whom he intended to marry. My first reaction was to recall a memory of a conversation we had when Tip was about eight years old. He told me that when he grew up he would want to marry somebody who was a lady, like me. There she was.

We had a week of camping on Cape Cod, to get acquainted and to make plans. The first problem returning to Québec was to find a new place to live. We found it fast and it was the first beneficial result of Susie's joining the family. Susie's best friend, Janie, had an aunt who had died and her house could be rented to us, she thought. We went to see it, loved it, but were told that it would have to be put in order first, specially because the family could not find Aunt Ethel's valuable diamond ring. I offered to help find it.

Janie, Sara and I went to the house together. It was in quite a mess. I suggested that Janie go upstairs to look in Aunt Ethel's room, because I was sure the ring would be some-

141

where there. We would start putting things in order downstairs. We were hardly there 10 minutes when Janie's voice rang through the house, "Welcome home!" She found the ring where she had been looking, looking for weeks without seeing it. The months and years we passed in that beautiful house made us increasingly sure that Aunt Ethel herself was the one who said that "Welcome" to us.

When we left for São Paulo, we had to find a place for Ruby. We had taken her to a kennel. Now that we had a house, we went to fetch her, and we found her in a sad state. She had glassy, unseeing eyes. She was shivering and circled the room, she circled and circled as if she were out of her mind. The owner of the kennel told us that she had been like that since a few days after we left. We packed the poor dog into the car, took her home and gave her a bath, to take away the smell of the kennel. She allowed me to treat her, did not show any sign of any will, she just shivered and shivered. It was a warm afternoon, I took her out to dry on the terrace.

The whole family was there, looking with compassion at that poor animal, gone crazy from grief. She now circled the terrace. I said, "The house is strange, she can't recognize a thing." She must have recognized my voice. She stopped. She came to me and put her head against my knee, as she used to do, and the strain slowly left her body. She stopped shivering, collapsed on the towel and fell asleep. From time to time she opened an eye to see if we were really there. After a short nap, she stood up, shook herself, went to Kathy, who was her special mistress, then greeted everybody in turn. She sniffled at Susie for a while, as if to ask who that was, and Tip introduced his bride.

Québec had changed a great deal since I first arrived, in 1948 when Duplessis was lord. I followed with interest the changes through the tragic battle of Paul-Emile Borduas, who died a broken man in Paris, then the efforts of Father Levesque, who became a beacon of education in Africa. Then came the insolent "Frère Untel", a Marist teaching brother, who criticized the educational system under that pseudonym. He was sent to Rome to learn his lesson and learned it so well that he came back to turn into Jean-Paul Desbiens, responsible for setting curriculum in the Ministry of Education (I worked on his committee for a while). Then Abbé Dion and Abbé O'Neill, of *Laval University*, put Christian conscience into play against the misuse of power and that brought an end to Duplessis' regime.

In the early sixties the "revolution tranquille" swept the land. And in 1965, "les trois colombes", Marchand, Trudeau and Pelletier entered the federal scene. Few could foretell at that time how much they would change the country. I was in my second year of the master's program at *Laval University* when the federal election of 1965 was fought. We were given an assignment to research public opinion in connection with the election. I chose to study the press to see how the interest in international questions was being dealt with in the English, as compared to the French, press. I expected to find that the French press would show more interest for international questions. The findings went far beyond my expectations. I found that the press, whether English or French, showed more interest in what happened in the international field where there was a sizeable French-Canadian population.

An English newspaper in Manitoba had a headline saying something like: "PEARSON TALKS ABOUT OUR INTERNATIONAL OBLIGATIONS to a capacity crowd in Winnipeg." The same event was reported in Vancouver like this: "HUGE CROWDS CHEER PEARSON SPEAKING about Canada's foreign obligations in Winnipeg." This country had a prime minister who won the *Nobel Prize* for peace in 1957, but the country as a whole was rather unaware of what was going on in the world.

During the few months I was in Brazil, the educational system in Québec underwent a radical change. Just to mention one instance, the *Académie de Québec*, an elitist college for

143

boys, turned into the *CEGEP Ste-Foy*, to prepare both sexes for either a career demanding two years of study, or for admission to university. Fernand Lemire, director of studies, hired me to became professor of social psychology and human relations in that CEGEP. My students needed a solid grasp of psychology because they were mostly re-educators, social workers, nurses, administrators, besides some who were preparing to go on to higher studies in psychology and education.

I had to put in another year at *Laval*, because my thesis was not typed and handed in when we left for Brazil. Typing and copying it would have cost 300 dollars, which I didn't have. This delayed my diploma, but gave me a lot more assurance.

Thanks to that unwanted delay, I could add the following Postscriptum to *A Proposed World Order: Bahá'í Teachings and Institutions*, in March 1968: "Work on the present thesis was finished in November, 1966. Since then, I visited Hungary and Germany after an absence of 25 years, travelled in Central and South America, and passed one semester at the University of São Paulo, Brazil.

"These experiences have fortified the conviction that the proposals of Bahá'u'lláh form the only existing body of criteria whereby the global disharmony can be organized into a working unit.

"Therefore, with all the humility that can accompany such a statement, I offer this thesis – knowing that it gives an inadequate picture of the world order of Bahá'u'lláh – as a general theory of supranational relations."

It added to my feeling of having achieved something of a valuable contribution to political science, when Professor Bergeron called my thesis a normative theory!

Our trip to Brazil brought suffering to all of us. Some prepared for good things to come. Some were lessons we had to learn. One immediate result was a "close shave" with a third marriage for me.

At a *Rotary* Convention we met Bart, a businessman from New York. Meeting my two girls, he said that he also had two daughters and that he was divorced. I said I was divorced too. Whereupon he said that in that case it might be a good idea for us to get married. Why not, I said . This was of course all in fun, but he offered to drive us to São Paulo, "to talk it over". By the time we got to town he had my address, I had his, and we were sure that we should carry on talking about that idea. He wrote from New York and when I returned to Canada he came to visit and things started getting serious. My girls were not happy with the idea. Kathy was very explicit; she was down-right against it. She could not express herself calmly; she told me that I behaved like a 15-year-old tramp. Talk like that don't help much, because they sound like unreasonable emotions.

But Leo Zrudlo, our good friend, said something that made me reflect. After meeting Bart, he said, "Angéla, you seem to be looking for difficulties."

There was a problem with Bart that did bother me quite a bit; he drank. When I told him that this bothered me, he offered to stop. He came to visit during Christmas and I went down to New York for New Years to meet his daughters and his parents. I was worried about his drinking problem and when Bart took me out to a lovely restaurant, I said that I would be more relaxed if he would have a drink only when it was really necessary for his business. He thought this was a great idea and ordered a Martini, I of course refused. He knew that Bahá'í don't drink. When he ordered a second one, I put my finger on the rim of his glass.

"I lost out to this one."

"You mean you made up your mind?"

"Yes."

"Then I can say that I lost out to a religion." Thanks to God, he did. After dinner we were expected at a Feast. Friends arranged a special "Unity-Feast", so that Bart, a non-Bahá'í, could attend. When we came to the home where the

145

Feast was to be held, I thanked him for the ride and let him go. I walked to that white door of a house never seen before, and I felt that I was coming home.

Being in New York made it easy to follow up an interesting contact I made through work at *Laval University*. One of the political scientists we read in the last course I had to take, was Kenneth W. Thompson, then with the *Rockefeller Foundation*. I liked his way of seeing the real problems. When my thesis was photocopied, I wrote to him about it and he asked for a copy. He read it and he wrote that if I was ever in New York, I should get in touch with him. He had the thesis, with red markings, on the table when he received me. We had a short but meaningful exchange, and kept in touch for some time. Last time I heard from him, he was occupying the Woodrow Wilson Chair at the *University of Virginia*.

Another important consequence of Brazil was my participation at the Panama Conference.

In February 1967, on the way to Brazil, Kathy, Sara and I stopped in Mexico City, because I would have liked to see Val Nichols, living then in the Yucatan. We called at the office of the *National Spiritual Assembly of the Bahá'ís of Mexico* where the secretary, Soliedade Bilbatua, said that Val had just left for Merida, after a *National Spiritual Assembly* meeting. Had we come a day earlier! It was too far and too expensive to contemplate a trip to her now. Soliedade then proposed that we plan to meet in October, at the Panama Conference. I said that I did not have money for that. Soliedade said that she did not have money either, still we should make a pact to be there! We shook hands, promising that we would both try to be there. Once in São Paulo, I sent in my registration.

When I returned to Québec, my commitment to Rotary only half fulfilled, they naturally stopped payment on the remainder of the scholarship. Thus I found myself at the end of July 1967 with no immediate job prospects. Only after settling in the house in Chaudière Bassin did I call on Gloria Wenk, to enquire what was happening in the Bahá'í commu-

146

nity. Big changes had happened; Québec City became a goal to form a Local Spiritual Assembly and Gloria and her sons moved from Myrand Avenue in Ste-Foy to Québec City, to help achieve that goal. Here I was, settled in a home outside the goal-area before knowing about the goal! After being an "inactive Bahá'í" during the Ten Year Crusade, now I gave the impression of not co-operating with the plans!

One day when the girls and I were discussing our situation, I said that I would have to cancel my reservation to the Panama Conference because I had no money. Kathy objected:

"You have never stopped doing things for the Faith out of financial considerations. Don't cancel just yet. If you are really unable to go, you can cancel it later." That evening Kathy was supposed to baby-sit at the Zrudlo's, whom I had not yet met at that time. There was a program at the Y.M.C.A. she would have liked to attend, so I offered to replace her as baby-sitter. The young mother, Janis, said she was glad to meet the mother of her favourite baby-sitter. Of course I like to hear my daughters praised and said that I was proud of them, even amazed at the advice I got from them about plans for the Faith and finances.

"How much would you need to be able to go?" asked Janis, and when I told her, "Oh, at least 600 dollars," she said, she would be glad to lend it to me. So I went to the Panama Conference and Janis and family are today Bahá'ís. I wonder whether it was the unusual attitude that made her look into the teachings, or was it an already Bahá'í heart who was ripened into commitment by helping a Bahá'í do something for the Faith?

Getting off the plane in Panama City, my old friend, Rowland Estall, greeted me: "How come you came here and not to Wilmette?"

I had no idea that there was a conference in Wilmette. There were announcements about the conferences held simultaneously in different places around the globe. I read them but Wilmette somehow escaped me. I had not yet visited Wil-

147

mette. It would have cost much less. Why was I then in Panama? The answer came next day, as we went up to the spot where the corner stone of the Panama Temple was to be laid. Two gentlemen were walking on the path in front of me. I heard one say, "There will be prayers in all the major languages of the Americas."

"Who is going to say it in French?" I butted in. They turned back, in consternation. They had forgotten French!

"Can you do it?"

"Sure."

"What's your name?" Angéla was easy, but Szepesi too hard to write, specially walking on a narrow path to the top of the mountain.

"Are you from Québec?" I was announced as "Angéla de Québec".

Apu, my father, the professor of French, maybe had a hand from amid the Supreme Concourse, guiding me to be at the right time, in the right spot, to see that French should not be forgotten as a major language of the Americas when that spot symbolizing the unity of North, East, South and West was blessed. Since then I think of "Angéla de Québec" as a favourite name for me.

When I packed for Brazil, I was thinking of going for a long time. It is warm there. I wouldn't need a winter coat and boots, I thought Gloria can use them. So I gave them to her. When we settled in Aunt Ethel's house, her family took what they wanted of her things and told us to use or dispose of the rest. There was a black fine woollen coat hanging in a closet with a pair of black boots underneath. It was the kind of a coat I was hoping to be able to afford one day, and the boots were my size, exactly the kind I gave to Gloria only these were brand new.

John and Audrey Robarts came to visit. They passed their 40th wedding anniversary with us. When I told them of the coat and boots, John said, with that wonderfully sweet smile of his, "I know of somebody who loves you, Angéla." To my questioning look, he said, "Aunt Ethel." Yes, Aunt Ethel, and it is reciprocal. She gave us her home and much more. I pray that she rest in peace unless she prefers to have even more work, more chances to help people. Aunt Ethel, the lady I never met in life, the owner of that special house in Chaudière Bassin, became our very good friend from the Other Side of the Gate. I have never seen a photo of her, but I am sure to recognize her when I get to the Other Side.

Yucatan
Summer 1969

Another consequence of our going to Brazil was *El Puente*. That was the name we gave to the trip of a group of my students of *Ste-Foy* to the Mayas of Yucatan.

One day two students, Louise Gagnon and Louise Maillot, stopped me in the corridor.

"Madame Szepesi, we would like to ask you to help us with a trip to Latin America." They explained that the Secretary of State offered grants to help students to travel abroad if they could present a good project and an adult accepted responsibility. As I had travelled a bit, they hoped that I might help with their project.

We set a date to discuss it and *El Puente* was on the way. We called the project *El Puente* or "The Bridge" because it was to give Canadian students a chance to meet the people of the country to which we were going. But which country? They were thinking of Chile. I knew no one in Chile, and besides it would be too expensive for travel, so we gave up that idea.

Then Val came to our help. She wrote how sad she was to have missed us in Mexico City. I answered immediately and told her about the project my students were planning and asked her opinion. She wrote back that the *University of Yucatan* would be a good institution to co-operate with and sent the address of the department of psychology. Dr. Castello Valez answered cordially and helped with all the preparations at that end.

At our end we prepared a good project and got a grant that would cover half the cost. We figured out how to cover the second half. We decided to form a group of 30 people, those who could, would drive down to Mexico City and then to Merida. This would save money and would be more enriching too, but we needed cars and drivers.

I bought a new car, a Renault 16, in which one could sleep on the road. Then I called Sandy who was again working in the Yukon and asked whether he would want to come along and drive my station wagon. Next day he was on the road to Québec. There were only four students who did not have either a plane ticket or a place in a car when a young priest called to ask to please let him come along. He had a car with four free seats. We told him that he was an answer to our prayers. Thirty students, among them Sandy and Sara, and four adults passed five weeks in the Yucatan, in the heart of the country of the Mayas.

When I was a youngster, a book in our library was *The Mayas*. I don't remember the author, only that I loved the book and that I thought that "Maya" and "Magyar" were similar; could this mean that we were related? I was attracted to the Indians even before I met one. Then at the Panama Conference, in October 1967, 1 met the first Indians! The talk that impressed me most was given by a Maya. He said a lot, and in seven short sentences.

Another memorable talk at that conference, addressed to the Native participants, was given by Rúhíyyih Khánum. She said that the Natives should not be shy about their culture, even if at school they learned only about the culture of the white people. Their history and their culture go back way before others came to this continent. The tree of their life has deep roots, and when the white man will eat the fruit of that tree, he will become a better human being.

I loved the women of the San Blas Islands whom I met. They were barefoot; wore golden rings in their noses, and did not know how to use the bathrooms on the ninth floor of the *Panama Hilton Hotel.* They watched me turn on the tap and wash my hands. The oldest one stood nearest and when she understood where one turns on the flow of the water, where one holds the hands, she told the next woman and so the information was handed down to the very youngest one. People are adaptable, and there is so much to learn!

When *El Puente* arrived in Mexico, the first thing we did was to get a general feeling of the country by visiting the *Museum of Archaeology,* in Mexico City. The students wandered in wonderment with the balmy warmth of the semitropics and the impressive new culture surrounding them. In the evening we stood in the middle of the *Praca das Tres Culturas,* with the ultramodern buildings, the Columbian church and the Pre-Columbian ruins. Standing there in the moonlight with a group of youngsters from Québec!

Our headquarters were in a pension in Merida. From there we roamed the countryside, the interesting sites that were already developed, and looked at each hill wondering what there might be still hiding under it. We swam in the ocean at Progreso and Sisal but our most memorable days were spent in the villages. Youngsters from Québec had never seen Mayan outhouses before, and I hadn't either. To go to the toilet we disappeared behind a wall in the garden. There were flat stones on which to stand and the turkeys came around the wall to watch. To get water we lowered the bucket hanging on a wheel above the well, then swinging it around until it filled, we pulled it up by turning the handle of the wheel. That one I knew; we had one like it in Kecskemét. We slept in hammocks. We took one end from hooks on one wall, hung it on the opposite wall of the hut, and climbed into a bed that was more like a swing.

We had photos of Canada to show and when we showed them to the people of Chablakal, they showed us how to behave on such occasions. There were at least 50 people in the room, children, grown-ups, men and women, but there was no noise or impatience or shoving. We stood on one side of a table and they formed a circle, with the smallest ones closest and the tallest ones behind. Nobody gave orders how to stand. They just formed the best group for everybody to see. The photos were passed from hand to hand. The big black eyes, those wonderful velvety eyes, showed warm but calm interest. We gave concerts to communicate with our music and they answered with their music.

One morning after a concert, I was sitting on a stone wall with a group of girls. They said that it would be nice to ask some questions from somebody, when an old Maya came over to say how sad he was that he could not come to the concert last night. His name was Don Secundino and he was glad to answer the questions the girls wanted to ask.

"What is friendship?" asked Solange.

"Friendship is strong, it is eternal, it is giving appreciation to somebody, not looking for qualities, but giving him qualities."

"What is love?"

"Love is the same thing as friendship."

"We mean the love you have for your wife," Solange clarified.

"Oh," said Don Secundino, "That is friendship with interest. You are interested to have her all your life as the most beautiful person for you, and to be the same for her."

"Do you believe in God?" asked Jocelyne.

Don Secundino asked me to repeat the question. When he was sure that he understood, he looked at Jocelyne with infinite compassion and said, "Poor little thing!" That

154

was all he would say in answer to that question. Then he said how good it was to have an interpreter because otherwise we would not be able to exchange our ideas. And he said that he was glad that we had come to visit his village. Michelle asked whether he found it strange that we drove around in cars, that is to say that we were rich compared to them.

"When we come into this world we have nothing and when we go out of it, we take nothing with us. Whether we have much or little in between, has no importance."

"Does that mean that you do not envy us strangers?" asked Louise.

"There are no strangers," answered Don Secundino, and we thanked him for having come to meet us. When I told Val about that answer, she said that now she understood why the Bahá'í of the village elected Don Secundino as chairman of the Local Spiritual Assembly.

Both Sandy and Sara found it easy to communicate in Spanish, although they never took any lessons. One evening, as Sandy and I walked in the unbelievably beautiful colours of the tropical dusk, I told him that I was happy that they had inherited my talent for languages.

"It is not a talent for languages, mother, it is a talent for understanding people. Once you understand people, the words just come."

That trip to the Yucatan gave me the first chance to have a good talk with Val, my spiritual mother. I was too busy to pass much time at her house, but I did take one evening to be alone with her, because I needed to ask her guidance. She had taught me that we should not try to convert people but be friends and love them and help them with their problems and to talk about Bahá'u'lláh only when they ask. There were things that bothered me with the way Bahá'ís were taught in French-Canada. 'Abdu'l-Bahá said that the hearts and doors of the French-Canadians were open but there were Bahá'ís who were banging on those open doors as if they were shut, and that turned people away from the Faith.

"Do you talk about it with those who plan?" asked Val. I answered that nobody wanted to hear what I had to say.

"Angéla, you have to work with the administration."

"I would love to, Val, but they do not want to listen to me."

"Angéla, you HAVE to work with the administration," repeated Val. I started to cry.

"Even if you don't understand, I must be wrong." Val also had tears in her eyes as she said,

"I know that you have great contributions to make to the Faith. You must go on pilgrimage."

As soon as I returned to the pension, I wrote to the World Centre to request a pilgrimage "on the advice of my spiritual mother". The answer came soon after our return to Québec, I was granted pilgrimage starting April 12, 1971.

For a while I wondered how I was going to be able to take time off from teaching to go on that pilgrimage. That problem was solved in June 1970, when I was notified that the school would not renew my contract. Then the problem became again a question of money. By the time I should have bought my tickets, I had no money to pay for them. I called the National Office to say that I would have to cancel my pilgrimage for lack of funds. The secretary said that they would review the correspondence and call me back. The treasurer called to say that the *Universal House of Justice* desired me to go on pilgrimage and to go to Hungary from the Holy Land, and asked me how much I would need. "About 600 dollars." They sent me a loan of 600 dollars.

The 600 dollars Janis lent me to go to the Panama Conference were easily repaid from the salary at the CEGEP. A visit from John and Audrey Robarts and the ringing circle of Remover of Difficulties we said, holding hands in my tiny office, was a great help with the difficulties I met there. But some difficulties must happen, otherwise we would not change course. A new contract would have made me permanent on the teaching staff. I was too different for the director, a re-

156

placement for the one who had hired me two-and-a-half years earlier. Taking a group of students to the Yucatan was too unusual for the rather conventional thought that prevailed under the new director. Bill Donnelly, who was assistant director at the time they let me go, asked me years later if I knew why the contract had not been renewed. No, I answered, I did not know.

"Did they tell you the reason? Were you given an alternative?" His question made me realize that I did have an alternative, but I did not see that I had made a choice. I knew that my personal style of teaching social psychology was different from the customary but I gave to my students what I considered they needed. I did not think of my position. It did not even occur to me that I could do it otherwise.

"Today we do not hire anybody who does not have your attitude," said Bill. "Your problem was that you were six years ahead of your time." I was, like my father, following and expressing my convictions, without calculating the risks this might mean to my career. For my growth, as a person, that trip to the Yucatan was of capital importance. I stuck out my head, without having an idea of how big a job I had undertaken and what the consequences for me might be. I helped youngsters to live their dream, and suffered a lot during and after the trip. I am glad I did not foresee it; it would have been a pity to have them miss those experiences. As a Bahá'í, the talk with Val, her suggesting that I ask for a pilgrimage to solve the problems I had with the administration, had profound results.

Val became a Bahá'í in 1936, in Los Angeles. She was deepened in the Faith by a remarkable woman, Beulah Storrs Lewis, who came from a well-known Mormon family of Utah, who had learned about Bahá'u'lláh through prayer and dreams before she ever met Bahá'ís. Val's brother, Artemus Lamb, beloved Counsellor for South America for many years, wrote to me that Beulah gave profound spiritual deepening to them, Val, Artemus and their mother, together with many

Bahá'ís in California. She was one of those early Bahá'ís who internalized the spiritual teachings of the Faith but had problems with their administration (It takes time to develop feelings and thoughts to achieve a balance between the two, especially because "administration" has such a negative connotation in the pre-Bahá'í world). Her spiritual daughter, Val, was already mature enough as a Bahá'í to give the right advice to me, her spiritual daughter, and suggest that I go on pilgrimage.

17 Fall and Winter, 1968 and 1969

Sandy came back from Europe a very different person from the boy I called "my bear cub" when he left Canada. Of course he had grown a lot. He visited Portugal where he was looking for and found the traces Tip and I had left. He saw embroideries he knew and loved. He, too, found the Portuguese warm human beings. After visiting a number of European countries, he went to Hungary. Armed with a map of Budapest, without knowing Hungarian, and without any help from the family, he went straight to Mother's and Emese's place and knocked on Mother's door! The family loved him and wrote to congratulate me on this fine sample of my children. He passed Christmas and the New Year with them. He met my beloved Gizi néni and wrote that he could see that she had had a great influence on me. He communicated amazingly well with the family, but Gizi néni was the only one with whom he had long conversations because they were both fluent in French. When he came back to Canada he did not come to stay with us; he took an apartment in Montréal. He shared it with a few other students and ex-students. He tried

159

to go to *McGill University*, finished first year and gave up. When he came to visit, he talked little, he played his guitar. I guess he wanted to say with music what he could not say with words. I could not understand his music and did not know how to ask what he wanted to say with it.

Kathy graduated from high school that spring and she did not know what she wanted to study. Al invited her to live with them in the Montréal suburb where he now lived with his new family. Kathy used to be Al's favourite and she accepted the invitation, but stayed only a week. Then she joined Sandy in his apartment on Mount Royal Avenue.

I was teaching at Ste-Foy. That fall semester was unexpectedly delayed by two weeks due to construction problems. I had been worrying about Sandy and Kathy and prayed for solution to their problems. When the two-week extra vacation was announced, I called them and asked if they would like to drive to Cassiar with me to visit Tip. Tip and Susie had been married now for a year and Tip was working in the laboratory of the *Cassiar Asbestos Mines*, near the Yukon border. Sandy was eager and asked me to pick him up in Montréal the next morning. We hoped that Kathy would come too. But she was like a mother to that rather sad group of youngsters, although they were all older. When I went upstairs to look for her, one of the girls living there looked at me with blurry but trusting eyes, "So it is from you that Kathy learned to cook?"

I tried in vain to talk Kathy into coming. She felt that those people needed her and that she had to care for them. Like mother like daughter! I wish she had thought of her own good but the example I gave her did not teach her how to look out for herself. So we left, just the two of us and made a mad dash for the North. While Sandy drove, I slept in the back of "Friday" the red station wagon. When I drove, Sandy slept. We arrived at Tip and Susie's log cabin in Quartz Creek near Cassiar in five-and-a-half days. Susie was washing outdoors and she was starting to show her pregnancy. When she saw us arrive, she gave out a shrill "Andy!" (Andy is the name

160

everybody, except me and old friends, calls Tip now). They did not expect us and it took them a few minutes to regain their wits. After a short breather and a cup of tea, the two boys continued the job Tip was doing, bringing electricity to the cabin. They were up each on a tall slim pine, fixing the wires when the phone rang. It was from Montréal and it announced that there was an emergency concerning Kathy. Sandy and I got into the car and headed for Montréal. Tip and Susie made a valiant effort at being cheerful as they waved good bye, saying "Drop in any time for tea!"

I don't remember much of our trip back and I don't think Sandy remembers much of it either, except that we were in an even-greater rush than going west. It took us five days to get to Montréal and three weeks to get Kathy out of jail. The other occupants of the apartment pleaded guilty to the charge of possessing marijuana and were released awaiting trial. Kathy said that she was not guilty. She had no drugs, she was only taking care of the apartment. She did not know that her awareness of drugs in a house made her guilty by association. Her case went before a juvenile court to decide in whose care she should be released. Al and his wife spoke to the psychiatrist, who gave the expert opinion that they should be given custody because they were in a better position to assure a stable family atmosphere than I. I happened to have my contract with the college in my purse that said that I was a professor of psychology and had a good salary. I showed it to the judge and he called an intermission to reconsider the case. After a short consultation he brought down his verdict, giving custody over the 17-year-old Kathy to her 19-year-old brother, Sandy.

During those three weeks Tip and Susie moved to Clinton Creek in the Yukon. Sandy decided to go up to work there again and Kathy wanted to help Susie with the coming baby. She was badly shaken by her experience in jail and by everything else that had happened to her recently. She loved Susie, wanted to be near her, and to be useful. I helped them pack into the Volkswagen, took a photo of her kissing Sara good-bye and waved after them as the car drew out of sight. That was the last time I saw Kathy.

This was in October 1968. Sandy and Kathy were planning to set up house together but soon Kathy moved to Tip's and Sandy was left to fend for himself. Kathy's letters showed uncertainty about it all and after a few months she moved to Whitehorse. There she worked as a waitress to earn her living and gave swimming lessons for fun. She took part in the *Yukon Games* and won a lovely parka, embroidered moccasins and gold nuggets. She seemed to enjoy herself. This was the time I called Sandy to come to the Yucatan with us. After *El Puente* returned to Québec, Sandy and Sara both started studying at the college where I taught. Sandy was thinking of studying medicine and took the pre-med sciences, Sara was in math. Mathematics of all things for my daughter!

Then, in October of 1969, an unusually long letter came from Kathy. She wrote that she was thinking of studying marine biology and was going to visit the *University of British Columbia* to look into it. And that she had other decisions to make and would come East to consult with me before taking them. She ended the letter by saying that she loved me especially because I understood her. This was not her usual style and I wondered what those decisions could be.

Then, on the 10th of November, a phone call came from Vancouver. It was an afternoon when I had no classes and was relaxing at home. The call was from the *Rescue Centre* of the RCMP: a two-seater Harvard trainer plane was expected in Port Alberni, but it did not arrive. The plane belonged to Edward Hodgkiss of Whitehorse who was piloting and Kathy was the passenger. The rescue went out to look for them.

I put down the receiver and leaned back thinking, "Kathy is dead. God has decided that she has suffered enough. She was always caught between competing emotions. She always wanted to see people happy, but if she was nice to one, the other would be hurt. God has taken her because He loves her." I got my prayer book and said a prayer of thanks. After a short rest, the assurance of her being dead left me. No, Kathy wants to make people happy on this earth and there is so much to do about that! No, God is giving her the chance of getting away from the rivalries and confusions and He lets her do her own thing. Whatever is happening, it is in God's hands and we should not even try to look for her because there was no way to know where she is. Everything is going to become clear **when the time comes**. The prayer to which I opened my book was called the *Day of God*.

Of course I could not tell the *Rescue Centre* not to look for them. They would not understand. Besides, how did I really know? The best was to say what I thought to those who asked, and to wait and see, and to pray. The search had been intense but gave no results. It was called off after about a month of publicizing their particulars, dragging the shore between Prince Rupert and Port Alberni, checking every possible radio-signal. Vancouver phoned again to say that the search was called off because the territory was too vast. There was no sense in looking any more. Before Christmas I received a letter from Mrs. Hodgkiss, the pilot's mother. She wanted me to know how much she felt for me and that she believed that our children were meant for each other. She loved Kathy from the first minute she met her when Ed took her to be introduced to his family. This was news but it did not surprise me too much. Decisions to be taken?

A young engineer, sportsman. His mother felt always secure in the canoe when he was maneuvering. Kathy was an outdoors girl, strong and nimble. Nice pair, but where were they?

Then, in February, I got a call that the plane had been found. It was on Roderick Island, an uninhabited island in the Queen Charlotte Islands. The rescuers were on their way with helicopter and tracking dogs. I was anxious for further news! They found the plane upside down in the trees. The logbook described that they could not land in Port Alberni because of fog, turned around to head back to Prince Rupert but ran out of gas. They force-landed, knocking into trees which took away the shock of impact. They got out of the plane, both unhurt. They set up camp making a tent out of the parachute and built a fireplace of rocks. They saw planes fly by but nobody spotted them. After seven days their food supply was getting low and, as there was no chance of finding food on top of the mountain, they left the plane to go down to the valley where they were sure to find game and fish. They listed what they had: food for four days, gun and compass, survival gear, etc. They were leaving, going west because they heard noises of marine traffic. The message sounded cheerful.

The rescuers followed their tracks with dogs and found a suitcase with city clothing belonging to both of them. Those were evidently too heavy to carry and not too useful, at that moment. Among their things was a camera with two Polaroid photos, one showing Kathy sitting in the tent, the other, a view from the tent. Small patches of snow were on the pines. A photo of Kathy when most people, I included, assumed her to be dead. What next?

18

Spring
1970 and 1971

The plane was spotted in February 1970. The rescuers found the terrain slippery, much too dangerous and called off the search saying that Kathy and Ed must have been buried by an avalanche. I was relieved. They should be allowed to follow their own way.

In March, I was in Montréal for a conference and friends asked me to talk to their teenage children who were involved with spiritualism and had just recently become Bahá'ís. The parents had no idea how to approach the question and were glad when I agreed to talk to them. As I mentioned, Imu, my grandmother, was a Theosophist and she made me comfortable with the thought of souls looking at us without our seeing them. I had a meeting with a half a dozen young people and told them what I thought of the contact with loved ones. We can be quite certain, I said, that those who loved us in this life, love and help us even more from the world beyond. We should be grateful for their help but never try to contact them. I gave the example of a baby growing in the womb of a pregnant mother, unaware of us. We would

165

never think of opening the womb out of curiosity because we know it would harm the baby and the mother. We should never try to look into the world beyond, especially because we don't know the laws of that existence. We could cause great harm to ourselves and to souls in the other world. We should live our lives here to the full, trust, do our duty and then we shall be well developed for the next world.

Let me quote from p. 157 of *Gleanings* from the Writings of Bahá'u'lláh:

"The world beyond is as different from this world as this world is different from that of the child while still in the womb of its mother. When the soul attaineth the Presence of God, it will assume the form that best befitteth its immortality and is worthy of its celestial habitation."

At a meeting in the *Windsor Hotel*, for which I was in Montréal, Rúhíyyih Khánum was the speaker. After her talk a young man asked about the anticipated cataclysm. She answered that we do not know what, when, how things will happen but we know what to do. Our duty is to build the World Order of Bahá'u'lláh. In that way people lost in chaos will see us assured, optimistic, because we will be guided by the *Universal House of Justice*.

"But how will the Universal House of Justice communicate with us if there is chaos?" asked the young man.

"The Supreme Concourse has a much more efficient delivery system than anything we know of," was the answer. In my head (or heart?) a bell rang that Kathy's fate had to do with that.

Kathy and Ed's disappearance caused a sensation. Radio and newspapers reported on the search in detail. When the plane was found, again, they reported on the two young people missing. Our many friends in Québec followed the news with interest and compassion. On April 11, Mother's cousin called. He was rather embarrassed, he did not know how I was going to react to what he had to say. A Hungarian lady in Québec, a widow, practised automatic writing. Well,

166

she said she had a message for me from my mother about Kathy. I called the lady whom I had met a few times at events organized by the Hungarian community. She told me that she had the habit of sitting with a writing pad, to allow her hand to be moved on the paper by her "guides", the spirits who contacted her. On this occasion she had been in touch with her husband who had died many years before. She asked whether there was anything they could do to help me get news about Kathy.

"Who do you want to help?" came a question and she answered, "Angéla, the Hungarian girl who was in Brazil a few years ago." A quick answer, "Wait a minute!" Then she heard a new voice say: "I am Angéla's mother and I would like you to tell her that the children are alive, well and happy, and that they will get in touch with her as soon as they need her. I would like you to tell her this because she is showing great courage but her anxiety is starting to undermine her health." The writer asked, "When did you leave this earth?" and the answer came: "Angéla was still a little girl when I left her."

The writer had never received such a message before, and when two days later she was again in communication, she said that she did not know what to do with it. Her husband answered, "It's time for you to obey your orders!" whereupon she quickly called my uncle and asked whether my mother was still alive.

"No, she left her when Angéla was still a little girl." Hearing the same words, she gave the message to be forwarded to me. I asked her exactly when this happened. She had received the message at about noon on April 9. Neither she nor my uncle knew that I was exactly 50 years old that day. As she spoke, I remembered little Kathy on my lap as we drove over Victoria Bridge in Montréal. It was winter; the bridge, built with tracks, made the wheels wobble and shook the car. Kathy became nervous. She held onto me and looked down to the frozen St. Lawrence river.

"Mommy, if I fell, could you save me?"

"Sure, Sweetheart," I answered, knowing perfectly well that if she fell and I jumped after her, both of us would die. I wanted to comfort her, just as my mother wanted to comfort me now. It is neither important to know where Kathy was, nor did it matter when we should see each other again, here or on the Other Side. What mattered was that I loved her and trusted her and that my mother loved me and wanted me to know it because she knew that I was in need of being comforted. I took that message as a very special birthday present.

I wrote about this "message" to my beloved Aunt Gizi, who fed me when my mother had little milk, and was always very close to her and to me, specially after Anyuka left me. She answered, very quickly. She was, of course happy that I had hopes to find Kathy alive, on this earth. But she cautioned me not to take these kind of "messages" too seriously. She would have been worried, had I swallowed "hook and sinker" whatever came through people who claimed direct contact with departed souls. She expressed what Bahá'ís generally hold true, that seeking contact with the other world is dangerous to our spiritual development. We are in this world, we have to develop while we are here, by making this world bit-by-bit more heavenly. We pray for those who love and help us from beyond, just as they pray for us. And we are grateful for their help.

I needed comforting in other concerns besides Kathy. In a way it was fortunate that I did not have to think of teaching during the 70-71 academic year, because the pilgrimage scheduled for April 1971 was nearing. How would it be possible to take time off, I wondered before. Now this was taken care of, but where would I find the means for our livelihood until then?

Sara was still studying at *CEGEP Ste-Foy*, but not in mathematics. She had changed to fine arts and started teaching English at Berlitz. Badly shaken, Sandy left college soon after Kathy disappeared. After a short stay with his father, he decided to try to fit into the business world. He had his beard and hair cut, put on a neat camel hair suit and took a job as credit representative for *International Harvesters*. It was too big a swing of the pendulum from one extreme to the other. I wondered what would come of it.

I tried many things. The most promising attempt was in handicraft development around the Gaspé for the *Ministry of Cultural Affairs*. I went on a preliminary tour to see the possibilities. It was a lovely trip in the late fall. I saw the beauty of the Gaspé peninsula, but got no job. My finances were very low.

One day I said to Sara, "To buy a bottle of milk and a loaf of bread, I would need a dollar. Would you go and see what is in the mailbox?" She came back with a letter posted in St. Louis, Missouri. A woman I hardly knew asked me to send her a Bahá'í pamphlet she saw in Québec and included a dollar for postage. Sara burst out laughing. Looking up to the ceiling, she said, "We *know* we are poor, You don't have to make fun of us!"

Next day there was a letter from Brewster, Cape Cod, where I had bought a piece of forest on a whim 10 years earlier. The real estate agent wrote that the forest has become valuable and was expropriated for many times the price I paid. If I wanted to keep it, I could appeal the expropriation. I did not want to hold on to my forest. It got me out of the hole just at the right time!

In January there was a gathering, a *Vahdat*, for Bahá'ís throughout Québec at our house in Chaudière Bassin. Sara had several friends who were either children of farmers or interested in that movement of the "back to living on the land", so fashionable among city youth at that time. Somebody brought up the idea of a farm which they would work as a co-operative. They talked about it till the wee hours of the morning and they were very convincing when they told me about it. They thought that from the Holy Land, after my pilgrimage, I could go to Hungary and stay as a pioneer as they could

169

fend for themselves. I agreed to help them find a farm. There were five to begin with, among them was Sandy, but two became soon discouraged. I stepped in to help. Sara and I went all over the province of Québec. We looked near Hull, in the Beauce, in the Eastern Townships, everywhere. We found nothing. I kept on praying. The house in Chaudière Bassin was already rented for April and we still had nothing in sight. By mid-March it was necessary to book the movers. I told them what there was to be moved, a piano among all the household furniture. The man asked where it was going to go. I had to think quickly. Sara came back one day from a trip to the Temiscouata which she found so beautiful that she got out of the car and made somersaults in the snow for joy.

"Mommy, you should have seen the grocer, I think it was in Cabano, the way he was cutting baloney for me, with so much care!" For where the move would be, I said, "Temiscouata". He told me how much it would cost and that I should call him by March 29 to say which day we wanted to move, April 1 or 3. Friends asked anxiously:

"Have you found your farm?"

"Not yet." Sandy called on the evening of March 26.

"Have you found the farm?" Told that we had not, he said, "Let Sara come up tomorrow. I'm going to find something to show her." His territory was between Rivière-du-Loup and Edmundston.

While Sara was on the road up, he called on an *International Harvester* dealer in Sully, Temiscouata. After their business, Sandy asked, "By the way, would you know of a farm for sale around here?"

"The farm where I was born and raised." Sandy went to see it, liked it and he showed it to Sara. When Sara arrived home that evening she was tired not only from the trip of that day but from all the trips and the search of months.

I asked, "How is it?"

"It's O.K." she said.

"Can we move in right away?"

170

"Yes."

"Can it be heated by wood?"

"Yes."

"Is it livable?"

"Yes."

"How much land?"

"One hundred and one acres."

"How much does it cost?"

" $2,377.24."

"Two thousand, three hundred, seventy -seven dollars and twenty four cents?"

"Yes."

I tucked her into bed and next morning I was at Sandy's place in Edmundston for breakfast. He gave me bacon and eggs and took me to see the farm. I signed the papers on March 30, Sara moved with a car full of essentials on the first of April. I packed the rest of the household and the movers took it on April 3. I left for pilgrimage, with a ticket to the Holy Land, to Hungary, and return to Canada, just in case.

Before departure for the Holy Land, I spent a few days in Montréal with my brother and with Emeric and Rosemary Sala, in Canada from Africa. On a drive in town I spotted a young Bahá'í we called "Haifa", because he was from there. I called out to him that I was on my way to Haifa. Joshua (that was his real name) asked me to take a photo of him to his grandmother, dashed up to his apartment nearby and brought a big envelope, with the address on it. The Salas drove me to the airport, where Emeric took out his wallet and gave me the change he found, exactly $30 as pocket money for my trip. He gave me the address of his relatives in Budapest and asked me to look them up for him.

In the plane, on my way to Israel, I mulled over the realities of my situation. Had the *National Spiritual Assembly of Canada* not lent me the money to buy the ticket, I would not be in that plane. Money was important.

We landed in Tel Aviv. It was Good Friday, Passover and there was a general strike in Israel. Another passenger, also going to Haifa, found a taxi and offered to take me. We drove into Haifa as the sun was setting over Mount Carmel. The golden dome of the Shrine made my heart jump for this wonderful birthday present, because it was April 9 and Good Friday, the most meaningful holy day of Christianity for me. I was in Israel through Easter, the day of resurrection, to start my Bahá'í pilgrimage on Monday!

The taxi drove the kind lady to her destination then asked where I wanted to go. I asked him to take me to an inexpensive hotel. He circled around for a while, then stopped on a residential street to ask a couple something in Hebrew.

I did not understand him but when the lady turned to her husband and said, "Let's take her in for nothing." I understood because she spoke in Hungarian.

"Are you Hungarians!?" They took my suitcase out of the taxi and invited me into their house and I became a beloved guest, sleeping in the room of her mother who had died recently. They were out for a walk to chase away their loneliness. They all had lost their families in the Holocaust. Next day they drove me to the address on Joshua's envelope.

I entered the garden where the family sat around a table and held up the envelope. When it became sure that I was at the right address, I took out the photo to show who sent me. The grandmother gazed in disbelief, then clasped the photo to her heart.

"Joheshua! Joheshua!"

They made me share their Passover meal and gave me Joshua's room to sleep in. Their daughter spoke English quite well and took me around to show the town. Her son was in elementary school. He told me how they practise keeping calm, go on playing, even when there is danger. I got a taste of the love of a Jewish family and the stressful situation in which they lived.

The first thing I received when I arrived at the *Pilgrim House* was a gift of welcome from the *Universal House of Justice*, an extra day for Ridván, the day of the administration. I said nothing about why I was on pilgrimage, only that my spiritual mother advised me to go. I wondered how the *Universal House of Justice* handled requests for prayers. On the afternoon when the House received us for tea, Amos Gibson, a member of the House, called me over. He said that I should not be shy to ask them to pray for me and proceeded to say that they read out, every morning, the names of those they pray for.

Then another member, Ali Nakhjavani, motioned to me and started to thank me for bringing him a gift from a Mrs. ???

"Are you not from Ireland?" He had mistaken me for a young pilgrim, Pat Montgomery from Dublin, my friend and constant companion from the first day. He broke into hearty laughter, put his arms around me and said that he was happy to meet me, even if it was by making a mistake. I wondered how he could take me for somebody who was young, short, dark haired, while I am tall and well beyond middle-age. Maybe the similarity of our personalities that made us seek each other's company made Mr. Nakhjavani mistake us for each other? Maybe that is how we will classify people in the future, by their personalities, not by size, age, colour?

When we went to Bahji, before we entered Bahá'u'lláh's room, our guide told us that the Covenant-breakers had removed everything, only the divan and a rocker were from His time. I was overcome by sorrow and crouched down on the carpet. Suddenly I felt as if a hand had touched my shoulder. It was a light caress, as if to say, "Don't be sad, I am glad you came." I looked up and saw the rocker, its arm just above my shoulder, at a distance a hand would need to touch, to comfort.

In front of the *Pilgrim House* there was a big asparagus plant with many red berries, each with a seed in it. I picked some seeds and once back in Canada, I put them in earth.

They grew. And they grew! I watched in amazement as it grew till it reached the ceiling and back again, as I had never seen an asparagus grow before. I called it "the administration asparagus" and when aphids attacked the young shoots, I crushed them, calling them Covenant-breakers.

One evening in Haifa, Ian Semple, member of *The Universal House of Justice*, cracked a joke on us. With a perfectly straight face, he said that recently a hitherto unknown tablet of Bahá'u'lláh's had been discovered. It began, "In the Name of God, the Most Humorous...".

Among the many memorable moments of that pilgrimage was the Ridván Feast in the garden of Bahji. Sweets sent from Morocco by the persecuted believers, were shared around the walks of His garden while the birds circled over our heads, as if in harmony with the prayers.

At the end of the last day, we went to the Shrines to say good-bye. First I visited the Shrine of the Báb, then went to 'Abdu'l-Bahá's.

As I prepared to kneel down, I heard, "You have no time. You have lots to do. Go!" I backed out of His Shrine, and went.

Fifteen years later, in the summer of 1986, I went back for three days to Haifa. My first visit was to 'Abdu'l-Bahá's Shrine. I entered with some trepidation. I was alone and a restful, warm stillness surrounded me. I knelt down and prayed. Then I stood up without meaning to.

Straight as I rarely do, I stood and called out, "Give me the glory of seeing the results!" Why did I behave that way, I wondered and knelt down and rested, rested for quite some time. I had quite a bit to rest from, because those 15 years between the two pilgrimages were not easy years to live.

After the first pilgrimage, in the plane to Vienna, was a large group of loud youngsters, were moving around chaotically as only excited teenagers can do Usually I am quite tolerant of such noise but this time it made me reach for my prayer book, to ask help in ignoring the noise. In Vienna I met the *National Spiritual Assembly of Austria* who were then in charge of teaching activities in Hungary. History plays strange tricks. For centuries "Vienna" meant oppression for most Hungarians. Now Vienna was responsible for the preparation of a just society! To make the lesson even plainer, that new rules were in play, the person appointed to see me was a young Czech believer!

How hilarious it seemed that I should be received by a young Czech to help me in my mission to Hungary! I thought of Ian Semple's *Tablet of the Most Humorous,* and how much there is to learn! I told Hanna, the young Czech believer, that I would stay in Hungary but I did not have a job there and no likely source of income. What I had was a return ticket to Canada for May 14. She asked me to let her know my address in Hungary as soon as I had it so they could communicate with me.

When I arrived in Budapest I was so exhausted that I did not go directly to my family. I needed a night to collect myself. I took a bed and breakfast room. The host wanted to practise his English on me. Finally I was alone! My head was full, my heart even fuller. I reached for my prayer book, "Please, help me!" and opened it at random. It opened at the Long Obligatory Prayer.

This was in 1971. I declared myself a Bahá'í in 1948, 23 years earlier. I accepted Bahá'u'lláh because I asked God to show me the way to peace. I tried to follow all the laws as an obligation that goes with the privileges. I said the Noon-Day Prayer. I chose the shortest one. I came from a Protestant, European intellectual background where prayers were not abundant. I felt that prayers could actually bother God. Once I looked at the Long Obligatory Prayer and decided that it was for Easterners, with all the movements. But now I asked God to help me. He obviously wanted me to use this one, so I started to read it. There was hardly any room between the bed and table, just enough to squeeze in the prescribed movements. I read it to the end, crawled into the strange bed and slept like a baby, the first good night's sleep in a long time.

At the home of my stepmother, a letter from Canada was waiting. It was from Tip. I read it eagerly, mother and my sister watching. The letter ended with "by-the-way" news that both he and Susie had declared themselves Bahá'ís and thus the local *Spiritual Assembly of Waterloo*, Ontario was formed. I exploded in tears, but smiled in the meantime at the anxious faces, not to worry.

After a good Hungarian lunch cooked by Mother, I went to see the room they found for me for the three weeks in Budapest. I rented it and sent the address to Vienna. The three weeks went very fast with visits to Emeric's uncle and aunt, to the few Bahá'ís then living in Budapest, to my relatives. As there was no news from Austria, on May 14, I took the train to Vienna and from the station, called Hanna, before heading for the airport.

"What are you doing in Vienna?" she asked, astonished.

"I am on my way to Canada, just called to give greetings from the friends in Budapest."

"Didn't you receive our letter?" They had written to tell me that they wanted me to stay.

I could not go back to Hungary once I had left the country. To be truthful, I was glad not to have received their letter, because I was worried about my 17-year-old daughter, left to fend for herself in charge of a farm. But it was a mystery, I was curious to find out how it happened. Bahá'u'lláh did not want me to stay in Budapest, that was clear, but how did He do it and why?

The answer to how He did it came soon after I arrived back in Canada. Hanna sent me their letter to Budapest and returned with the note "Address Unknown". I looked at the address that was unknown. It was my fault! My room was at 37 Balzac Street. I forgot that 7 is crossed with a line in Europe, otherwise it reads as 1. I, proud of my ability in cross-cultural understanding, forgot that small but significant difference between Europe and North America! There are still things I have to learn about the two sides of the world.

When I next consulted with the friends in Vienna, the one in charge of Bahá'í teaching in Hungary was Mehmet, a Turkish believer from Cyprus. A Turk, he learned at school that Hungarians and Turks were related, brothers, whereas I had learned that Turks occupied Hungary for one hundred and fifty years, and were horrible barbarians, etc.

In the library of a friend in Kecskemét, I noticed a book I had received as a prize at the end of a school year, *The Stars of Eger*, by Géza Gárdonyi. Eger was the scene of battles between Turks and Hungarians. I read that book of glories and heroism again, but it was not heroism I saw in it this time, but a testimony to man's ability to treat others as beasts.

Hanna, the Czech, Mehmet the Turk were not my enemies. We did not even have time to ponder the tragedies of the history of our nations. We were busy consulting on what was to be done today!

19 Sully, Temiscouata
1971-1989

When I called Sara to ask how she would feel if I returned to Canada, she sounded truly glad to hear me say, "Come to get me in Montréal on the 14th." Things did not work out as well as she had hoped. The task was too much for her. And the life of a businessman in a camel hair suit was too much for Sandy. They were both at the airport and I could feel something in the air that I knew I wouldn't like. We had a meal with Emeric and Rosemary Sala. I gave them the love of their family and friends in Budapest, and we headed for Sully.

Sandy took me for a walk around the farm. He pointed to a field and said, "The marijuana plantation could go there." I stopped and asked, "Did you want to hurt me?" These words brought the conversation to an end and the end of Sandy's stay at the farm, the end of the camel hair suit and marijuana.

A few years later, when I first thought of selling the farm, he said, "Don't sell it! Finding that farm was the only good thing I did as a credit representative!"

Sara still wanted to try to succeed. She found friends to help her and she seemed glad when Tip and Susie called to ask me to join them in Waterloo. They were now the parents of a two-year-old, Peter. They decided to further their studies, came down from the Yukon and went back to school in the department of integrated studies at the University of Waterloo. My visit with them resulted in my becoming a resource person for that department. It was a new idea. Nobody really knew how it would work and everybody had strong opinions.

I was an unconventional teacher but the situation at Waterloo was too unconventional even for me. I was at a loss. Then Sara gave up at the farm and came to Waterloo, frustrated and hard to get along with. To top it off, my health was bad. I was hemorrhaging continuously. At one moment I thought that I was going to go out of my feeble mind. The next moment I realized that I could control how I felt. I lay on my bed, turned towards the wall, lost, confused, crying.

Suddenly I looked at the wall, as if I had just discovered that it was there, and asked myself, "Do I WANT to be unhappy?" That was the end of my misery. I decided that no, I did not want to be unhappy.

I drove out to Tip's house. Peter was standing at the door. He had awakened from his afternoon nap. His pyjamas were unbuttoned. He was looking for Susie. When he saw me, he called out, "Oh good, Oma, now you can help me!" I buttoned up his pyjama pants and gave him a hug. It felt good to be a useful grandmother.

Several good things happened during that year in Waterloo. I was elected to the Spiritual Assembly of Waterloo, in a by-election created when Andy and Sue moved out of town. Changing of the generations. Next came a visit from Peter and Janet Khan, from Australia. They talked about how members of the *National Spiritual Assembly of Australia* loved each other. It was beautiful! And I met a couple who became my steady friends, Bill and Phoebe-Anne Lemmon. Then came

180

the Welland Conference on April 9, 1972 where Lloyd Gardner surprised me by asking the friends to sing "Happy Birthday" to me. Dear Lloyd, the one who sent an affidavit of support to Lisbon for me, so I could come to Canada!

Sara took a job with *Talking Books* for the blind, remaining in Waterloo, while I went to the farm as soon as I could. When fall came, I did not feel like trying Waterloo again, but I did have to find a way to earn my living. I was not used to praying for money but one morning I sat down in my favourite chair and prayed that I should not have to leave Sully on account of money.

MONEY. I never regarded money as important, until en route to pilgrimage, high in the air from where things on the ground usually look very small, I found myself thinking that I would not be going to the Holy Land had I not been able to find the money for plane fare. First the thought was a rebellious one, that it is unfair that a lack of money should hinder people from achieving what they want. Then, for the first time in my life, I made the statement of fact that, yes, money is important! If we want something we have to prepare for it. The first step is a wish, the second is its materialization, and for that material means are needed. I had never regarded money as important because the possessions of my family went up in smoke at the end of the First World War and I learned that there is no security in material possessions. Maybe it was a kind of defence mechanism for my father to talk in a derogatory manner of people who "run after money". I grew up to feel disdain for money, as something dirty, not to be talked about in good company. It became clear to me that money is important, when I sat in the plane to Haifa. Yes, money is important but only as a means; what is crucial is that the purpose for which it is used be valid.

As I meditated and prayed for money, the phone rang, André Bard, the insurance agent, called to ask whether it would interest me to teach English at the college. "The college", a school for boys with problems, was five minutes from

181

the farm, on the next road. I signed a contract with them that very afternoon. The director of studies was full of compliments. He thought that I would be their most qualified teacher.

That happy state of affairs ended very soon, when a student left the college after a drive with me. On the last Friday in September, the boys offered to put up my double windows. I told them that I had to go to Trois Rivières. They could come next weekend to help. After class a boy came to ask me to take him along. He said that he would like to come to have a chance to do some thinking. He was a bright boy who asked all sorts of questions. I asked him why he was in this institution. The boys were mostly orphans, or from broken homes, or boys who had been in trouble. This boy did not seem troubled to me. He said that it was the director of studies who asked him to come.

"We are good friends. At times I pass a weekend at their cottage."

When we got back he thanked me for the ride. It was a great help, he said, and had allowed him to make a decision. Next morning his place in class was empty. And the director of studies was cold as ice with me. This time I wanted to keep my job and tried everything to please him. The more I tried, the less I succeeded. At Christmas I received notice that my services were not needed any more. They gave as reason that I was not a capable English teacher and that I was unable to keep discipline. Those would be valid reasons to break the contract of a teacher but I knew that they were not valid in this case because they were not true. I knew that something was very wrong but only a year later did the real reason become clear. In the meantime the police investigated complaints and one day the newspapers reported that the director of studies, with other Teaching Brothers, was found guilty of gross indecency against the boys.

The reason for the icy treatment and my discharge was that the boys had confidence in me and that was of course threatening to people who abused them. How naïve could I be!?

182

The boys did tell me, "Mrs. Szepesi, please marry the director of studies so that he will leave us alone!" I thought that they were talking as students so often do, just for fun. I couldn't imagine what was unimaginable to me. Had I not had ups and downs before in my life, this could have broken me. But I was seasoned in disappointments and practised in floating on top of stormy waves.

The house and the farm, of course, had something to do with my composure. If you can look out over the mountains, it is easier to look beyond the corruption of people who should be guardians of virtue.

Bijou Charest built his farm on bedrock. He and his wife brought up eight children there and, when none of them wanted to farm any longer, they sold it and moved to the village. The couple who bought it did not make out and the odd price of $2,377.24 I paid, was what was left from their debt. They just wanted to get rid of it. It was a gift to me from heaven. From the window at night, I saw the lights of Rivière Bleue down in the valley and of St-Eusebe up on the slopes. The road to La Resurrection wound upwards, like a sparse necklace. I could not see La Resurrection but I knew that it was there, just beyond the horizon. My forest smelled like the forests of the best summers of my childhood. From the highest pile of rocks Bijou Charest and his children gathered when they cleared the land, I could pray as nowhere else. I pray in three languages, English, French and Hungarian. Not that God would need translations but because the Guardian translated the prayers into English, my heart is in French Canada, and my roots in Hungary.

The two years that followed were full of new friendships, with young and old from the village and from the surrounding villages. I am different, I come from afar, speak another language, but the people of Sully became like family to me. I loved the church of the village. The priest gave me a pew although he knew that I was a Bahá'í. The church has very good acoustics. The Beethoven song which I sang in the church of Igló, where I was baptized, sounded beautiful when I sang it at a few weddings in Sully.

"The Heavens Laud the Glory of the Eternal..."

Life in Sully was similar to life in Igló before the two world wars. Everybody knows everybody. Families are related. Those who go away to study often come back to practise. Even those who live away come back to help out at harvest or to get their meat for winter. There was a stability around there, making me thankful to be accepted and loved after so many years of insecurity. But love is not enough to live on. I had to find work. Yet, all I found were activities to do for a lady who can afford to be a volunteer.

While looking for a job, I also tried to get some order into my things. One day I sorted old photos and a folded paper fell out of a box followed by a photo of my mother.

"Anyuka wants me to look at that paper," and I opened the paper. It was my father's last letter to me. Apu wrote it after Sara was born and I remembered that it made me uncomfortable when I got it. What he wrote sounded like reproaches. It did not sound like that now; it was rather a sad message of good-bye. With a shock, I realized that he had been taken to the mental hospital very soon after he wrote it. The letter did not seem to have been written by an insane man but by a very sad one, one who gave up fighting a losing battle. Why did I not notice that before?

It was only in December 1998 that I learned that Apu was not taken to the asylum for being insane. My brother Attila and his wife Martha came to say bye-for-now before going off to sunny Florida for the winter, and Marti spoke about the evening before Apu's death. She had been trying to understand what he was trying to say and had been asked to leave at 9 p.m. sharp: discipline was strict. He was found dead, in front of his bed. The basement of that hospital was rented to other hospitals, to send their dying patients there ... !

In the summer of 1971, soon after I returned from pilgrimage, a letter came from the *National Spiritual Assembly of Canada.* It called me to a meeting; the purpose given was to talk about the community farm my children planned to operate. I arrived at the appointed time and was met by the whole Assembly. There was no talk about the farm at all, instead of that, I was told that it had come to the attention of the Assembly that I had been engaged in backbiting. I was asked if it was true that I have made critical comments about people and events. I felt as if I had suddenly become paralyzed.

According to the Bahá'í Writings, backbiting is a grievous sin. Bahá'u'lláh forbids it in *His Most Holy Book*, the Kitáb-i-Aqdas, in the same sentence with murder and adultery. No wonder I was speechless hearing that accusation. When I finally found my tongue, an exchange followed, which made it clear that misunderstandings must have happened. I requested a prayer, and we went for a cup of coffee.

During coffee, Ted Oliver, an old friend, came to sit beside me. He wanted to tell me that he was glad to be there, because although he had known me for years, now he really had gotten to know me. And this made him happy.

His friendliness eased somewhat the anxiety I felt. Ted was then Auxiliary Board Member, his approval made me feel less hurt by the accusations, by being told that I was backbiting and having a bad influence on young believers. A number of my students became Bahá'ís. What was it that I did do wrong? Maybe John Robarts was right when he said that I have a sharp tongue...

John and Audrey Robarts were the other couple — besides Emeric and Rosemary Sala — to whom I felt very close ever since I first met them. They suggested that we should settle in Québec City. We did not follow up because Al felt that Montréal offered more chances for a job. They applauded our moving to Verdun to open that community for the Faith. Audrey was the one who suggested the discussion groups on child psychology for parent education. They invited me to stay at their home when I went for the Peace Conference, in Toronto, in 1952. In 1953, they understood my sadness at not

185

being able to go to the Marquesas. John gave me one of his warm hugs right on Mountain Street, as he ran to do the last errands before they left for South Africa. He assured me that the time would come when I would also be able to go off to teach the Faith to waiting souls. Their daughter, Nina, has a ring that she calls a sister to the ring I wear, the one Lua Getsinger had made from the stone 'Abdu'l-Bahá gave her before the turn of the century. Nina's ring used to belong to John's aunt, Grace Robarts, Mrs. Harlan Ober. When Nina saw my ring, she said, sadly, that she had broken the stone in hers. I suggested we try the jeweller near my home in Québec, maybe he could fix it. He did, and the way he did it, made the gold cover the broken part and exposed what was intact. It was in the shape of Africa!

John settled my problem about money. In our early years, I had helped to provide for the family and gave every penny I earned. Once, I was so anxious to contribute to the Bahá'í Fund, that I packed up what was really mine, a few pieces of jewelry I inherited from Anyuka, and sent them to Lloyd Gardner, the national treasurer. I asked him to sell them and give the money to the Fund. Lloyd sent the little package back with a beautiful letter, which said that what I had done made him really happy to be our treasurer, but the money he could get for my old pieces was less needed than the intention! In the early 70s, soon after my pilgrimage, the Robarts family came back from Africa and John (appointed Hand of the Cause by Shoghi Effendi shortly before his passing) undertook a cross-Canada trip to talk about the nature of the Bahá'í Fund. Until then, I had had some of the confusing feelings many people have, about the fund. I wanted to build the New World Order...! He said that what is needed is moderation. If I give away what is really needed by myself and my family, others will have to take care of me. And that would not be fair to others, nor comfortable for me.

In July 1974, a mini-summer school was held at the farm. The subject was the relationship between science and religion, one of my favourite subjects. About 25 friends came, from all over Québec, the Maritimes, even some from New England. We had a wonderful weekend, warm, friendly and uplifting. I felt that I had finally become useful, of service in the community.

Next weekend a young English girl came to visit. She had recently declared herself a Bahá'í and was full of joy at having found the Faith. But, she said, there was something that bothered her. There were two people in her community whom she did not like. When she told me who they were, I had to laugh. I also had trouble getting along with the same people. "It must be because we both grew up in Europe," I said, "and some North American manners rub us the wrong way. We have to love everybody, but we cannot like everybody. This is why Bahá'u'lláh came. This is why we are Bahá'ís, to unite the many very different people of the world. With time and working together for our common future, we will learn to get along." We reflected, read a bit, and prayed before going to sleep.

A few days later Sara called and I could hear from her voice that she was worried. "Mother, what did you talk about with Elizabeth?"

"Oh! It caused trouble?! Don't say any more!" I sat down right away and wrote a letter to the *Local Spiritual Assembly* of the community to which she belonged. I knew that the two believers we were talking about were on the assembly. But I wrote to the *Spiritual Assembly*, which is over and above individuals, an ideal body, ordained by Bahá'u'lláh, to heal our ailing society.

I described our conversation, assuring the Assembly that we were not talking to criticize anybody. We wanted to clear away problems we met. These problems come from our different upbringing. Dislikes for behavioral patterns which we find strange can separate us, but only while we are ignorant about them being prejudices. Once we recognize them for what they are, they can harm no more. I do not remember what exactly I wrote, but I requested the *Local Spiritual Assembly* to help me assure the two friends that I think highly of them and would not want to hurt their feelings. And I begged them to help me repair whatever harm I may have caused.

I trusted that the *Spiritual Assembly* would help me settle this problem, and waited anxiously, hoping that they would call me to consult about it.

This was at a time when "the new race of man" about which Shoghi Effendi was writing, was a promise of the future. We, all, were "children of the half-light", trusting in God and His Messengers, but not yet able to even guess at the perfection of Bahá'u'lláh's World Order. The importance of *Local Spiritual Assemblies* was repeatedly stressed by the Guardian, but could hardly be grasped by the believers. No matter how perfect the instruments are, an orchestra can only produce fine music, when the musicians are skilled. This, of course, takes time, and a lot of practise.

A few weeks later Sara spent the weekend with me. We were sitting on the terrace when the mail came. I went to the box and returned with two letters, one for each of us. Mine was from the *National Spiritual Assembly of Canada*. When I finished reading the first page, I read it out to Sara. It said that because I had again indulged in backbiting, they had no choice but to remove my voting rights.

The removal of voting rights is a very severe action, now used only in cases where it is clearly necessary. When a believer breaks a law that was made for the protection of individuals and the unity and tranquility of society, the Assemblies have the duty to call his or her attention to the error, and help to correct it.

Turning to the second page, I read, now to both of us, that I was not to discuss the matter or to talk about it to anyone. And I had just read it to Sara!

Next Monday a letter came from the *National Spiritual Assembly of Austria*, then responsible for Bahá'í teaching in

Hungary, asking me to translate 'Abdu'l-Bahá's *Tablet to Dr. Forel* into Hungarian.

The fact that I had read the news of losing my voting rights to my daughter, before knowing that I was not supposed to talk about it to anyone, told me that I was doing something wrong, while I was unaware of it being wrong. And the *Austrian National Spiritual Assembly* asking me to translate a Tablet by 'Abdu'l-Bahá into my native tongue, showed me that I could be of service to the Cause even if I had lost my good standing in the Canadian Bahá'í community. "This is God working. I have to be firm and to remember that everything that is happening serves the Faith, and that it will become clear when the time comes!"

As soon as I received that letter, I wrote to the Universal House of Justice, that the problem for which my spiritual mother suggested in 1969 that I ask for a pilgrimage, had now come to a head — with the removal of my voting rights. A copy of this letter was mailed to John Robarts. The answer from him came very fast, with an emotional phone call.

His voice was trembling as he said that I should ask the National Assembly to review this decision. I said that I did not feel that asking the Assembly to change the decision is what I should do, instead, I should ask how I could regain my good standing. He agreed and promised to pray for me.

Soon I received a letter bringing the answer from the World Centre. When I found it in the mailbox, I noticed, with amazement, that holding it in my hand did not provoke the grip of anguish in my guts which used to accompany the reception of important letters. As I walked up to the house, to open it in my praying-chair, I thought, "Even if they say that they do not want ever to hear my name again, IT IS ALRIGHT."

The letter written on behalf of the *Universal House of Justice* said that I should feel assured that they would pray for my guidance and protection at the Holy Threshold. I let the letter fall on my lap, and then had a long, good cry.

The committee appointed by the *National Spiritual Assembly* to inform me of the steps I was to take to regain my voting rights advised me that I would have to seek treatment with a psychiatrist. It does not have to be a Bahá'í, they stressed, just a competent psychotherapist.

By this time I knew that only a Bahá'í could help me, because my son took me to a psychiatrist at the time of the first warning, in 1971. He asked me why I had come to see him.

"Because my children think that I need to."

"Do you think so too?"

"Not really, but it cannot harm."

"What is the problem?"

"I am unable to communicate with the Bahá'í administration."

"What does that mean? ... Can you bring me some recent correspondence?" I showed him the last letter I wrote to the *National Spiritual Assembly,* asking guidance about continuing or not my academic career. He read my letter and the answer to it. Then he leaned back in his well-padded chair, looked at me with a satisfied smile, meaning that he understood everything. "Is this ALL you received to THIS? This is what administrations are like. What did you expect?" And he shrugged his shoulder at my naïveté.

He looked at "administrations" as uncaring, while I looked at the Bahá'í Administration as all-knowing. He did not ask me whether I gave enough information to receive a real reply to my query. How on earth could anybody receiving such a request answer anything else but, "Sorry, dear, you will have to decide that question for yourself???"

There followed three sessions, during which we played a game of fencing between optimists and pessimists. Neither of us convinced the other. It became clear to me that it would take a Bahá'í psychiatrist, one who is on the wavelength of the New World Order, to help me solve this problem.

Soon after my voting rights were removed, my back started to act up again. Since the operation, in 1963, to remove a herniated disc, it was quite alright, but now it hurt so badly that I made an appointment with the closest chiropractor. I drove over the beautiful mountain road between Sully and Notre-Dame-du-Lac. The view was superb but my back hurt so badly that a sigh broke out of my deepest insides. Looking up at a cloud, I said "Apu! Now you have to come and help me!"

Dr. Doucet looked at my back and said, "This took a long time to get like this. It will take a long time to straighten out." All the doctors had said until then was that the deterioration was progressive, non-reversible. This was the first time that I had heard that my back could improve. I believed him because I wanted to believe that my back could get better!

On the drive home a long forgotten memory popped into my mind. Sitting on Apu's lap, he told me the story about *Méhecske*, the Tiny Bee.

"One day Tiny Bee fell into the water and she was going to drown. A dove noticed her, picked a leaf from a tree and dropped it on the water. She climbed up onto it, dried her wings and was soon able to fly away. Some time later she noticed a hunter pointing his gun at the dove. 'No!,' she cried, 'I won't let him kill the dove who saved me!' She quickly flew to the hand of the hunter and stung him. The hunter dropped the gun and this time the tiny bee saved the big dove's life."

He had told me that story not once but often. I was sure now, even if for many years I had not thought much about the Apu who held me on his knees and told me stories. Memories of bad moments did not let the good ones get through, prevented me from remembering the good in him.

"You better be a good strong dove now, Apu, because I really need your help!" I said with trust to a white cloud on the blue sky above the mountains.

20   Chelsea
1974-1976

Sara came for a visit to the farm and this time she had a special purpose. My daughter felt concerned for her mother. She did not want me to turn into a hermit. She worked now in Ottawa, on the federal program of bilingualism and she thought that I should leave the farm and my solitude, and join her. While she spoke of my need to be with her, I objected. But when she said that she would like me to take care of her for a while, of course that was a different proposal.

I rented the farm to a nice young lady. (She stayed at the farm for six months, and a few years later she called one evening to let me know that both she and her husband had became Bahá'ís, and that this was because of the books she found on my bookshelves.)

We found a little white house in the Gatineau Hills and I soon found an interesting job. The director of a special school in Hull for students with learning disabilities, after seeing my curriculum vitae, asked whether I would be comfortable as a specialist in fine psychomotricity. I asked him to tell me first what that was. He explained that gross

193

psychomotricity was physical education, where the whole body is involved. Fine psychomotricity has to do with the co-ordination of the hands and the senses. It can be any kind of activity, as long as it helps co-ordination. I had taught re-education and handicrafts, so I thought that I would enjoy it, and signed a contract as a specialist in fine psychomotricity, to start teaching after Christmas. This was early December and I expected to hear about plans, preparation. When no call came, I went to the school one morning to see what the new job would be and how to prepare for it. The director was in the corridor and greeted me joyfully: "I am so glad you knew that you were starting today! I was afraid that I had forgot to tell you. We have five minutes. Wait for me here!" and he dashed off. Then he ran back to get me and he walked me into a classroom. There were about a dozen children amid piles of paper, paints, xylophones and guitars, all in a holy mess.

The director said a few nice things about me and assured the children that they were going to be very happy with me, then he left. The children gazed at me and asked, "Where is André?" This is how I found out that before Christmas a young man taught them guitar, finger painting, and xylophone. They in turn learned that now they had a white-haired lady to teach them ... whatever is she going to teach? Good God!

One of the things I used to teach my students in re-education was that children with learning disabilities have to be prepared slowly and carefully for any change. In the situation in which I found myself, there was very little of the necessary conditions for a successful re-education. The months that followed tested my ability to quickly adjust to the unexpected. I had four groups of children in that school and three in another and had to find my own solutions to the problems.

Fortunately there was a group of devoted teachers to work with. We could consult and often found clever answers, like when Gisèle cleaned out a room and showed me boxes of material and asked if I had some use for them.

194

"This might be a good idea for some of the girls," and I sat down to try the burlap and thread. I was in the corner of the teachers' room, next to the corridor. A few students saw what I was doing, gathered and asked to have some too. What I thought would be interesting for girls turned out to interest six-foot tall boys! Soon they made their own designs, chose their own colours and they were having fun. Horses' heads were the most popular among the budding embroidery artists. And messages, such as "I love you", in all colours and types of stitches.

One thing became evident very soon about these students: they were motivated when they could be useful. There was a boy in one of the classes, Denis, who did no work in any of the regular subjects but was very clever with his embroidery. One of the others wanted to give his mother something for her birthday, I suggested that he ask Denis to help. Denis became an angelic helper. He not only finished the masterpiece but he found white paper and ribbon to pack it beautifully. Next day he surprised Margot, the teacher of math, by asking a question! But things were really in a mess. The director promised things and did not keep his promises. Some teachers wanted to make a complaint against him. Our group proposed to get together with him and help straighten things out.

"Why are you so solicitous about him? He is not trying to be nice to you. As a matter of fact, he called a meeting for tonight to cut one of you to pieces," said the assistant director. And he told us that there was a meeting of the parents' committee to discuss one of us.

"What?! I was not notified!" said Jean-Marc who was on the parents' committee and should have known about it.

We all came to that meeting in the evening. It was March 21, the Bahá'í New Year. It was called to discuss me and my methods because a mother complained that her son was made to embroider. Her son, born after three girls, should be using hammer not needle! The director, instead of a talk

195

with me, wanted to show that he was a good director who protected his students and the parents. But the parents asked pointed questions about the promised individual treatment and the use of funds for supplies. I told the mother who started the whole thing that her son made only enough stitches to let me see that he had good co-ordination. Once I saw that, I let him read the books which interested and benefitted him. At the end of the evening the director was asked to prepare a report on the use of funds. The mother, no longer upset, praised me for initiative and creativity in my task as educator. A few days later the director resigned.

In that school I came to see the enormity of the unease in education, at close range. Everybody knows that there is something wrong with how teachers, pupils, school boards, parents, principals, school buses, cafeterias, budgets, curricula and laws relate to each other and to the rest of society. We all know that a big change is needed, but where and how? It is possible that the best leaders of tomorrow are today among the "children with learning disabilities". The president of the student council helped me form this opinion.

On an excursion one of the boys was hurt. They called the school, I answered and went to take him to the hospital. The president of the student council happened to be near. I asked him to come along. I took advantage of the ride alone with him to ask a few questions.

"Why are you in this school?"

"Because I do not know how to read and write."

"Is it because you are not able or because you are not interested?"

"Not interested."

"Does it not bother you that people think that you are stupid?"

"Je ne prends pas ce qui ne me convient pas" (I do not take what does not suit me), he answered. I looked at him and he looked at me. He was not fresh or snappy. He knew that I had asked him a real question and he answered truth-
196

fully. I felt a wave of admiration for this youngster of 15 who knew that the poor opinion of others did not have importance for him. That boy came from a well-to-do family. His mother and father both worked to provide what their children needed, or so they thought. What seemed valuable to the parents did not answer the needs of the children. The way these children relate to what most people consider worthy of effort is different from what people are accustomed to thinking.

At the end of the year the director of the personnel at the school board asked what could I teach besides fine psychomotricity. I said, "English."

"Good, we will take you next year to teach English and you will take courses in special education, to be safe in a special school."

I went to Sully for the summer and Sara stayed in Chelsea where she had a job. She wanted to go back to school in the fall, in second-year history at the *University of Ottawa*. In mid-August I got a call from her. Would I come back to Ottawa a few weeks early, because she was asked to be interpreter at a Bahá'í Conference in Antigua and wanted me to help her prepare. At the airport she said, "See you next week," but when I saw the plane vanish in the sky, I felt that it would be some time before I saw her again.

Charles Mondelet
1801-1876

Next week, when Sara was supposed to arrive, a cable came instead. Rowland and Vivian Estall, pioneers to the French Caribbean, had asked her to stay with them on Martinique. Is it alright with me? It was, under the condition that she continue her studies. The only thing she could study on Martinique at that time was law. So, instead of taking history at the *University of Ottawa*, Sara became a student of law in Fort-de-France. And I started as English teacher in Masham, and as a student in special education at the *University of Québec* in Hull.

My first subject was *Organization Scolaire de Québec*, with Hubert Lacroix, a study of the school laws. It could be done in a seminar fashion, otherwise he would give it to us ex-cathedra. We preferred to do the research ourselves and present our findings to the class. He put the dates of the important school laws on the board and told us to choose one we wanted to handle, and to form teams to do it. Another member of the teaching staff in Masham, Pierre Austin, teacher of Christian education who became my friend as soon as we met, also took the same course. We formed a team, choosing the School Law of 1841. I suggested that one, because the date was the closest to 1844, the beginning of the Bahá'í Era. I was curious to see what Canada and education looked like then. This was the beginning of my love affair with Charles Mondelet. And the beginning of Pierre's love affair with the Bahá'í Faith.

Charles Mondelet was a lawyer in Trois Rivières, and later became a judge of the Supreme Court of Québec. He was a patriot and an advanced thinker, way ahead of his time. He saw the need for education and wrote a series of letters in the newspapers to explain why a system of public education was needed and what it should be like. His *47 Letters On Elementary and Practical Education* is considered by historians as the intellectual preparation for legislators to establish school taxes, and the population to pay them. The School Law of 1841 was enacted by the first Parliament after Upper and Lower Canada, that is to say Ontario and Québec, became united. Mondelet saw education as the assurance for a country to be free of corrupt rulers, therefore a general necessity for all civilized nations. In Canada he saw a special need for education because of the two languages and religions.

"The true patriot, the sincere wisher of his country's good, the man who looks to the happiness of himself and his fellow men, in this world and a better state in the next, is bound to exert himself to educate, or procure the means of educating the people.".... "All good men must discard whatever prejudiced opinions they may have formed ... Let us therefore, whatever may be our origin, our religion, our politics, join heart and hand in the noble cause of education. On the success of our efforts depends our happiness, but the failure of our efforts must be followed by worse consequences than the most timid are likely to apprehend."

The foundation of all knowledge is in moral development, Mondelet said. Therefore school should start every morning with religious education, of a kind that is valid for all. Priests and ministers, together, could certainly find enough material in the Bible that could be given to all children for their spiritual elevation.

He addressed himself to the distrust between the French and English Canadians, and suggested that there should be two schools established in each community, possibly in the same building, one in English and one in French. This would result in the French parents sending their children to the English schools and vice versa, because they would see that there was no reason for mistrust and would see the benefits to their children's success in the world. The spreading of English as an universally spoken language would — paradoxically — result in the rich and elegant French language being learned by all educated people. "The moment the masses are enabled to convey their thoughts, meanings and wishes by one and the same language ... the end will be attained, and the sooner the better ... to make of us all one people."

Educators have to discourage all prejudice among their students, Mondelet said. If it is found that they meddle in partisan politics, they should be fired without pay.

"The instructor should not be allowed to intrigue, canvass or become a political brawler, nor convert his school into an electioneering club." He should teach his students, pave the way to peace and to the acquirement of knowledge, to know and exercise in time the rights of free men and fulfill the duties of their station in life. The teachers should be the best developed, most respected and best paid members of the community.

"There can be no profession more honourable and useful than that of a competent teacher; he should be treated as the guardian of youth..."

"The study of geography is of great importance ... to show that a constant intercourse and mutual assistance between all the nations of this globe are necessary." Mondelet said this in 1840! "You may try as many systems of education as you possibly can imagine; you may seek to improve the mode of tuition and ... secure the most efficient aid and assistance ... you will never succeed ... unless you ground your work on the sole basis it can safely be expected to rest upon, and that is REMOVING DISTRUST AND RESTORING CONFIDENCE."

Pierre, my partner in research, teacher of Christian education, studied at the same time 'Abdu'l-Bahá's Paris Talks. Now he exclaimed, "Mondelet was a Bahá'í!"

The Parliament enacted the law of 1841, obliging property owners to pay taxes for schools. But two amendments were entered: one gave permission to a group who may want a school only in their language, the other one gave the same right to any religious group wanting a school solely for that religion... As soon as the taxes began entering and the schools were built, the bishop of Montréal and the governor started to use the schools as a battleground. We know the sad results. The schools which were established in a hurry to handle problem learners, became tips of the iceberg.

By the time the first examinations were under way, Charles Mondelet had not even been asked to oversee the results. He did not become discouraged or bitter, he did not waste his time and energy to attack those who were not able, or did not want, to understand him. He aimed at the progress of his people, he worked for it in ways he was able to do. He gave talks about the emancipation of women, trusting the future to them.

Charles Mondelet made me see what went wrong in education in Canada. There is no use in bandaids when the whole body is sick. It also made me see that I did not have to worry, there are certainly others in this nation which produced a Charles Mondelet a century and a half ago, who would see to it that education should serve the best interests of those who pay for it.

Mondelet saw his country as an example for other nations to follow to bring harmony and co-operation among peoples who speak and believe differently but are united by the bonds of respect and trust. He was so sure of this role for Canada that he was not impatient. He knew that it would come one day. He was a true gentleman, an intelligent, farsighted and patient thinker. He made me see that I did not want to carry on in education as it was then. Rather, I considered myself an educator of the future, educating those who are obliged to put on the bandaids while we look for the cure. He trusted the future to women, the mothers, first educators of children.

The more of Mondelet's writings we read, the more Bahá'í books Pierre was eager to borrow. As he gave one back, he said, "They all say the same thing."

"Are you getting bored?" I worried.

"No! Truth is truth, no matter from where we look at it."

He started attending the Toeg's firesides in Hull. Latifa Toeg and her three sons were happy to answer all his questions. By the time March and the Fast arrived, Pierre wanted to keep it. And by the time it ended at Naw Rúz, the Bahá'í New Year, he was ready to declare his belief in Bahá'u'lláh. As I was still without voting rights, I could not recommend him, so we asked Phoebe-Anne to do it. This was a great lesson for me, it made me see that I was not alone, not solely responsible for the progress of the Faith. If I am not able to do something, another will carry on. This is not my Cause, nor the Cause of the Bahá'ís alone. It is God's Cause for the whole of mankind, and He will enable those who will help it to progress, according to His plan.

When I exchanged the solitude of the farm with living with Sara in Chelsea and teaching in Hull and Masham, I also found the way to comply with the recommendations of the National Spiritual Assembly, and my ardent desire to do what was necessary to regain my status as a Bahá'í in good standing. There were two Bahá'í psychiatrists living then in the area: Dr. Hossein B. Danesh, in Ottawa, and Dr. Abdu'l-Missagh Ghadirian, in Hull. Dr. Ghadirian accepted me as a patient. I will never be able to thank him adequately. He was patient, warm and wise. I felt totally confident in the success of his treatment. He told me in one of the sessions that people have respect for my intellect. "You have a well-developed mind. Now it is time for you to develop your spirituality."

It took maybe a week for this statement to reach my consciousness fully. I am what the French call an *esprit d'escalier*, meaning a "staircase spirit", one who remembers what he should have said upstairs when he is going down, one who takes time to grasp things.

I was driving home to Chelsea from the school in Masham, when the enormity of this statement fully hit me. I had to park at the side of the road, to allow the wave of surging blood to calm down. I felt as if a huge weight had been taken off my shoulders. "I am respected for my intellect? I don't have to run, to read more books, to learn more-more-more?" Like one who never feels rich enough, has to earn more, save more, I felt that I never knew enough, had to catch up with the most important theories ... What a relief! But! What does spirituality mean? The one I should develop? I used to think of myself as a spiritual being. Did I not stick up for my religion when the family made fun of my being a Lutheran, and going to church on Sundays? Maybe that is not what being spiritual means ... I would have to learn what being spiritual really means ... I have been trying to figure that out ever since. It is a challenge, a long road. Hopefully, it will never end.

Sandy found something that suited him better than a business suit. He became French editor of *All About Us*, a collection of poems by Canadian children from coast-to-coast. Then he met Susan and they came to the farm where I spent my vacation. They helped me start renovations. Braving the height and steep incline, they took off the old roof.

Sandy went back to school to become a teacher. Tip and his family were back in the Arctic, and Sara asked me to join her on Martinique. Before taking the plane, I had to make another sort of a trip.

204

About 10 days before I was to leave, I came down with a cold. Everybody had the "three-day-flu", said the doctor. He gave me medication and told me to go back if in three days I was not better. I was not, and he prescribed something stronger and told me to see him on Monday morning if I still had fever. That Monday was when I was supposed to take the plane. Sunday evening my fever was higher than ever and I was coughing, in bed, utterly miserable.

I sat up, very unhappy and weak, looking at the plants on the windowsill, thinking, "Here goes my two weeks at the seashore." And suddenly everything became clear! During the years of confusion, when I was groping around in my external and internal chaos, I would say to Al, "If I could only have two weeks at the seashore, by myself, I am sure I could figure things out," and he would say, "You would make friends with the mussels," meaning that instead of figuring things out, I would try to save the mussels.

"So this is what you are up to!" I said to the flowerpots, as if they were the dark forces playing a trick on me. "You want me to go on being miserable, never to be free of confusion?" I said to my own fears. "Nonsense! I am not going to be sick! I am going to have my two weeks by the sea!" I made a big mug of lemon tea, took two aspirins, said a very decided Healing Prayer and covered up. I woke up at two, completely drenched, changed my bed, got another mug of lemon tea, two more aspirins and another Healing Prayer. I woke up at six, without a fever. When my neighbours came to drive me to the airport, I was at the door, with my suitcase, ready for two weeks by the sea.

In the plane, at 30,000 feet above the earth, I mused about Freud's defence mechanisms. He says that people often use illness when they are not up to something but cannot face it maturely nor admit that they are not able to handle it. It is safe to say that sweeping that illness away was a drastic step on my long road towards maturity. My favourite definition of maturity is knowing what abases or elevates one, and choosing the latter.

205

Another thought to muse over at that high altitude was about a neat trick God was playing on me. I was 28 years old when I met the Faith and left Europe. Now I was 56, ready to leave North America after exactly 28 years. He made me a European pioneer to Canada, while I knew nothing about North America, or about the Bahá'í Faith. I was about to step into the unknown again.

Soon after I arrived in Martinique, a telegram brought the news that my voting rights had been restored and that the *National Spiritual Assembly of Canada* greeted me as a pioneer to the French Antilles.

22 Martinique
1976-1979

Sara was at the airport and she came in a white Fiat which she had bought that morning to greet me in style. It was, of course, second-hand but we loved her and called her *Kislány* which is Hungarian for "little girl". She took us to the beaches and to the beautiful island of mountains covered with poinsettia, which grow to tree size and are called "six months green, six months red", through the groves of bamboo and mango, by walls covered with bougainvillaea in many colours, "married" because that's how they are happiest.

The people are every possible colour. Some are "white", some as black as black can be, and everything in between. Some have Negroid features but green eyes or red hair. There are a few Carib Indians and many East Indians, with their shiny wavy hair. There is so much mixing that a family of six might look as if each member belonged to a different race. The language of the people shows the imprint of slavery and French education. When I hear them speaking Creole, I hear the sounds the slaves caught from the masters' shouting instructions. When they speak French, they use the most refined adjectives, coming straight from Lafontaine. They cannot pronounce the letter *r*, and that gives a special softness to their speech.

Martinique used to be the distributing centre for the slaves from Africa. Traders from North America came here to make their choice. Society seemed to me both post-colonial and post-Communist. Most of the economy was still in the hands of the "béké", the descendants of French colonialists, while there were many Communists in municipal offices. In the seventies, when I was there, the mayor of Fort-de-France, the capital, was Aimé Cesaire, the well-known poet of Negro feeling, an old Communist, who gave back his card in protest when the Soviet army crushed the Hungarians, in 1956. "Cancerous materialism" is a term Shoghi Effendi used, which I never saw as graphically illustrated as at the entrance to Fort-de-France at rush hour. Fort-de-France was built before cars came to make our lives supposedly more comfortable. On the road to St-Pierre I had a moment of great fright, when I wished that I were not in a car, but on the back of a mule or a horse. It was a steep road, I was in a hairpin turn when the clutch did not catch and I looked down to the sea while I groped for the brakes. A car does not know danger and will not protect me where an animal would. Should we not wait till the road is safe before we use technology?

The Martiniquais are warmhearted, hospitable. Shaking hands on meeting is obligatory, and if your hands happen to be dirty, you hold out your elbow to touch. People kiss, sometimes on both cheeks, and if they want to make it really friendly, they add a third kiss. We enjoyed the humour expressed by sayings like *Pa ni problem, piece, piece*, meaning that there was absolutely no problem, or *Chien pa ka fe cha*, which in French would be "Chien ne fait pas un chat", meaning that the dog does not have a kitten for a puppy, or "like mother like daughter".

Sara did not enjoy studying law and suffered from the strain. She took a part-time job teaching English at the *Chamber of Commerce of Fort-de-France* and she fell in love with a young

Martiniquais. I was fond of him as a person, as a friend, but when he started courting Sara and she responded, I was worried. I could not see them happy for more than a few weeks. I was convinced that they would soon "wake up". Sara would feel that her unfinished education was limiting her to a small island, away from her natural habitat, and the young man would feel that her superior education, many-sidedness was a threat to his masculinity. When Sara asked me to give my consent to their marriage, I asked her to wait.

No matter how mature the relationship between mother and daughter may be, a situation like that is not easy. I would like to believe that I have a good balance of devotion and detachment about my children. Of course I wanted them to be happy, but I also knew that they would have to find their own way, blunder through their own mistakes. I loved Sara very much, but did I KNOW what would make her happy? She pressed me and my confusion grew. One wants something very badly and doesn't know how to reach it. I came down with pneumonia. First it was just a cold, a great tiredness, I felt quite good with it, and told friends that I was enjoying the chance to rest. Sara became worried when the fever dragged on and took me to the hospital, where a mild pneumonia was diagnosed. They pumped some antibiotics into me and sent me home, threatening that I would have to be hospitalized if I did not get better. I didn't get better, just felt O.K. about being sick, not having to think.

But thinking, of course, went on. In a slowed-down, less frantic way, I was continuously weighing, considering pros and cons of a marriage of this kind for Sara. She told me that it was her life, not mine, and that I should hurry up and let them marry right away. The doctor wanted to hear from me by five p.m., to decide about the hospital. Sara left for her English classes at two. My thoughts came to rest on my father's quandary about George. Was it the fact that this young man was coloured that made me find him not right for Sara? Could it be that I was not free from racial prejudice? That was a horrible thought and I reached for my prayer book for help. I opened it at random; it opened to the long Prayer for the Departed. I knew that I had to say it for Apu.

When I want to really pray, I chant my prayers. As soon as I started singing, the room around me disappeared and I saw an open coffin with my father inside. I started to cry.

"I lost my father!"

I sobbed like a bereaved child. I sobbed and sobbed to the end of the long prayer, then I fell asleep. When Sara came home at five, she found me still asleep, with the fever gone. When I woke up, I wrote a note of consent to her marriage and told her that I gave it because she said that it was her life, not mine, and that I wanted to stay alive and well. She gave it back within a week and told me that when she gets married, she wants a real consent from me. She decided to go back to Canada to continue her education. Today both she and the young man are happy that they did not marry each other.

Had Apu and I exchanged thoroughly about George, would he have said that it was because he was Jewish that he did not want me to marry him? Or was it because I was very young and he knew that I needed to develop first? And — oh, horrors! — had he given his consent, would I have married George or would I have changed my mind? I did not want to pursue this line of thought just then. I had to think of Sara's departure and to organize my life after she was gone.

To earn my living, I did some psychological counselling, but that did not turn out to be a money-maker. The people who came to see me nearly all came with spiritual problems. It was hard to help them without mixing religion into the advice, and one cannot be paid to teach the Faith. Psychological counselling should be "neutral", not to take advantage of the situation.

I struggled with the problem of what to do, as I sat in Ginette Montabord's car, while she was at the bank. Next to me, on the seat, was a volume of the Bahá'í World. I opened it at random, it opened at the obituary of Greta Jankko, a Finnish Bahá'í whose name I had met before, without really knowing much about her. Now I read it eagerly. She was a *Knight of Bahá'u'lláh* for the Marquesas Islands, where I had wanted to go in 1953! The Finns are regarded by Hungarians as brothers, from the ethnic and linguistic roots. Now I felt I had a true sister, a Finnish Bahá'í who had taken over where I could not go. She also translated the Writings into her mother tongue. Yes, we have to build the new world, because that alone is the real help. I wrote to Canada, to the *International Pioneer Committee*, that I was unable to earn a living on Martinique. Their answer was that they wanted me to stay and therefore would deputize me, if I agreed.

I rented a studio on the beach of Anse-a-l'Ane, and there followed 19 months of security and well-being I had never felt before. I spent very little money, but felt rich because I could do what I really wanted to: translate the Writings into Hungarian. I could talk about the Faith to anyone who asked on the seashore where I lived and in the villages where I visited. Whenever I became tired of mental concentration, I put on a bathing suit, called my young neighbour Martine and her dog to come for a swim. I hardly ever used the car any more. There was a ferry to town from the beach, right in front of my terrace. I found that much more agreeable than the drive on the hot road. The ferry was so pleasant that at times I took it for no reason other than to relax, to feel the rocking of its engines, to smell the salty air, to listen to the sounds of the conversations, to watch the fish jump out of the sea and the sun go down into it.

As for trips to other parts of the island, there was the station of the "collective taxis", close to the ferry in Fort-de-France. I found that a much better way to travel, to meet friends, than the lonely rides. When I realized that the car was idle, with its battery all dried out, I asked Zeus if he would like to have it. Zeus lived in Morne-des-Esses, a lovely village up in the interior, which got its name from the winding road, with all the "S" curves on it. He had a theatre group called *Ja-Ca-Ta*, which means *It's Time*. He wrote plays, some dealing with the problems of alcoholism and superstition.

"Why should black people be afraid of ghosts when white men are not? Look! What you saw on your way home after drinking, and thought to be a ghost, was only a banana leaf, waving in the moonlight." Zeus was 19. He was delighted to get "Kislány" as the first car of his life, and I received a valuable lesson about how to handle the problem of battery fluid. Zeus saw that the battery was empty. He fetched a green coconut, right from a palm tree before my terrace, cut a hole in it, and poured the juice into the battery. The car put-putted away merrily.

Zeus had a little niece who was born sometime after I met his family. The grandmother wanted her to be named Angéla because of the good influence I had on the family. She said that the violent ones became gentle when they became friends with me.

I did not know it but, when I set foot in Morne-des-Esses, I went to the centre of *cambois*. *Cambois* is the Martiniquais version of "voodoo" or black magic. I was never one to dwell on black magic, it did not interest me, but putting my foot into its centre had consequences. A young woman who lived next to us in Fort-de-France had problems of her own creation. She fell in love with a married man and was hoping that he would leave his family to marry her. Sara and I tried to help her see that she was going down a road that would lead to grief all around, but she was too confused to see. One night she asked me to go to a movie with her. When we got to the cinema we saw not the expected film but the "Antichrist". Once there, we stayed and watched. It was a film about evil and a lot of the symbolism connected with it. For example, when an unchaste priest reached for the Chalice, a horrible toad oozed out from it. I had never seen anything like that and was under the effect of it for days. Then it became clear!

I was walking over to the house of the woman mentioned above. The passage was dark, and the noises around me reminded me of the horrible things in that film, and there was an uncomfortable pressure of fright in my guts. Then, suddenly, I laughed out loud!

"You want to frighten me?! But that is children's games! Alláh'u'Abhá!" The noises that made me frightened a minute before became the familiar tree frogs croaking in the calm tropical evening.

On the beach I could meet Canadians, Germans, Swiss, Australians, and of course French and Martiniquais. Yachts anchored in front of my house, and on them one could meet the world's wandering people. On the beach I could gather beautiful shells and corals. One day I went for a long swim by myself to a yacht anchored way out in the middle of the bay. I lulled a bit to rest, then decided which way to swim back. I was close to a steep shore where I have never been and considered swimming there to look around, but changed my mind and decided to swim back to the familiar beach of the *Hotel Calalou.* That hotel belonged to a Canadian couple, Claude and Helene Dallaire. The cook, André Charles-Donatien, a Bahá'í, made the best calalou, a typical Martiniquais soup made of what most people would consider weeds. A delicious soup!

I swam slowly and was aware that I was rather far and alone. I could get a cramp or something. The worst that could happen would be dying, and that would not be so bad either. I turned on my back, looked up to the sky and swam with a feeling of complete security. When I got to the shore, people greeted me with great agitation. Did I know nothing about last night's earthquake, and that its backlash had just reached our bay? I looked back and saw that the water was in turmoil on both sides of a narrow path which connected the spot on the beach where we stood and the yacht. On that narrow path, I had just swam to safety. The worst spot of the undertow was next to the steep shore I nearly went to explore.

213

"You can say, thank you!" said a handsome man, and that was a good beginning for a conversation on dangers, security and world affairs. He told me that he was a banker, educated in Switzerland, on loan to Canada at the moment. A member of the *Club of Rome*, he told me that the affairs of the world were in the hands of 15 families, who held the strings to the world's money supply. He might have told the truth or he might have been fooling. But I know that many houses on Martinique did not have water or electricity and that it was not polite to ask to use the bathroom, because there might be no such place in the house.

Claude Dallaire, owner of *Hotel Calalou*, lent me a book. He thought that it would interest me because it was written about Hungary, a family's life through the two world wars. The title was *Csárdás*, written by an American woman. She talks about the disastrous effects of World War I, on the Serbian front, on fine young men. I had never heard about them before, but she wrote about the atrocities Hungarian troops committed, violating women in the villages, torturing and killing them amid cheers of drunkenness. She says that many of those soldiers became emotional wrecks from those experiences.

I remembered a big colourful skirt in our attic in Kecskemét. It was of a rough texture and we ripened our winter pears on it. We called it "the Bosnian skirt". I could still hear Mother's voice,

"Go get a few pears from the Bosnian skirt." Where did the skirt come from? I wished I could ask Apu about it. When he died, the doctors said that his illness was progressive paralysis and that it started way back when he was serving as an officer on the Serbian front. I had always felt that he was a victim of the war, but it took a book written by an American woman, lent to me by a French-Canadian, on the beach of Martinique in the Antilles, 60 years later, to put the pieces together.

Martine, my neighbour, and I lived through Hurricane David, and it was frightening. It was terribly painful to see a yacht, which you knew belonged to a family who came out each weekend to enjoy it, ride wave after wave, trying to stay on its anchor, but slowly moving closer and closer to the shore, end up on the rocks, wave after wave assaulting it, until it was broken beyond repair.

We were in well-built houses, not in danger. One night Martine came over to my place; next night I went to hers. We passed those two evenings, without telephone, by candle light, in the middle of the howling hurricane, in unusually serious conversation. We spoke of Mont Pélé, the volcano. We had been to St-Pierre, the old capital of Martinique, and had seen the ruins of the once glamorous city and the pictures in the museum, from before the eruption of 1902, which completely devastated the city, killing every soul except one man, a prisoner in an underground jail. Nature had given enough warnings about the coming danger. For days there were rumblings, and on the day before the eruption, a thin flow of lava destroyed a building. The population was scared, wanting to flee, but the governor prepared an election, assured the people that there was no danger, and they should stay. Some listened to the signals from the volcano and fled, but most of them stayed and died with the governor in a few seconds of hot gas and ashes.

Surrounded by uprooted trees, washed-away beaches and broken boats, in our houses stripped of all greenery, chopped to shreds by the hurricane covering the walls and windows with a thick layer of green foam, Martine and I talked about the affairs of the world. We tried to listen to the signals. We hoped that we would respond to them and not stay to vote for unimportant issues when the big issue is at hand.

It was in Martinique that I became more aware of the close relationship between mind, body and spirit. When I was 12 I had been diagnosed with scoliosis and was told the condition could only deteriorate. I had the operation in 1963 to remove a herniated disc from my spine. In 1974 a chiropractor first told me that there was hope to straighten out my spine.

A Bahá'í travelling teacher came to Martinique. She stayed at the National Centre in Fort-de-France, but found the town much too hot for comfort, so I invited her to stay with me in my studio on the breezy beach. I am one of those people who take a long time to become fully awake after a good night's sleep. The first morning she started chatting away at an early hour. I told her I awaken slowly, but she didn't understand. Next morning, when she started chatting, I told her the Chinese story about the soul leaving the body to roam freely when one falls asleep, and it needing time to get back into the tight quarters of the body when the sleeper awakes, else the sleeper feels uncomfortable all day. The third morning, when she still started the day with a flow of talk, I told her that it felt as if she were pounding on my temples. In the afternoon I heard her say to Ludy Johnson, a fellow pioneer, "Poor Angéla has awful headaches in the morning."

I realized that I had three choices: to tell her to be quiet in the morning; go somewhere else to live; or endure the chatting. I wanted her to have a good impression of me, so I decided to endure the chatting. A few weeks passed, and my back started to hurt. It became so great a pain, I decided to look for help. I found no chiropractor, but made an appointment with a "kinesitherapeut." She looked me over and remarked on how tense my spine was. As she massaged the tension away, my mind put the pieces together. Not enough milk as a small baby, a case of rickets as a young child, not allowed to express grief, or ask for tenderness... Became a good gymnast developing strong muscles which were able to push the spine straight and deny there was a problem. No wonder that poor spine became crooked to the side and twisted around itself.

That evening as I said the *Long Obligatory Prayer* on the terrace "...My back is bowed by the burden of my sins..." I stopped and gazed at the sky. It seemed to be all lit-up!

Bahá'ís do not look at sin with the attitude of *mea culpa*, but see sin as the result of ignorance or illness. Education and healing are needed, not punishment. One who is educated in the right spirit will be enamoured of virtue and look at committing a sin as the worst of punishments. My ignorance caused my back to become distorted! Now I came to understand that accepting a situation not in harmony with my needs caused my back to ache and become crooked. And if I could cause the pain through ignorance and denial, knowledge and acceptance could straighten it! With the help of the kinesitherapeut, swimming and a lot of prayer and reflection, it was possible.

So mind, body and spirit started to learn a new harmony in me, to sing a new, if unfamiliar song.

One day I was on the terrace, working on my translation. It was spring, although one does not notice seasons there. An unusual movement caught my attention for a second, but it disappeared and I concentrated on my work again. Then it came again and I looked up to see a swallow zigzag by. Swallows by my terrace on Martinique! I jumped up and watched as they swooped down one after the other, picked a few insects from the palm trees and then headed for the *North Star*. They were flying home for the summer. In a few days — or weeks — they would sit on the wires by the barn in Sully, like notes on a sheet of music. I ran for my camera and, with tears down my cheeks, I took photos of small black spots among the palm trees of Anse-a-l'Ane. Only I knew that those were swallows on their way to Sully for the summer.

Down there the *North Star* nearly touches the horizon. *The Big Dipper* is only visible for seven months. At times I could see the *Southern Cross* from among the flowers of the bougainvillaea. The fragrance of the frangipane mixed with the salty air of the sea. I picked limes from the tree to make

217

my morning drink and finished my lunch with golden papaya ripened on the tree. At times I thought of people who spoke of pioneering as sacrifice! It was beautiful, it was enriching, but I began to feel that I had enjoyed enough of it. I started to feel the urge to carry on, to return — like the swallows — to the place from where I came so many years ago.

Then one day Rochane Ghadimi arrived, coming from Peru. When he heard that I was a Hungarian, he asked what I was doing on Martinique, while people in Hungary where he was on business recently, were thirsty for the Message of Bahá'u'lláh. I told him that I was a deputized pioneer to Martinique.

"If I deputize you to Hungary, will you go?"

"Of course."

"Come to the airport to see us off tomorrow morning." Next day, at the airport, he put a nice sum, in cash, before me.

"Write to the *Universal House of Justice*, tell them I want to deputize you to Hungary and, in case they agree, ask when you can leave. If they do not agree, send them the money to send somebody else." The announcer called out his flight, he embraced me and left. And I left for Hungary soon after.

23 Hungary 1979-1980

I had left Hungary in 1941. I had gone home 25 years later, in 1966, for a visit of three weeks. In 1971 I again spent three weeks at home. Those two visits were much too short; during them I had remained always a guest. This time I was to stay long enough to feel really at home, to see things from the inside.

From Martinique I flew first to Canada, to visit my children and to pack warm clothing. Sara was at the airport in Ottawa.

"Do you want to come to my graduation?" When she came back to Canada from Martinique to continue her education, she had enrolled in linguistics. I knew that a few months ago she had gone into medicine, but I didn't want to ask, "What has happened to your studies in linguistics?" because I was afraid that she would answer, "Oh, I had enough of that and quit."

No, she had finished linguistics, graduated with the gold pin of the rector for highest standing. Then she started medicine! I was a proud mother.

During my three-and-a-half years on Martinique, I had to come to Canada only once, on business. The drive into town from the Ottawa airport had been a shock, an unpleasant culture shock. After the teaming warmth of the islands, the neat cool acres of lawns without a soul on them, the wealth and good grooming of Canada hurt me. It seemed wasteful, unfair. I had been happy to return to Martinique, to hear the carillon of the Fort-de-France airport, see the hibiscus and, yes, even the flying cockroaches that laid their stinky eggs in my favourite scarf.

This time I experienced the change very differently. I saw the order, the cleanliness and spaciousness of Canada as a promise for a cleaner, richer, juster future when the little girls, like little black Angéla of Morne-des-Esses, would have the comforts that useful technology could supply, such as water and electricity, and could grow into educated, competent members of an emancipated world.

It was the end of September of a most colourful Canadian fall. Sara drove me through the blazing Gatineau Hills. Under the copper-gold arch of the maples in our former garden of Chelsea, she showed me the photos of a summer meeting in Vancouver of Emeric and Rosemary Sala and all my children and grandchildren (Kathy was of course not there. We said nothing about her, kept our thoughts to ourselves.). We did not cry. I guess we felt too moved to cry.

After a few days with her, I went to see Sandy. He had finished his degree in education and was now teaching in Alert Bay, British Columbia. They showed me the awe-inspiring totem poles of the Kwakiutl people. Jacob, a year-and-a-half, with nearly white blond hair and sky-blue eyes, enjoyed berry-picking from my back when I took him walking by the moody waters of Sandy Cove.

I visited Tip. He was finishing a degree in social work and community development in St. Paul, Alberta. After a few years as settlement manager in the Eastern Arctic, he felt the need for further studies. Now they were packing again to go back to their beloved Yukon. Peter did not need me to button his pyjamas any more, he was practically an adolescent. Sophie, with whom we picked the last of the fall strawberries, reminded me of myself as a little girl of eight.

When I was in Hungary on my first short trips, I had been surprised by the well-being and cheerfulness of people. In Canada there were so many stories in the papers, and told by expatriates, about negative things that any positive sign was an unexpected joy. Now, in 1979, I was not surprised, just looking for the explanation.

I went to Kecskemét, where I had been brought up and I looked up Marie. She used to be our cook. When she married, her husband became our gardener. Their eight children were born in the gardener's house on the other side of the lawn. Marie crossed that lawn one night during the war on a dangerous mission. She decided to save some things for me. My family was gone and the house was occupied and used as officers' quarters. She knew that there was a big old wooden chest in the maid's room and that in it were things I had inherited from my mother. She climbed in through the window, took a box full of the silverware which belonged to my great-grandmother, climbed back out the window and buried the treasure in her yard. When she heard of my first visit home, she took the box to my family, to be given to me.

I did not have time to look her up before, but now I made sure to start with a visit with her. I rang her bell and she came to the door. She looked of course very different from the young woman who used to impersonate "Father Nicholas" on December 6, or the cook who spoilt her pancakes because she knew that I liked them that way. Had I not known who she was, I would not have recognized her in that well-groomed old lady. She was not expecting me and I was also very different from what I used to be. She looked at the stranger in the open door. When I told her who I was, she clapped her hands and cried: "Little Miss! Please be so kind as to enter!" (Hungarian is a complicated language, it is difficult to give back in English the way people talk to those they hold to be of a higher class.)

"Don't talk to me like that Mari, times have changed!" I said, and she promptly switched:

"Then come right in and look at my pictures!" And she laughed and hugged me and showed me pictures of her travels to Turkey, Egypt, Russia, Austria and Switzerland. She showed me pictures of her children and grandchildren, all fine-looking people. And I showed her pictures of my children and grandchildren, and she found them fine-looking too. I was not "The Miss" anymore and she was not "The Cook". We were two old friends who had lived and loved a lot since we last met and had much to tell each other.

I looked up the girls who used to be my friends at school. They were mothers, grandmothers, some widowed, some happy, some sad. I visited graves of dancing partners who died on the front.

And of course, I sat by my mother's grave which she now shares with Apu. I clipped the ivy so that the two white marble tombstones could be seen and I planted rosebushes for both. I walked on the streets, some still paved with the yellow bricks I never saw anywhere else in the world until I was in Trgu Mures, in Romania, in 1991. They are glazed and they look slippery in the rain, but they felt good under my feet. There are still pigeons all over town. One flew low above my head and a small white feather fluttered down after it passed. I held out my hand and the feather landed in my palm. I took it to mean "Welcome!" and "Peace!" and I put it in my prayer book.

I went to see the school where Apu used to teach. It had hardly changed. The school where I studied had not changed much either. It still reigns over the main square of Kecskemét. Not far from where it stands is what used to be the synagogue. I had never entered the synagogue, although I had passed by it at least twice a day. It is now transformed into a building dedicated to science. This time I entered and walked around and thought of the souls who used to worship there but are no more.

I went to the Lutheran church where, sitting next to my mother, I learned that "God is our strong fortress". At that time only the thin steeple could be seen from the square, because shops were hiding most of the building. Those shops had been removed recently and the church was in full, lovely view!

I found two friends of my mother still alive, both over 90. One of them, Joli néni, used to be the subject of my envy. She would walk to town between her two handsome sons and to me she seemed elegance personified, with the two young gentlemen at her side. I could now walk like that with my two sons, if all three of us could ever be in the same place at the same time. The other one was Mici néni, wife of my father's best friend. Her husband was an outstanding scholar and also a poet. Mici néni recited for me her late husband's poems in a strong voice. I was spellbound by the vigour of this very old lady, reciting long poems by heart, as if she had some inner voice guiding her memory. The poems were mostly about faith in the power of God and in the goodness of man. Many had biblical themes and talked about the imminence of Christ's Second Coming, to bring justice to the whole earth. A volume of these poems was in the process of being published. I was surprised to hear that it was being published not only with permission but with support from the authorities. This, in a country where religion was supposed to be proscribed?

"Oh, that's the bad propaganda we get," was the answer. It used to be that religion was frowned upon, but no longer. Actually there was a strong movement to teach the Bible because of the need for moral education to counteract alcoholism and suicide. Children showed me their school books. They learned that consultation was important in the life of the community because that's how progress in social development would succeed, when all concerned become involved in decisions. What surprised me most about these books was that they said that Marxism was a step towards the united, classless society. A big step, but only a step.

Three of my teachers were still around and I went to see them. They happened to be the teachers who were key-people in my upbringing: our "class-head" or home-room teacher, the teacher of Hungarian and that of English. Kató néni used to be our home-room teacher when I was 10-18 years old. She taught mathematics, and, I did not like mathematics. She, in turn, did not like young ladies to be late for school, arriving on bicycle, in tennis shoes, with flushed cheeks, obviously late on account of a game of tennis. Our relationship at that time was a graceful conflict of personalities, graceful because of our common respect for discipline. It was fun to meet her now, still very much herself. We exchanged gracefully, in a warm but aloof manner, like a good game of tennis.

My teacher of Hungarian language and literature was now living in Debrecen. I travelled there specially to thank her for teaching me so well, that after so many years of hardly using it, I was still able to translate the finest and most poetic Bahá'í writings into Hungarian. Besides good parents, good teachers are a special gift from heaven.

I went to thank Mária néni, my first English teacher, because she opened the English world to me. Whenever I hear somebody say that one cannot learn a language in school, I can present my case to prove the contrary. There were no English newspapers nor radio nor TV, I still learned it so well that at 21, I could be sent to Lisbon to report what was important for my country in the English-speaking press, because I had good teachers.

Education in Hungary is scientifically-oriented, but such questions as what is right, wrong, just or unjust, lasting or passing are also important. I often heard the word *text*

224

meaning, "It is easy to talk, what are the actions and the results?" Unfortunately, I also often heard the word "useless". Some Hungarians tend to feel their powerlessness, like a small boat or a drowning bee, on the troubled waters of the stormy sea. People in Hungary look to Canada, as leader in world affairs, with great respect, with hope and trust.

Not far from Mother's and Emese's place, stands a house that belonged to Ármin Vámbéry, the first Hungarian Bahá'í. There is a marble plaque on the wall, because he was a famous orientalist. In 1979 that building had three occupants, the Peace Council, the Patriotic Front and the U.N. Association, groups working for the most important areas of internal and international aspirations. For the historians of the future it may become intriguing to connect the present use of that building with its past history.

It seems very significant to me that the national anthem of Hungary should be a prayer. It asks God to bless Hungarians with joyousness and plenty; to hold out a protecting arm when they are fighting with an enemy; to bring happier days to those who were torn by ill-fate for so long; because this nation has already paid for the sins of the past and of the future. This remained the official anthem during all the years of Communist rule. I find it significant that Canada's national anthem should also make mention of God.

Rochane Ghadimi was right when he said that I would be comfortable in Hungary. I could have good conversations with most everybody, buy flowers on every street corner, I could swim in relaxing hot springs, go to concerts, eat whipped-cream-topped pastries with friends who love me, but I could not stay. Not yet, anyway.

In the train one day, between Kecskemét and Budapest, I was looking out the window as the train passed a row of army barracks. On the corner stood a Russian soldier, a sentinel, in disciplined attention. He was young, maybe 19 or 20. A peasant woman sat across from me in the compartment. As the train passed, she turned away from the window and looked at me with her soft brown eyes and said: "The poor boy! He would so much prefer to be home with his family."

This time I was supposed to stay in Hungary, but to do so beyond six months, because I was a Canadian citizen, the request had to be made at the Hungarian embassy, in Ottawa. Therefore, I returned to Canada, entered my request at the embassy and was told that it would take four-to-six months.

Tip and family then lived in the Yukon, in Whitehorse. They invited me to stay with them while I waited for the permission.

First I had to take care of the farm. Back in Sully people greeted me saying, "You did say that you would be gone for five years!" So I did, although I have forgotten about it in the meantime, with all the travels since I left. People were happy to greet me back, but the chipmunks were not. They were mad when I made them leave the house. Everything was in order, pictures on the walls, dishes in the cupboards as if the owner had left the week before. I was lucky, I was protected. I decided not to stretch my luck any further and to rent the house before I left it this time.

With much to do, I threw myself into it with joy because Sandy was coming East with Jacob. Jacob was now over two years old. I expected them, and it gave me wings. Then came a phone call, they were not coming to the farm. Jacob was tired of travelling. Could I come to meet them in Québec? It was not the kind of visit I had dreamed of, but it was good to see the calm, intelligent little boy, looking at everything with his thoughtful eyes. We said good-bye at the bus station in Montréal and I did not feel like going back to my lonely farm right away. Normally I did not feel lonely there, but this time I felt like passing a week with friends in Québec.

When I got back to the farm, I found a man sitting on the steps. He said, "I have been waiting for a week because I want to settle here." He heard from neighbours that the house was for rent. I knew that I could not make a living there, and

226

I had to work for another five years before I could retire. I told people that I would like to rent the farm to a family who might not pay much but would make improvements.

This young man sounded capable and he said, "I am a constructor, I shall build a comfortable little house of field stones for you, on your favourite spot." In that case he could count on the big farm house for himself and family, because I prefer a comfortable little house. We agreed, and I left Sully for the Yukon.

24 Yukon
1980-1982

Tip and Susie wanted me to be another loving adult in the house because they were both working. That is to say, I was to be a grandmother, a useful one for the whole family. Thus, after three-and-a-half years in the tropics and the greater part of a year in Eastern Europe, I landed in the Arctic, in the centre of a culture I had wanted to know. And I could be a grandmother in the bargain!

Tip was waiting at the Whitehorse airport and the first thing he said was that next day we were going to a wedding. I got to know their friends right away. It was a wonderful way to become a part of the Yukon! The bride was the sister of a girl I knew from Martinique and the groom was a young Native pilot, I was anxious to know because I had heard lovely stories about his family. It was the wedding of Mark and Leslie Wedge; a moving wedding, reminding me of a Japanese wedding I attended at *McGill University*. The two young people who marry have the whole community around them, supporting them, sending them off on their own voyage over the sea of the future, but not leaving them alone to brave the storms.

At the end of the reception the young couple gave gifts to their parents and friends with words of thanks or whatever seemed relevant. I received a little vase with white and yellow flowers, and the words were, "To the one who came from the farthest."

Soon after I arrived, there was a winter school in Anchorage to which Tip and family went. I preferred to stay and have a rest.

**Hand of the Cause at Rawdon, November 1982
Left to right: John Robarts, Audrey Robarts,
Angéla Szepesi, André Bergeron**

Peter and Sophie were already young teenagers. We had fun collecting rosehips and making them up into a syrup against colds. Peter enjoyed pushing me into the snowbank and Sophie offered her cat to hold in case I felt lonely when they were at school. I loved to hear Susie delight in the meal on the table when she came home from work. But they did not really need me and I was not a professional grandmother. Soon I felt that I was not really needed in the house. I wanted to get a job, but did not want to start something and have to quit suddenly.

My dilemma was solved by a providential visit to Whitehorse by Jamie Bond. Jamie was still a student when we first met at the *Laurentian Bahá'í School*. He married Gale, a Hungarian girl. When Jamie heard that I was struggling with a question connected to pioneering in Hungary, he thought that this should be put to the *Universal House of Justice* for guidance. He helped me write a cable to Haifa, to ask whether I should accept a job in the Yukon, or go to Hungary when permission came, even if I had no job in view there. The answer came, and it said that it was essential to become self-supporting in Canada before leaving for Hungary.

This was the turning point in my relationship to money and also to myself. The *House* wanted me to become self-supporting in Canada! They wanted me to be comfortable, independent! I opened the newspaper and answered the first ad and got a job as secretary-treasurer of Teslin, to start on April 21, Ridván, the feast of the Bahá'í administration! I had never liked to do anything with numbers or money. But Bahá'u'lláh clearly wanted me to tackle this job, therefore He would help me if I asked. John Robarts said that in a difficult situation, one should use the Remover of Difficulties, a prayer revealed by the Báb. To say it once and, if it did not work right away, say it nine times, 95 times; if still no result, say it 500 times. Mine was a pretty difficult situation, therefore I decided to start the day with 95 Remover of Difficulties. It worked.

On the 50th anniversary of my graduation from high school I learned that the teacher, who taught us mathematics all through the eight years, was known as a poor teacher. This was known by everybody except me because my father did not allow anything critical about teachers to be uttered in the house. Had I known that this teacher was not a good teacher, I would have probably not developed the opinion that I was not good in math. Yet, had I not felt that this job was so hard for me that I had to have an hour of "Removers" every morning, I might have not gotten into the habit of saying them.

Thank God, I became addicted to an hour of Remover of Difficulties to start my day! It worked so well that within a year I had the accounting organized according to Canada-wide municipal codes and everything on computer.

Teslin is on the Alaska Highway, on that fabulous highway constructed during the Second World War, and, is one of the stories I specially liked to report to Budapest. Now I lived on it and came to love its every bumpy mile. The population of Teslin is mainly Indian. They were the only people living around there until the highway was built, in 1942.

On my first day at the office old David Johnson came with his cane and a five dollar bill, to pay for his water. Water was supplied to the houses by a tanker truck. A minimal fee of five dollars was charged to each house, to provide three deliveries per week, up to 1200 gallons per month. When I entered David Johnson's payment, I noticed that he had had only two deliveries in the past month and the quantity was 312 gallons. Then another Native came with a similar situation. When the third such case paid his five dollars, I said to him, "Titus, you only had water once last month and took only 68 gallons."

"I don't need more," answered Titus.

"But you pay for three deliveries per week, for 1200 gallons a month."

"I don't need more." He told me that he only took water for a tank in his cabin, in case there was a fire. When he needs water, he gets it from the lake. And he told me how he used to work as a fire-fighter when he was young. It was different then. Young people now prefer to play around, not like it used to be.

After a few more futile attempts to explain that paying five dollars gave right to more water than what they used, I realized that there was no sense in trying to make these people see that they were paying unfairly, because they just could not equate water with money. Money is a piece of paper, water is real. It's like somebody trying to make me equate

232

money with love. I felt elated to be among such human beings once I understood that "incapacity"!

There were of course things in their ways which made
me sad. I saw too many drunk people. Recently back from
Hungary, I could see how similar people here were to my
own countrymen. Both have the dubious honour of having a
very high rate of alcoholism and suicide. I guess it is difficult
to be sensitive when one feels weak and powerless.

I sat one evening by my window. It was in June when
the days were long, the sunsets beautiful, the sky still light at
11 p.m. A village boy, Eddy, whom I specially liked, was weaving his way home. He was very drunk. There was something
familiar about the way he was going first in one direction then
in the other, with uncertain steps, as if he were looking for
somebody or something, never finding it. I realized with a
start that the way he walked reminded me of my father. Yes,
Apu walked a bit like that. I guess I was lonely for him now.

I sat by the window, thinking of Kathy. One late fall
evening, when she was five, we were driving back from the
forest where we picked fallen leaves to enrich the earth around
our new house. I was enjoying the last lights of the dusk, when
I heard a barely audible whisper, "I feel jonjy."

"Are you lonely, Sweetheart, because Tip and Daddy
are not with us?"

"No, just jonjy." She just felt sentimental, nostalgic. As
I registered that I was truly lonely for her, a car stopped before my house, and Louise Profeit LeBlanc and her three
daughters got out. They came to see how I felt in Teslin. One
of the girls held out her hand. There was a small ceramic
heart on her palm. "It's for you."

I often have to take long rides by myself, and friends
ask if I am lonely. No, because there is a small brown ceramic
heart, close to the clutch in my car. It keeps me company.

A few weeks later I was invited to pass the weekend in
Carcross, camping with friends. Carcross has its name from
caribou crossing while going to new pastures. The night I ar-

rived, there was a spectacular display of Northern Lights, a perfect arc of solid white light arched over the valley the caribou used to pass.

Next morning I woke up early inside my tent. I was still half asleep when I had a half-dream, half-vision. I was a small child and I was running after Apu because I wanted to ask him to forgive me for something, but he just kept on walking, getting farther and farther away so that I could not catch up to him. I suddenly thought to myself, "Maybe he does not know that I am running after him."

Could it be?! Maybe at that time, in my early childhood, when I could not ask him to forgive me because he did not wait for me, he was not even aware of me behind him? Maybe he was in a rush to get to school, or maybe he had something on his mind? Could it be that my worst fear of Apu not loving me was due to nothing but a lack of understanding? Was I hurt, unhappy for nothing? What a beautiful feeling!

One day Leslie Johns, an artist, a great photographer shared with me his beautiful pictures. When my turn came, he stopped at one that showed Kathy and Ed. It was a composite photo Ed's mother had sent me shortly after they became lost. Leslie asked, "What colour was their plane?" (There were two planes missing about the same time.) When I answered that it was yellow, he said that his mother and he were convinced that the couple in that plane was taken prisoner by a Russian or Chinese submarine. In those years of the Cold War submarines were active in Arctic waters.

Leslie's mother, Dora Wedge, is known for her uncanny intuition. In 1948 she dreamt that a white-haired man called her to walk up to a building that had white columns. In 1963, when she entered the house of pioneers, Ted and Joanie Anderson, she recognized 'Abdu'l-Bahá as the one who called her. Could she be right this time?

When I was on Martinique, a friend who was reputed to be a psychic told me that Kathy and Ed were prisoners because of some kind of animosity. I thought that she captured the "vibes" of a jealousy, because there was a young man who hoped to marry Kathy. I did not give serious thought to her talk about captivity then, but now I remembered what she had said. That friend, Mado, gave me a present, a golden pin with an antelope head from the Ivory Coast as a good-bye gift when I left Martinique. Now I sent her a pin of an owl Leslie had made from moose-horn, and wrote her what Leslie told me. Mado answered immediately, that she had received a vivid impression concerning Kathy when she received that pin. She felt Kathy told her that they were in Soviet Russia, under heavy guard in a pavilion. They were teaching English and French. They had applied for repatriation but did not expect it soon. Could it be? We may find out one day. If anyone knows my Kathy with the two-tone brown eye, please let me know where she is.

In Teslin I lived in a log cabin. It was one of the oldest houses, built by an R.C.M.P. officer a long time ago, people told me. How long ago, I asked. Oh, it was in the thirties! How relative things can be! The house where I was born was renovated at the turn of the century and under an arch an inscription was found: "Renovated in 1725." I still liked my "old" log cabin.

People who have never seen the Yukon cannot imagine the riot of flowers which appears as soon as the snow melts. Nature wants to catch up fast. Overnight wild roses cover everything. Then come the others, like the lupin and the fireweed. I started a garden thinking that I enjoyed digging the earth, even if there was not much chance to reap. I ate red currants in August from the bush I planted in June.

The most beautiful flower I found where the *North Star* is right above our heads, was the spirit of unity shown by the Natives. They do things together, whether it be administering the affairs of the village, or believing in God. When they say, "we", they mean all humans. When they want to refer to Indians only, they say, "our people". They have a kind

235

of family feeling that we would gain by imitating in our "civilized" world.

I noticed one day that people walked slowly and held hands. There was something different about the way they behaved. I was on the phone with Pete Sidney of Whitehorse and told him about it. He asked, "Did somebody die in the village?" Yes, and after the funeral there was a potlatch.

My window looked out on the Band Office and the long house. I saw the people go to the potlatch and wondered whether I could go. I asked Pete about it. He answered with a question, "How do you feel about it?" I thought that he did not understand my question, so I elaborated, asking if it was proper for me to go. He said again,

"What do you feel like doing?" So the next time there was a funeral, I went to it and the potlatch. Nobody made any fuss about me, nobody said excitedly, "Oh, it's nice you came!" I was one of the people, one of them, or rather one of us. So much so that a man who went around giving away dollar bills, gave me one too. I think that they might find it strange that I should make mention of this, as if it were something extraordinary.

One night I took part in a prayer meeting at the house of John Peters. His father, Tom Peters, an elder close to 90, looked around the room, at the people of different races and religions and talked something like this: "Once we are up there" — and he pointed his old finger towards the sky — "we will see that we all belong together, and we will say, what a pity that we didn't know it while we were still down there!"

My work with the accounts and other administrative duties of Teslin was not the hardest task for me. The relationship between whites and Natives wore me thin. This was specially hard because I was not impartial; my sympathies were with the Natives. I found it far too difficult to accept the attitude of whites, accustomed to being boss, while the Indians were accustomed to being ignored.

I encouraged the Indians to express themselves, to make themselves heard. That of course was not permissible for the secretary-treasurer of a Local Improvement District, set up by the white administration. It made me suffer and it made me vulnerable.

I told Sara about it and that I found the tension too much to take. She said, "I will let you leave Teslin only if you come to Ottawa." At the right moment, the old secretary wanted her job back and I was told to go. I was relieved. Now I could carry on, with this experience added to my life. It was not the end of the wonders yet. When I told Doris McLean, in Whitehorse, that I was glad that I had time to cross Canada by car and that I was leaving on August 10, she said, no. I was to leave on the 8th and go to the Blood Reserve with them to an *International Indigenous Council.*

"But Doris, I am not a Native."

"You are one of us. Besides, you are coming," said Doris. I did not regret having given in to her. Those four days as one of 16 people, in a convoy of four cars, were some of the most delightful days of my life. They took care of me because I am old, only the way they said it, "elder", is kinder.

As I don't see well at night, Frances offered to drive my car. I never slept so peacefully while somebody else was at the wheel. My old "backseat driver's psychosis" left me for good. They made fun of me because I wanted to camp, while they preferred to sleep at motels. They gave me an Indian name: "Wanna-Camp-Angéla". And they laughed at me. They were in the majority and they won all the time.

It happens that one meets somebody for the first time but it is as if he were an old friend, or a beloved family member. Mentality connects or separates for sure. When one meets somebody with whom one can be in a deep exchange as soon one meets, that is wonderful and this is what happened when I met Dave Porter. He was then Vice-Chairman of the *Council for Yukon Indians* and he came to a meeting in Teslin on his way to Watson Lake.

237

I first met the gentleman who was with him, a German. I had little chance to practise my German, so I started a conversation with him. Dave came around to say that they should get on the road and they had to have supper too. I did not want to cut the conversation short, so I invited them for a supper of goulash at my place. At the table my German friend faded into the background as Dave and I took off in a conversation that became an hour-long crescendo. When they left — because they had to carry on — and went to the door, Dave looked up where I stood on top of the steps, with those slanting bright eyes and said, "I have to go to Ottawa next week."

"My daughter lives in Ottawa," I said.

"Is she like you?" he asked.

After they left, I asked myself what that expression on his face meant when he asked, "Is she like you?" I have been told that I tend to come on too strong. Some people find it much too strong. Did Dave's expression mean, 'Who is this two-ton truck disguised as an old lady?"

No, Dave did not find me too heavy, maybe because he is a heavy weight himself. The last time I met him it was in Ottawa. I was on my way to work. As I drove through the intersection from Rideau Street to Sussex Drive, there he was on the sidewalk.

"Dave!"

"Angéla!"

People swore and tooted as we set a date for lunch next day. We talked about Teslin, about the progress with the land claims, about his children, the month he hoped to pass hunting in Inuvik, about my sister's expected visit from Hungary, about integrity in a system of political parties. Above all, we shared our conviction that it is worthwhile to work for a better tomorrow.

In the meantime he became a Member of the *Legislative Assembly*, one of 16 legislators of the Yukon, as well as heading the *Economic Development Corporation* and the radio and

TV for the Natives. At 29, he was an important man. I asked him what he wanted me to pray about for him.

"That I get a big moose and a fat sheep for winter," he answered, without a minute of hesitation. I laughed out loud on the sedate Ottawa street. He can count on my prayers, especially because if he gets a big moose and a fat sheep, his neighbours will not go hungry either.

Sara called me to Ottawa now for the second time. The first time we lived in a little white house in the Gatineau Hills. Now she shared a co-op in Sandy Hill with five others and I became the seventh and oldest member of the household. From the solitude of the farm and the privacy of the log cabin in the Yukon, it was a great change. From the moose and salmon diet of the North to a vegetarian diet, from chopping my wood to waiting my turn for the bathroom, it was a change. I like changes. It is fun to get along with people very different from myself, each with their own hang-ups, their own qualities. To be faithful to my never dull life-pattern, from the co-op where I slept on a mattress in Sara's room, we moved into a luxurious condominium, into an apartment on the 18th floor. Sara was in her last year of medicine and the terrace looked out on what is called "Medical Row", towards Alta Vista and Smyth Road.

I found a job on the first try. Jobs had started to get rare even in Ottawa but I landed one. Not an ordinary one either but one which supplied a missing piece of the puzzle

241

of my world. I had never been in touch with the world of factory workers; now I became a fore lady of the evening shift in a knitting mill. It sort of jumped at me from the billboard of *Employment Canada*:

"Foreman or forelady, to work between 4 p.m. and midnight." I like to have mornings to myself and the salary sounded alright, so I called.

"Would a 62-year-old lady do?" The voice with an educated British accent said, "She might. Come to see me next Monday."

Next Monday I sat in the office of Roy, the plant manager, and found out that he also had an M.A. in political science, with speciality in international relations, specializing in East-European affairs, of all things!

He hired me and I had to become acquainted with the workings of the different departments because I was to be evening supervisor for the whole factory. Even before I finished my first day, before knowing anything of the department I was in, I learned that it was the other department's fault that things were not going well. And that it was the management's fault that the other department was allowed to get away with murder. When I reported to my immediate superior what I learned in the first week, I learned from him that it was the rest of the management's fault that things were not as they should be. Here I made a decision: I have to work for harmony between different parts of that company. This is a general attitude with me and it is also the best way to achieve a good atmosphere in a workplace, which in turn should create greater productivity, say the social psychologists.

I threw myself into my job with an ardour that made Sara smile and say, "It's nice to hear you talk about the factory. You have always been good in situations where you could help the underdog." She meant the workers, but I regarded the owners as much oppressed as the workers. They could have started a meaningful dialogue but they were themselves so tense and insecure in an economic climate, full of pressure, that they were not able to see things in a new way.
242

Roy and I had a few good conversations. He hired me because he hoped that I could help him bring about a people oriented approach to management. When we talked about world problems, we agreed fully, but when we turned to the problems of the firm, the conversation usually deteriorated into his pain and frustration about the years of trying in vain. My concept of the company was that it was a unit, with different parts looking for the co-operation that would be to everybody's benefit. Roy thought that I was naïve. I decided to work hard and show him that it was worthwhile to trust.

I was, of course, a square peg in a round hole, but I found so many interesting things to learn that I did not notice quickly that I was not well-suited for the job. There were so many hard things to do that I was exhilarated with the feeling of achievement at the end of my workdays. Although I am an idealist, I am also practical, task-oriented and organized. In the factory I had ample chance to practise those qualities, but I could do little to improve human relations. The situation was one that I would not have expected in the Canada of the 1980s. People had power, because they had money. "My money" was important, all important; "my work" was not; "my person", "my feelings" did not enter into any consideration.

I don't give up easily. I found enough promising signs to hope that the good changes were right around the corner. We had a course on attitudes to cultivate in supervisors. This made it clear that the position of supervisors was a crucial one in building loyalty on which depends the success of a modern enterprise. I thought "Wonderful, this will give results." It did not. There were upstairs people, with air-conditioning and computers to check the financial situation. Then there were the downstairs people, where the physically hard work was done in heat or cold, in noise and dirt and hatred. The upstairs people were important, the downstairs people could be replaced as soon as they did not like it. There were enough people looking for work. Everything was pitifully and needlessly inhuman. Everybody was caught in the web of tyranny by money and machines. It was as if there had been no advances made since the galleys carried the slaves from Africa to Martinique to be sold to buyers from New Orleans. The conversation of the workers was outside-oriented. The factory and their jobs in it were something to be endured because of necessity. The quality of their contribution had no importance as long as it did not affect their paycheque. The bell rang at the end of another day as they earned their living with the sweat of their brows.

Still, they at least had work and received wages they could say they had earned. At the grocery store on my way home one day, as I awaited my turn at the cash register, I noticed a hesitating hand. It picked up a small chocolate bar and put it back again, then picked it up again, then resolutely put it back in its place. The hand belonged to a young man who paid for his groceries with a slip of paper. I peeked and saw that it was a $20 voucher from a welfare agency. The young man had a fine, clean face but a down-beaten look in his intelligent eyes. I imagined that he would be happy to change places with one of those workers who got wages at the end of every two weeks and could say that he earned his living.

That factory gave me first hand information about the economic realities of an archaic situation in a technologically advanced world. Of course, this situation could not last. It might sound simplistic, but I was convinced that the animosity would be recognized and eliminated by the owners as undesirable from every point of view. Love is a big word. For many it is a dream, a utopia. But love is the basis of life. Hatred is the cause of death, and also of failure in the business world. One does not have to be a religious dreamer to know that people who exchange their ideas well are happier and achieve more.

While I was working in that factory, I was also in touch with the social life of my compatriots around Ottawa. I saw and heard enough to become convinced that Canada is really playing a very special role in the world as the breeding ground of a civilized humanity, where all can learn to replace grudges by goodwill. Canada, truly, is the icebreaker. Those who arrive with hatred in their hearts are free to carry on their grudges, but the next generation is bound to see things more clearly.

As a child, I learned that Czechs and Romanians were thieves, my enemies. In the factory, the two people who were kindest to me were Roy, grandson of a Czech emigrant and Dan, a Romanian. He came from the south of Transylvania. He remembered a few Hungarian words and liked to greet me with a "Jó reggelt". The fact that he said "Good morning" when he saw me arrive in the afternoon did not dampen my joy. The enemy is not an enemy any more once he becomes a friend. So that I would really learn this lesson in understanding, the gentlemanly official of the government, who was checking the conditions of safety for the workers, was a recent immigrant from Yugoslavia. He still had the accent of that country, the third one I was taught to hate and whose king was assassinated with some help from my first husband.

Sara graduated from medical school, had a nice party in our high-rise apartment, bought a car, packed it to cracking and drove off to Calgary to start her year of internship. Before she left, we had a long heart-to-heart, adult woman-to-woman conversation. It amazed me to hear her reactions and perceptions.

For me, Sara's reaction to my telling her how many children I should have brought into this world is the most memorable communication between the two of us. First, she seemed deeply shocked. Then her expression suddenly changed. Her voice cracked, like a cowboy's surprised whip. "I have always wondered how come you are such a good teacher! They are helping you!"

Sara's room in the high-rise apartment was soon taken over by Emese, my sister from Budapest. She had never been in America before; it was fun to introduce her to Canada.

Our first trip of course took us to the Yukon. We arrived this time straight into a big get-together of the Johns family. Maraya Johns was a fabled Indian woman who was blind and passed much of her days in prayer. Doris, her granddaughter, told me how she would find her in prayer when she went to visit. She would play for a long time, till her grandmother finished praying. When asked why she prayed so much, she answered that she will have many descendants and has to pray for all of them. Her descendants were now gathered at Carcross, and they had invited us to the celebration. Had this been another wedding, Emese would have merited the gift "to the one who came from the farthest."

Emese was happy to meet this large Native family. She was especially impressed by Johnny John's deep voice as he said his favourite prayer: "...Oh God! I will no longer be sorrowful and grieved, I will be a happy and joyful being..."

Next day, Angéla Sidney, one of Maraya Johns' daughters, showed us how to clean fish. Angéla and I developed a warm friendship, finding many things in common of which our name was only one. She spoke Tagish, besides Tlingit, and remembered many old stories. People loved to listen to her and learned a lot from her. She was nearly blind, but when her son gave her three big salmon, she had no trouble cleaning them. She did it with a tiny pocket knife, not bigger than her knobby index finger. She chose a flat rock in a small brook, laid the fish on it and let the water carry away the stuff she threw out. We helped by holding the fish so they would not slip away. When she finished, she looked up at Emese with only one eye open, let out an impish, crystalline laughter and said, "This is how an Injun woman cleans a fish!"

In the early summer of 1991, one afternoon I was working in my garden. Without any idea why, I left the spade and went into the house, turned on the radio and heard Vicki Gabereau announce that the news had just arrived that Angéla

Sidney, the last Tagish-speaking Canadian, who was awarded the *Order of Canada* for preserving that language for posterity, had died that morning in the Yukon.

"Thank you, Angéla, for letting me know that you arrived safely and that you are well." And I went back to continue my work in the garden, to grow flowers and healthy food while still in this world.

Emese enjoyed meeting all my friends, but Tip and family were the main attraction of Whitehorse for her. She knew Tip from photos I had sent home since he was born. She followed the growth of the baby in a carriage into the small boy playing in the sand on the Portuguese beach, then into the little gardener grinning over his flowers with the trophy he had won in Verdun. She saw the photos of the serious big brother in the family picture, and the young husband taking his bride to the Yukon. Now she met him, a man of over 40, with silver threads in his black hair over slanting eyes. And Tip met his aunt, a serious, mature woman but full of good humour, interested in all that she could see. We swam and dined in the Takhini hot springs. Emese loves all beauty.

As Tip climbed out of the pool, shaking the water out of his hair, Emese whispered to me, "The men in our family are usually handsome, but Tip takes the palm." She found Peter and Sophie charming in their adolescence. Listening to Sophie express her ideas made her say, "Early maturity seems to be hereditary with you." I took it as a very welcome compliment. In our family it was a mark of brains to quickly and cleverly point out what was wrong. It was wonderful to be with a member of my closest family who saw the good and the beautiful and was not shy to say nice things!

Emese noticed how differently Hungarians and Canadians treat their guests. In Hungary the hosts would be always attentive to their guests, here she was treated with little fuss. We had a few good visits, conversations, friends were invited to meet us, but the life of the family was not disrupted, we just blended in. But when Susie, my daughter-in-law, handed me the keys to her car for a two-day trip to the north,

247

Emese nearly fell through the floor. She had never seen anything like that before! There were lots of cars in Hungary by then, but nobody would have shared them the way Susie did! The trip was something out of the ordinary too. We went to Elsa and Keno and met a Hungarian miner family and got lost on the mountain above Keno. We were beyond nowhere; it felt as if we were at the top of the world, wondering if we ever would find the way back. Of course, we did and on the way Emese had her first swim in Canada, in the Stewart River. The water was cold and she shivered happily when she got back into the heated car.

From the Yukon we flew to Calgary, where Sara was waiting. She showed us her hospital and the reception area, more like the hall of an elegant hotel or a greenhouse. The open-door library made Emese drool in admiration. She was used to the *Lenin Library of Moscow* where she had to wait for a permit amid armed guards. Sara packed us into her Toyota and we headed for Grand Forks, B.C. to Sandy and family.

Sandy was the only one of my children who had met Emese before. But of course he was very different now from the boy of 17 who went shopping for boots with his aunt in Budapest.

The weather was kind and we could continue tasting the rivers and lakes. Christina Lake, near Grand Forks, was perfect for swimming and surfing. Sara had her surfboard on top of the car and she sailed off, Emese swimming out after her. I played with Jacob and his little sister, Celeste, who in their innocence had absolutely no fear of the water.

I noticed the groups of young people on the beach, surrounded by beer bottles, behaving foolishly. This was a familiar sight but this time it struck me beyond all proportions. Maybe I was tired, maybe it just had to boil over, but I suddenly saw my father's wine and brandy, the tranquilizers I took, the drugs my sons were playing with and the memory of the helplessness, of lonely anguish grabbed my heart like an icy hand.

I was hardly able to control my feelings until we got back to Sandy's house. Once there, I went to our room and collapsed. Emese found me in tears and asked what the matter was. I blurted out, "George ... I would have left him had Apu not objected." I did not mean to talk about George. It just came out like a boil that bursts. Emese was a small girl, only four years old, when George died, but of course she knew about it. Now she asked whether I had ever talked about this before, had I told anybody that I think that I would have broken off our engagement, or maybe never would have become engaged had my father not been so categorical in his refusal to consider my love for him. No, I had never spoken about it with anybody, and had not meant to this time either.

"It will do you good to let it come out," said my wise sister. And she added: "Did it ever occur to you that George would have likely died in the gas chambers?" She couldn't have said anything more comforting.

From Grand Forks, Sara drove us through the Rockies, back to Calgary airport to catch our plane to return to Ottawa. That 18-hour drive through "the world's most beautiful roads", as Emese called them, was a big gift of Sara's, to show everything that could be shown in the short time we had.

Back in Ottawa, I took Emese to meet my friends the Tolstoys. In Grand Forks she met some of the Dukhobors who had come to Canada with the help of Leo Tolstoy. Now she met a family related to him and could compare the Russian spoken by her friends in today's Russia with those who lived for years in Canada. And of course, she could try out the swimming in all the lakes we managed to find in the Gatineau Hills. My work starting at 4 p.m. was really handy now! Then I took an extra week off and we went to Sully.

The people who rented the farm had not started to build my little house yet, but there was another two years to go and I did not feel like pressuring them. They fixed up the old chicken coop as a chalet "in the meantime", to serve as a place to keep my things and to house me on my rare and short visits. I was a bit disappointed with the way they took care of my things, but did not stop to bother about the unpleasant things of life. There were too many lovely things to share with Emese, above all the love of the people in the village. She brought slides of Hungary and a big group of friends gathered to see where we came from and to meet my sister.

The way news went around and people came, on very short notice, made Emese remark, "You love many people and many people love you."

August 20, 1983
Emese's photo on the Traverse de Levis
coming from Sully

We went swimming in Lake Temiscouata, in Lake Pohénégamook, and my friend Anne-Marie took us to her cottage on Beau Lake. This added another three to the lakes Emese tried out in Canada. And we had some more good talks. Mother told me when she was visiting in 1964, that my father used to treat Emese very much the same way he treated me. She mentioned this, not as something important, but for me that off-the-cuff remark was a revelation. It made me envy Emese. She had a mother to protect her, to let her know that it was not all her fault. Now we, two daughters of the same man but of two very different mothers, with such different experiences, could talk about him and about life.

It was a blessed week which ended on August 20, St. Stephen's day. He was the first king of Hungary, an "apostolic king", crowned in the year 1001, with a crown sent by the Pope because he converted his people to Christianity. In Canada, the end of summer is marked by Labour Day. In Hungary people talk of the beginning of fall as "after St-Stephen's Day". It was appropriate that I should say good-bye to Emese on that day. She went back to Budapest, to continue her work as a professor of Russian language and literature. She met the world in Ottawa, she said. Canada she came to know in Whitehorse, Calgary, Grand Forks, Toronto, Montréal, Québec and Sully. She loved Québec best, maybe because she met some of my old students and was taken for a ride on the back of a motorcycle to see the illuminated Chateau Frontenac. The buildings of Budapest bathe also in light on summer evenings. She returned to Hungary, to continue her life and her work with new insights. While here, nobody asked her whether she was a Communist or not. Everybody loved her and knew that she was my sister.

In the factory things were not getting better. No matter how much faith I put into my work, decisions were not affected by my efforts. Roy fired me at Christmas and he left the firm after the holidays. Here I was in Ottawa, looking for a job once more. I had one more year to go till my 65th birthday. I decided that I must pass that year in a meaningful way, not just to make money until my pension arrived.

I called Jean-Marc. He was one of my closest friends at *Laval* and we have kept in touch ever since. I followed his steady advancement and he followed my meandering during all these roller-coaster years. Jean-Marc had no doubts that I would find a job if I really wanted. He gave me valuable tips and I started knocking on doors. I had many good conversations, met terrific people but landed no job. My meetings were confirming, refreshing, but they made me see that I was a marginal, and that I was okay as a marginal. The important thing was to find out what to do with my marginality.

One day I had a chance to discuss this with Lewis Perimbam, vice-president of the *Canadian International Development Agency*. A year earlier I had heard him give a talk and liked what he had said, so now I asked his secretary to have an interview with him. He received me cordially and we communicated easily on the wavelength of two non-Canadian-born Canadians who have complete confidence in Canada's future. It was easier for us, we both felt, to see this country's greatness and to talk about it, than for people who were born Canadian. We actually had a duty to talk about our faith in Canada. When he heard that I was looking for a job for another year, he said that he planned to collect opinions of Canadians from coast-to-coast about their country and to publish it under the title *Homage to Canada*. What did I think about that?

The more I thought about that project, the more I felt that I would rather ask certain Canadians, people who had worked abroad. I went to see Gabriel Decaire who was head of the Briefing Centre of C.I.D.A. That centre prepared co-operants before they left for their posts in Third World countries, and collected their impressions after they returned. I told him that I would like to ask some questions from ex-co-operants who had been abroad with *Canadian International Development Agency* or *Canada World Youth* and to make a book of the answers. I would ask them what they hoped for before they went, what their disappointments were at their posts, and on their return, and what they would like to do for Canada now, after these experiences.

"Very good idea," he said and set up a meeting for me with Nicole Senecal, head of C.I.D.A.'s Public Affairs. Nicole was an hour-and-a-half late for the appointment and when she arrived she was exhausted. It was March 2, 1984. Pierre Elliot Trudeau, who became the most prominent of the "trois colombes" or "three doves" of 1965, had resigned February 29 as prime minister of Canada. Nicole had passed her day in "fire-fighting".

During the hour-and-a-half while I waited, I looked out over the Ottawa River and the view of the Parliament buildings spurred on my thoughts. On arrival I was nervous, I wanted a job very badly. Sara was on my mind, she was worn out from her studies. I wished so much to call her and invite her for two weeks in Martinique! But after a while of looking at the Parliament buildings, I became more interested in what those returned Canadians would want to do for their country than in finding a job. I wanted badly to put them in touch with each other, to have them exchange their thoughts, to encourage each other. I expected that they would talk about the frustration of watching the best efforts come to naught because of internal strife. Then I remembered the time I had reviewed the press during the 1965 federal elections. At that time I had expected to find something and what I found far surpassed my expectations. Maybe those Canadians who went abroad to work with other nations had come home with deeper insights than I had foreseen?! By the time Nicole arrived, I was burning to find out. I was not worried about a job any more. I wanted to hear what those Canadians thought necessary for their country, here and now!

I told Nicole that if I could not do this and have a job doing it, I preferred to go home and write my book. When I left her office, she was tired, discouraged, as so many honest people in government are now, and I said good-bye trying to cheer her up.

Of course, I had to write my book! I would find a calm place. Sully! I had the chicken coop, which would be comfortable enough. The phone rang, Micheline Descent, an old student, called from Ste-Foy. They had plans to add to their house and would like me to occupy the attic. I knew the lovely attic. We had a meeting in it with a famous anthropologist and Emese last year. The view from that attic is similar to the view from *Laval University* which always uplifts me. Yes, it would be a good place for writing. Next morning I told my friend, Phoebe-Anne Lemmon, about Sully or Ste-Foy to choose from.

"Your choice will be more difficult, because I am calling to ask you to come to live with us to help care for Mother."

There was no problem of choosing this time, because I knew that she did need help with Sophie, her 93-year-old mother. Sophie was bright and witty, but unable to care for herself any more and could not be left alone. My mother would have been exactly her age. I know and love Phoebe-Anne and Bill Lemmon. I knew that it was there, living with them, where I could best start my book. It would do me good to live for a while in a family atmosphere for which I was not responsible. Besides, they lived in Farm Point, close enough to Wakefield where Lester B. Pearson is buried. I could go to his grave for inspiration. And Farm Point is close to Ottawa.

Wakefield Cemetery, August 1984

While I lived in Ottawa I was active in the Bahá'í community. The local Spiritual Assembly appointed me as one of five members to the Community Development Committee. As part of our community development we visited all believers, and I had the good fortune to meet Mechthilde Behmer. With a name like that she had to be German, and was. We became friends. She introduced me to Tai Chi.

Tai Chi, the gentle Chinese exercises, have done a great deal for my health and mental well-being. They helped to improve my back and straighten out my spine ... and spirit. This became the continuation of my lesson in Martinique, and the next helper with my spine. Thank you Mechthilde!

From Phoebe's I could continue my lessons in Tai Chi and the meetings with the *Association for the Advancement Of Science in Canada* (A.A.S.C.). This gave me a chance to join forces with people who wanted to see technology play its fitting role in the peaceful transformation of society. For nearly 140 years, Canadian scientists had known the A.A.A.S., or *American Association for the Advancement of Science* and its journal called "*Science*". Recently people here had decided that there was a need for an approach particular to Canada which concentrated not on the development of science itself, nor its usefulness to industry but to improving the condition of human beings. The Capital Region chapter of AASC was formed and I became one of its enthusiastic workers.

That work started to become really interesting as we planned the program for the year. The program committee was consulted about the areas most likely to be of interest. We held a brainstorming session, wrote on the board the different problems that should be looked into. There were 16 areas such as "automation and unemployment", "soil erosion", "air pollution", "acid rain", "energy future", "cost of medical care", "research and decision making", "the nuclear threat", "the arms race", etc., when I interjected:

"As I look at the problem-areas we have pinpointed, it seems to me that most would be taken care of if we concentrated our attention on education. People should learn from early childhood that the main aim of science is to serve the happiness and well-being of man."

Max Bacon, chairman of the meeting, exclaimed: "But that's utopia!" We all looked at each other, stunned, then burst out laughing, Max laughing the heartiest. We realized that his reaction was the best proof of the need for a change in our education. We ARE in utopia! We have gone to the moon, what holds us back from making the other aspects of utopia come true?

26 Sully
1984 and After

The first draft of my book was finished, Sophie needed to be hospitalized, and there was no hope of a job so I decided to go home to Sully. This way I should be around to supervise the construction of my small field-stone house, I thought.

The people who rented the house were not at the farm when I called. I was told by the neighbours that the wife's father was ill and they had to go back, temporarily, to their home near Montréal. I called there. They did not know when they would go back to Sully. If I wanted to pass the winter there, I should live in the farm house, because electricity and water go from there to the chalet. The couple went to Sully to prepare the house for my arrival, but when I got there, they were gone. I found the place in an unbelievable mess. It smelled bad. Everything was covered with dirt. But there was water and electricity and the roof was over my head. I went out to the fields to smell the earth, the clover, the hay and I cried to the sky, "I am happy to be home!"

It probably helped a great deal that I did not drive to Sully by myself. Firooz Hatam Ardestani and his cousin, Mohammed Saidi, drove me from Farm Point with a van, with some furniture. They saw the state the house was in, but looked through, and above, things. After a frugal repast they helped to carry some really obnoxious things out. When they were ready to turn around to drive the long trek back to Ottawa, Firooz embraced me and said, "You will be happy here." I am sure that they said a few prayers on their way.

It usually takes me little time to make myself a comfortable corner from where to attack the rest. This time it was particularly important, because the house was full of rats. They came for the filth. The furniture I brought was mostly Sara's, what she did not take to Calgary. This was a lifesaver, because most of my things were gone or broken. I made a corner with a lovely Chinese rug, a comfortable bed, clean sheets and good-smelling towels in the bathroom. Then I bought rat poison and watched the rats go for it. I am not afraid of rats, because I saw lots of them at *McGill's* Donner Building, where they were used for experiments. I knew that it wouldn't take long for the poison to work.

First thing to do was to get the double windows in place. I could not find the windows, so I called the people near Montréal. The husband answered, the young man who said that he would build me a house on my favourite spot.

"Where are the double-windows?" I asked.

"Oh, they are broken; I would use plastic sheets."

"None of the faucets work," I said.

His reaction was: "What did you expect to find, a palace? You are richer than we are." It was only at that moment that I realized that I had trusted people I should not have trusted.

Some time ago, my son Tip handed me a flavourful compliment. I don't remember the occasion but I sure remember the compliment: "I have never met anybody, mother," he said, "who had your ability to fall into a bucket of shit and come out smelling like roses." This time the buckets were really full of the stuff. I liked difficulties, said Leo Zrudlo. Did I? I got to work and neighbours came to help. It took some work, but we cleaned the place. By the time snow covered the piles of rocks Bijou Charest and his sons gathered when they cleared the land, the house was comfortable and the only other occupant besides me was a cat. A nice, big one, who liked to eat rats!

One calm evening, when the snow took on a light blue shine at sunset, I stood by the kitchen door, looked out on the fields and savoured the peace.

"Poor people, they must miss this peacefulness now," I said and then pulled back from the window, looking at my reflection, with my hands on my hips.

"What?! Have I nothing else to think about? I should feel sorry for them, as if I were guilty because they have lost this place? Angéla, be fair to yourself!"

This was a crucial moment. I found the missing piece to the puzzle inside of me. I discovered, for the first time, that I felt guilty when others did not behave well towards me, *as if I had deserved it.* I already knew that when somebody was mean to me, I tended to be unable to pray for a while. Like a child who holds his breath when he is angry. This time it was clear that I did not deserve the treatment those people gave me. There was nothing I could accuse myself of except that I did not check closer on their respect for the obligations they took towards me.

I always assume that others are as reliable as I would like to be and that it is their responsibility to check up on themselves. My attitude is that of the farmer who wants to plough his furrows straight. If he watches the furrow of his neighbour, his own will be crooked. I have my own furrow to watch. I don't want it to be crooked, and I believe that others also want to have their furrows straight. Of course this attitude might bring disappointments, but I don't intend to change it. I just promised myself to look closer the next time.

Since 1974 my trips to Sully were short, not enough to notice other than logical changes, such as a new house built in the village or a little girl grown into an adult. After an absence of 10 years, I noticed now a remarkable change in the behaviour of the people. My neighbour who used to be rough and rushed all the time, now took time for a smile and a chat. When I asked what had happened, I learned that there were courses of human relations and personal development in the region. And, as so many did, my neighbours also took part. They came to chat one evening and invited me to join the next course. I went to the demonstration and listened to the animator. In the interval he came over and asked who I was. I told him that I used to be a professor of human relations in a college. When I sat down to listen to the rest, I was rather annoyed at myself. Did I have to tell him that? It might make the young man uneasy. It did not make him uneasy at all. On the contrary, he asked me specially to join the group because I had valuable contributions to make. That convinced me of his sincerity. I joined and what I gained was beyond all expectation.

I saw that there were profound social changes going on in Québec. This course was a private enterprise; people subscribed to it of their own free will, out of interest, not because somebody told them that it was good for them or that it was their duty, but because they thought it helpful and wanted to have what it offered. What it gives is an attitude of trust in oneself and in one's neighbour, and in the future and in what is humorously referred to as "the Guy Upstairs". People learn to admit that they are sensitive and affectionate and that it is alright to express it. It is wonderful to see the effect of "I love you", uttered to complete strangers. At first people are taken aback; it surprises, it's new. But it does not take long to notice how good it feels to be able to answer, "I love you too."

On my birthday when I became 65, supposedly an old person, I decided to become a mature child and have a visit with my father. I took out his last letter and sat down comfortably to read it. I wanted to see what he would have liked me to understand when he wrote it.

"My precious little Bug," it starts. Funny that I had never seen how sweet that was. It made my heart all warm. There followed a page which earlier had turned me off because it sounded like recriminations. This time I looked for my father who loved me, not the critical Apu, so I jumped over it and went to the end of the letter.

"Now there remains even less likelihood that I may live to see you again and that the mutual explanation I have so often dreamed about, should happen. Therefore I shall pray for you and yours even more fervently and I embrace you with much love. 1954, 5, 27, Your Father."

Strange, the love, the yearning and the faith had been in the letter ever since it was written, but it took me 31 years and a lot of suffering, to see it.

I had always felt that Apu's problems were caused by war in the world and disunity in the family. I wanted to work for understanding between all people, so that what had happened to him should not happen anywhere, to anybody any more. I was not aware of his love for me because he did not know how to show it. But in my search for the solution, his story about the Tiny Bee guided me. I remembered only a short time ago that he had told it to me, but my aims were always directed by the knowledge of the lifesaving love and interdependence between the big, rich and strong on one side, and the small, poor, and weak, on the other. Much of my character was moulded on his knee, and what I like most about myself came from my father. It was wonderful to feel that he loved me. Those who have always felt the love of their parents, cannot know how good it is to finally feel it. Now I can relax and grow old in peace.

There, in the Nuremberg of 1932, I first heard, "We are right. They are wrong. We have to fight them." Already then I preferred to feed the pigeons instead of learning the battle songs. Then, at 43, at the time when I went back to school to become qualified to talk about what I think is needed to build a just world, I received a piano as a gift. Now that I have written my book, and said my say, I can trust the future to other bees and to the doves. I can relax and learn to play the piano, just for my own pleasure.

Or can I? The time is not quite here yet. I could not enjoy my music while there are people in the richest countries of the world who do not dare to reach for a chocolate bar.

This little girl, born in the ruins of the First World War, in a rich house, of a family for centuries devoted to the common good, was a refugee in a cattle car before she could walk. As I learned to walk, in a temporary dwelling, I learned that there were cockroaches to be stepped upon. I would shout with a child's glee and squash them dead. Then my parents bought a home and a garden and an orchard and I learned that not all small things that ran around should be killed, because what looks like a cockroach to an ignorant child, might turn out to be a day-old chick. When I was a year-and-a-half old, already I wanted to help. I tugged on the blinds to let the light into the room for the doctor who delivered my brother. I have tried to help ever since, I pull on blinds, first among them, on my own.

I have to be true to myself. The time for rest is not far, but it is not here just yet. Maybe now I have to go back to Hungary, to tell them to work and have patience for a little longer. The dawn of a new era is soon.

27   Québec
1984-1994

Those 18 years during which I owned that piece of the earth Sara wanted to have and named *Le Hobbit*, a house surrounded by acres and acres of land, gave me the chance to grow up, to read the Writings, to meditate, pray, suffer — yes, suffer a lot. All change is hard, and I had lots to change. There was much to discard of what I had learned, in the way I felt about the world and about my place in it.

The village of Sully is today part of Pohénégamook. It lies in a mountainous region of Temiscouata, next to the Maine, U.S. border, close to New Brunswick. The population is homogenous, French-Canadian, Catholic. Before I moved there, friends in Québec warned me to be prepared to meet suspicion, even hostility. There was none of that. On the contrary, neighbours asked my permission to pick wild strawberries on the fields, as they did while there was nobody at the farm. It was fine with me, specially because they came, mothers with their children, and I could make friends with them easily. The village priest came to visit and to ask many questions. He celebrated the Mass at the farm on my birthday. It was a stormy April day, but 54 villagers took Holy Communion, with the photo of 'Abdu'l-Bahá looking down on them. I occasionally went to church, sitting in the special pew the priest gave me. The first time I sat in that pew, close to the front of the church, I had a strange experience. I had that feeling one occasionally gets when somebody looks at us intently. I looked up and my eyes met the eyes of the statue of Christ... I only stopped using that pew after a conversation that made it clear that the priest did not regard my religion as valid as his. This happened after the funeral of a lovely young woman who had killed herself. I told the priest that if he had parishioners who did not believe in their religion any more, and he saw that they were distressed, he could send them to me and I would try to help them regain faith in God and in life.

"You don't want me to tell them that Bahá'í is as good as Catholic?" I never went to occupy my pew again and entered the church only when friends specially invited me to be with them.

One event to which several neighbours had tried to get me for some time, is *Le Rencontre*, or *Meeting*. Finally I did go. As I entered, they were just singing,

> "If you believe, you will see the Glory of God.
> If you pray, you will see the Glory of God.
> If you love, you will see the Glory of God."

If Bahá'ís don't associate with people, how will they know where to look?

The fact that I attended these meetings gave me an opportunity to meet the archbishop of the region and talk about a publication to which I had tried to call attention for some time. In the regional high school, in Cabano, I had replaced an English teacher. There was a booklet in my desk entitled *The Labyrinth*. It gave short descriptions of different sects and religions that had confused the believers. Among them was the Bahá'í Faith. At the end of the booklet there was a comparative chart which showed how these beliefs were similar or dissimilar to the Catholic Credo. If they believed the same, they were given a full-moon, if they did not believe at all, they had an empty circle. For us Bahá'ís, they gave a half-moon under the question of believing or not in Christ. I tried to call attention to the errors contained in that chart at book fairs and through teachers of religion at the schools I was connected with, but nobody listened to me, nobody took it seriously. When the chance opened to speak to the highest authority of the church in the region, I took the booklet to him, with the circles filled to the best of my knowledge with correct information. I told him that I did not want my friends to receive incorrect information about my beliefs, because it would distress them if they found out that they were misled.

The Jehovah's Witnesses started to be active in the region soon after I bought the farm. I always try to exchange with anybody who wants to talk about religion, but once I lost my patience with two young ladies. They were dismissing what Buddha taught, saying, "That comes from a human being." I opened the door and said, "Sorry, I do not allow you to say things against another religion in my house. I know about your beliefs, I admire the devoted people standing on cold street corners to call people to God. Don't attack others without knowing what they believe in!" Not long afterwards another couple came, just as I was preparing to go on a teaching trip. I had lots to do, but felt something inside and said, "I am very busy, because I am about to leave in connection with my faith. I would not take time for anybody else, but because you want to talk about God, come in and sit down."

This is how a meaningful exchange between me and the Jehovah's Witnesses of the region began. Next time they came, they talked about the Kingdom of God to come, and I told them that they would not know how right they are, until they learn about Bahá'u'lláh.

They were already in the car when the husband got out, came back and asked, "What was that name you said? We do not want to change, but we do want to know about things."

He wrote down Bahá'u'lláh's name. Next time they came, they had just read a good article about the Faith in the French *Readers' Digest*. They remarked that many things were similar between their beliefs and ours.

"But what does a Bahá'í do, all alone, far from everybody?"

"I pray a lot and talk to people like you," I answered.

The people who came to the farm to talk to me were of all ages with the majority, teenagers. They sat around and asked questions about the parts of the world I knew and they would like to see one day. They spoke about their troubles and hopes. There was a boy who did not get along with his mother. I told him to think of her as somebody who needed his friendship. And I allowed him to play the piano. There was a girl who was interested in theatre. I told her that 'Abdu'l-Bahá said that the pulpit of the future would be the stage. In 1992, the village of Sully was celebrating its 75 years, and I was invited. As I walked to the tent where the opening ceremony was to start, I said to my friend, Anne-Marie, in whose house I stayed, that I wondered whether anybody would recognize me. Hardly did I utter these words when a lovely young lady ran up to me,

"Is that you, Angéla? I am Danielle, do you remember me? I think of you often. I am a teacher now and I want to be like you. You know, I was 15, and it is important at that age..." She was the young girl who was interested in theatre 20 years before. The young man mentioned above was then managing the family business and is his mother's partner and help.

A beloved spiritual son, Louis Brunet, became a Bahá'í at the farm. He was raised in a Catholic family, but had been away from any religious practice for years. Soon after declaring, he was surprised to see me getting ready to go to church. Next time he came with me. After the service, he sat silently while I drove. We were nearly home when he found his tongue, "Every word has meaning!" This showed me how deeply he was touched by the spirit of the new Revelation from the same

266

God. When somebody catches the spirit, a first sign is often a recognition of values in their previous religious teachings which they have either forgotten or never before recognized.

My neighbour told me about a book she was reading, a 10-volume account of an Italian seer, Maria Valtorta. She apparently received visions and dictations during the Second World War. Her work was published under the title, *Il Poema del Uomo-Dio*. It was translated as *The Gospel As It Was Revealed To Me*. I was just reading how Bahá'u'lláh talks about the suffering of Mary, the mother of Jesus, and told my neighbour that I would like to read that book. She did not follow up right away, but called me on the morning of next March 2. Just as I was beginning the Fast, she called — out of the blue? — to ask if I really wanted to read what Maria Valtorta had written. My Fast that year had a very special, wonderful quality. I read how the parents of the little Virgin Mary cared for her, how she cared for her little boy Jesus, what her garden was like, what she made for clothing, for food, all the normal, human cares in a divine story. Then the three years of His ministry, the many teachings He spread on His walks in the country we also call the Holy Land. The part Judas of Iscariot played in the divine tragedy, and how Mary went to comfort Judas' mother after both their sons had died. I was filled with admiration for that Spirit that tries again, and again, to rekindle the people who were supposed to believe in Him, to be ready to recognize Him in His new attire, to be able to see Him as He speaks to them today in a new human form, under a new Name, as He said He would.

The guidance of the *Universal House of Justice* to become self-supporting in Canada before returning to Hungary became reality since 1985 when I got a pension and could afford to do what I really wanted to do. What I wanted to do was to be involved in everything that went in the direction shown by Bahá'u'lláh. There were two developments at that time in Québec that caught my attention. One was in education, the other in social affairs.

When I was asked to replace an English teacher at the regional high school in Cabano, I immediately noticed a marked change in the atmosphere. There was an effort, directed from the *Ministry of Education*, to have consultation between teachers and school administrators on one side, and students and their parents on the other. With the long habit of the distance between these two sides, one side dominating, the other accustomed to being dominated, to being led, this development needed much effort to bring it to fruition. The important thing for me was the fact that changes were on the way. The English teacher I replaced was burnt out — as so many sincere, capable teachers are in a bad system. She felt that she had to follow outdated guidelines instead of teaching as she knew she should. When she saw that I had succeeded with a method she also would have liked to use, she overcame her inability to face her task and returned to her post. She gained so much self-confidence that, when the post of principal became vacant, she applied and returned as principal of the same high school.

The other development was an innovation in social affairs, the establishment of the C.L.S.C. network. C.L.S.C. means *Local Centres of Service to the Community*. As soon as I heard about it, I saw that there were needs this network could address, but that these needs had to be expressed. The government supplied the structure, now the population had to learn to use it. This of course takes time to be noticed and understood by the population that has been accustomed not to be served, but to be directed from above. I got involved and ended up as chairman of the committee for the creation of a C.L.S.C. in our region.

I also became interested in the work of the A.F.E.A.S., or *Association Feminine d'Éducation et Action Sociale.* I wanted to help local women to see that there is much power in their hands and that they can use it for good. By the time I left Sully, many were in leading positions in the community who until then felt shy, devoid of capacity. They only needed encouragement to blossom.

268

Soon after I returned to the farm, France Coté, who met the Faith in Switzerland, returned to Québec from Haifa. There she was nurse and companion to Ethel Revell during the last year-and-a-half of her earthly life. She had a collection of slides of the Holy Land and offered to share them with me and my neighbours. I invited people from the village and surrounding farms to see slides of the sacred spots of the religions that call Israel their Holy Land.

France came from Rimouski, by bus; I went to pick her up. The bus was late. By the time we returned, the farm was surrounded by a fleet of trucks and cars, our public waiting for us to let them into the house and start the show. With great good humour, lots of excuses, we all streamed into the house and France started out. First she showed a few slides of famous sites of Christianity and Islam, then she went into an introductory talk, with slides to illustrate, how the Bahá'í Faith started, and where it was today.

This was not what I had invited my neighbours to see and I tried to let France know that people came to see holy sites of Israel, not to hear a talk about our Faith. France just went on, not hearing my intervention. There was nothing I could do to stop her. I was rather embarrassed until it came to me that there was no need for me to get upset. France is a French-Canadian, she was talking to her own people. I went to the kitchen to prepare refreshments and to talk a bit to Bahá'u'lláh. I borrowed a phrase from General De Gaulle who said to Maréchal Pétain, "Débrouille-toi, mon vieux, avec les Allemands!" — "Take care of the Germans, my old friend!" as he left for Africa. I said, "Bahá'u'lláh, please take care of Your French-Canadians!" And I prayed for God to help me to smooth things out in case there were broken pots to mend. There were no hard feelings and France and I had a good laugh afterwards about how God organized her bus to be late and for us to have no time to consult before her presentation.

There was another occasion to invite neighbours to hear a Bahá'í. This time I made it plain that we were going to talk about what the Bahá'í Faith was and who Bahá'u'lláh is. This event was not prepared in advance, at least not by me.

I decided one day that it was time to write a new will, and headed to the notary in the next village. I noticed a car coming towards me, with a pair of familiar faces in the front seat. Pierre and Nicole Austin! My dear spiritual son who became a Bahá'í while I was without voting rights, the one we had to ask Phoebe-Anne to recommend; the one who taught Christian education in Masham, with whom I worked on the seminar where we met Charles Mondelet's letters on how education in Canada should be organized. He was the one who exclaimed, "He was a Bahá'í!" when he himself had just heard a few things about the Faith! Pierre could see the Bahá'í thinking in Mondelet, long before he declared. Mondelet's being a Bahá'í was so clear to Pierre that he does not even remember the event as an important one any more, while for me it had the quality of a major discovery.

Now Nicole and Pierre were on an impromptu trip around the province and just happened to come by when I needed somebody to sign my will as witness, and to give a quickly organized presentation on *What is the Bahá'í Faith? Who is Bahá'u'lláh?* Quite a good group gathered on very short notice, among them three ladies who came with a decidedly suspicious attitude. They were not going to allow any crazy ideas to be spread around here. When they left, they had sweet, friendly smiles and we all felt the spirit of unity pervade the air. Pierre's straightforward presentation left no doubt about who Bahá'u'lláh was, but no doubt about it either that He is no stranger and no enemy of sincere Christians.

For me, the talk Pierre gave to the people who were friends to me in this faraway corner of the globe, was the spiritual equivalent to my renovating the house.

The house was built solidly by Bijou Charest who raised it out of the virgin forest. When I bought it, it was worth little, it was badly damaged by careless tenants. I had it renovated, made it a comfortable and dignified place on the solid foundations. When I needed to, I could sell it to buy a house near Ottawa, near my children, so that I could start commuting between French-Canada and Hungary.

In Lisbon, in 1948, where I first heard the name of Bahá'u'lláh, I also heard the first French-Canadian name: Louis Bourgeois. He was the architect of the Mother Temple of the West. Near Chicago, in Wilmette, a town named after the farmer, the first permanent settler, a French-Canadian, Antoine Ouilmette, with his Indian wife, Archange Chevalier, raised their family there. The building symbolizing the merging of all previous religions, was erected there. Its architect was Louis Bourgeois, born in St-Celestin, county Nicolet, Québec.

On Mount Carmel, Haifa, above the cave of Elijah, who predicted that God will one day rule over the earth from that sacred mountain, a building designed by William Sutherland Maxwell of Montréal (one of the Maxwell brothers who were the architects of the landmark of Québec, the *Chateau Frontenac*) was erected to house the earthly remains of the Báb, Bahá'u'lláh's forerunner.

Landmarks illumined at night, they shed their light on the path that leads to a bright tomorrow.

While I taught English in the school where I met Pierre, I translated 'Abdu'l-Bahá's *Tablet to Dr. Forel*. I had not used Hungarian for about 25 years, and had never translated Bahá'í Writings. When I sat down to start it, the possibility of misunderstanding 'Abdu'l-Bahá's thoughts haunted me so badly that I had to write to the *National Spiritual Assembly of Canada* for guidance. I asked whether I could feel competent to translate His thoughts. (Tradutore or traditore? = translator or traitor?) They answered that they thought me competent to do it and that they would pray for my success. This was a real lifting of spirits, and still it took a dream to get me started.

It was before the Christmas vacation. My son Sandy invited me to pass it with them in Victoria, B.C.; my daughter Sara invited me to pass the holiday with her on Martinique. I ordered a ticket to Victoria and one to Martinique, to decide later which one to buy. Then I had a dream. I was walking with two Bahá'í ladies in an old, beautiful garden. Under the towering trees, the grass was young, tender. We passed a lonely-looking young man who sat on a bench. We came to a restaurant and I said that I was hungry, let's go in. The two friends were not hungry and went on, I went into the restaurant and found that the waitress was Hungarian. I was ordering from her when the sad-looking young man I saw on the bench, entered. When he heard us talk in Hungarian he exclaimed, "Then we can communicate!"

I cancelled both tickets and passed my Christmas vacation working on the translation. I mailed it to Vienna on the morning we went back to school.

There were many things God did to shape my life, without my being aware of them. This, of course, is a statement that could be made by everyone. Our life becomes glorious when we come to see, one after the other, His actions that prepared our way.

After my first pilgrimage, in 1971, I visited a cousin in Budapest. She was my mother's goddaughter and also a painter. I told her about the beautiful portrait of 'Abdu'l-Bahá done in Budapest by Robert Nadler, which now hangs in the seat of the *Universal House of Justice*, on Mount Carmel.

"Nadler Robert had great respect for your mother," she said. When I heard the name like that, as we say in Hungarian, with the family name first, memories flooded my mind. As a child, I often heard that name! My mother was one of Nadler's students, then one of his colleagues. In April 1913, she was still a student in his studio. Did she meet the Master when He passed nine days in Budapest? Even if she did not actually meet Him, she worked in that studio, with His portrait on the wall! I always knew that my mother helped me from the Other Side, that she stood by me in crucial moments and that she led me to the Faith. I wonder now, am I a first, or second generation Bahá'í? I am looking forward to asking her about that.

My mother and father also seem to have done things for me quite recently. The first to come to my knowledge had to do with money, of all things. Before going on my second

274

pilgrimage, the short one, in the summer of 1986, a letter came from Kecskemét, it was written by a lawyer. He had been appointed to take care of my interests, and would I go to see him the next time I was in Hungary? When I entered Dr. László Szentkirályi's office, he smiled.

"First of all, Madame, I have to tell you that I do not understand your case. In this country, during the past decades, most people lost everything they had. They were thrown out of their homes, lands, they were chased away, without a penny, on their bare bottoms. In your case however, they say that you have this and you have right to that. I have to admit that I understand your case only if I say that God has mixed Himself into your business."

"It is quite possible," said I, smiling back at him. We became instantaneous friends. We still are. He is now one of the town councillors and a respected, responsible man. He hopes that I can come to visit real soon, because he finds that I give him strength and faith in the future. God has truly mixed Himself into our affairs.

I was buying postcards. The lady behind the counter asked where I came from, who I was. When I said my name, a small thin woman I did not see, jumped up from a low stool by the wall.

"Finally I found you!!! You will not believe how long I have been looking for you and where I was asked to give news when you are found! In Moscow, a member of the group I went with, when he heard that I come from Kecskemét, asked whether I knew where you were. And to let him know as soon as I can. Wait, his name was ... Nemény ... or something like that. You were together at university, now he is a professor at the same university, only now it's called *Karl Marx University of Economics and Political Science*. He lives in Budapest, and wants you to call him." Next time I was in Budapest, I called the only Nemény in the telephone book. His wife answered.

"Vili is going to be so happy that we have found you! He is in Warsaw today. Say, what are you doing next Monday morning? Vili is defending his big doctorate at the Hungarian Academy of Sciences. Could you be there at 10 a.m.?" Monday, sharp at 10, I walked up the red-carpeted marble steps of the venerable building of the *Hungarian Academy of Sciences.* On top of the stairs waited a white-haired gentleman. We looked at each other questioningly, then threw our arms around each other.

Out of one of those tricks that God is so good at playing on us, the secretary of the Academy misunderstood the hour of this event. Instead of 10, he came at 11. Thus we had a full hour to catch up on 45 years and I had time to read the abstract of the thesis he was to defend. Its title was: *A General Theory of Planning*!

The good news my lawyer-friend had for me was that I still owned a piece of land of what used to be our orchard. When the family sold it, one-sixth, my share, could not be sold, because I was abroad. Now a part of it was expropriated for a street and I had money coming to me. As it came from my parents, I spent a part of it on them. The cemetery where they were buried was now abandoned and soon to be turned into a playground. I had trouble finding the graves, everything was so overgrown. I had to climb over branches, discarding layers of ivy, until my hand met a solid surface! On white marble appeared Apu's name. I arranged for their remains to be exhumed and transferred to the new, common cemetery.

In a small white coffin, good for a child of four, what remained of the bodies of my parents was gathered into a white shroud. I spread petals from the Holy Land over them and a new funeral was held, with Marie, our old maid and two daughters of my parents' best friends at my side.

**75th birthday and publication of 2 books,
celebrated in Kecskemét – April 10, 1995**

Friends in Vienna told me that there were three Bahá'ís from the United States studying at the *Kodály Institute of Music* in Kecskemét. It was an extraordinary event, the meeting with Silvana Neal, Maggie McLellan and Shirley Robertson! They spent a whole year in this town where I passed my childhood. We only had time to touch. They were leaving next day. Silvana was planning to return next year and we promised to meet then.

The last thing she said was, "See István Vidák at the *Toy Museum*! I wish we had met him earlier!"

Of course I went to the Toy Museum and met István, his family and many enthusiastic people. They said that I came at the right time, that I was "God-sent". They needed to translate into English the list of articles going to an exhibition leaving for Prague next day. They thought it would take the whole night. It took us less than an hour.

"Can you come to the *International Yurta Camp* to be our interpreter?" A happy collection of yurta-builders from Australia, United States, Finland, Sweden, Russia and Germany met for a week of work and fun out on the famous plain where the wide-horned white cattle still graze and white-skirted horsemen crack their whips with relish, to the amusement of tourists from all over the world. We slept under felt tents, ate food cooked over open pits, spoke in many tongues, spun cord, made felt from scraps of wool, cut poles and built portable homes like nomad people did for thousands of years.

When I had a free moment, I worked on what the Bahá'ís of Budapest asked me to do for them. It was a translation of the Statement on Peace from the *Universal House of Justice* that needed corrections. István asked what I was doing.

"You should ask Antal Hideg to help you. He is a fine translator. He is tied now to his wheelchair and might be happy to work on something like that." I found Antal Hideg, a hemophiliac, translator and educator. He was willing to help me with the Peace Statement. Thank God, the translation was very bad, so we had to go through every sentence several times. We worked four solid days. This way we both got a lot out of it. Anti came to know Bahá'í thinking and I gained a most valued friend.

It was in the summer of 1986 that I started commuting between Québec and Hungary. That year I passed two months in Hungary, the two summer months. In 1987 and 1988, I was there for four months. Then, the *National Spiritual Assembly of Austria* asked me to stay for six months, to be on hand for the first *International Book Fair* to be held in Budapest, in October 1989. That created a problem, because the farm, now newly renovated, could not be left for that long, or the freezing cold would damage the plumbing. I called my children, to consult. It took us five minutes to reach a decision.

"Sell the farm and come to live closer to us," one of them said and we all agreed. I gave the house to an agent to sell; Sara found a house in Campbell's Bay, Québec, across the Ottawa River from her Ontario home. I took the essentials to stay in my new home for five days, on my way to Hun-
278

gary. The farm was sold; Sara and Tip moved my things before I came back for winter.

In Kecskemét, among family and friends waiting, was Anti Hideg. He helped me with more translations, then guided me to write the first book I finished, my autobiography in Hungarian. (Excerpts from it were published in an anthology of Hungarians living abroad, in 1993. The book was published in 1995.)

With publishers Mr. & Mrs. Feher, grafist Gabor Ulrich and Iren Filep of the NSA of Hungary, holding my translation of excerpts on Bahá'í economics, compiled by Hooshmand Badi'i, of St. Vincent, West Indies."

When I said good-bye to Anti in November 1989, he said, "Don't be sad that I did not become a Bahá'í! This tender faith needs people who can talk for it, without being members. Come back soon!" When I went back in six months, I found him occupying the chair of deputy-mayor of Kecskemét. From the lonely cripple, living on a pension, he had become the second-in-command of a town of 120,000 people. He was in charge of everything to do with human beings: education, health, culture and social affairs. That a person like him, still in his wheelchair, could rise to a position of that importance, showed me clearly in what direction things were going in Hungary. It also shows how God prepares people to serve Him.

In October 1993, I got a call from a friend in Kecskemét. When I asked her if Anti was still deputy-mayor, she said, "Yes. He is the lion-tamer. He chose that role, God bless him!"

Pécs University, Hungary – August 13, 1989
Angéla and Dr. Mária Ormos

A copy of that corrected translation of the *Peace State-ment* travelled with me when I went to visit an historian who wanted to ask questions about my first husband's role in events between the two World Wars. Dr. Maria Ormos, rector of the *University of Pécs*, wanted to know about Tamás' relationship to Anton Pavelic of Croatia. She wrote a book about the Marseilles assassination of 1934, mentioned Tamás in it, now wanted to know more about him. We passed two delightful days together, two grandmothers, both involved in the same
280

events, from two different perspectives, with the same eagerness to find the truth.

At one point I asked her how was she able to do so many things in one life. She answered, "I am quick." It was August 12 and 13, 1989.... . After she got the answers I could give, she asked what this "Bahá'í thing" was. I told her a few things.

"Do you have something written in Hungarian?" I gave her the translation of the Peace Statement. She took me to the guest apartment of the university, wished me good night, and said that she would be back in the morning.

In the summer of 1989 Ormos Maria was not only rector of an university and a noted historian, she was also one of the most powerful people in the country. She was a member of the Presidium of the *Hungarian Communist Party.*

Next morning she was back with more questions, not about the events of the past, not even about the Bahá'í Faith. She asked my opinion about problems she was concerned with, such as agrarian politics, private property, the Gypsy question. She wanted help with the problems she was responsible for.

When the time came for me to leave, she was sorry that we did not have more time together. She walked me to the bus and embraced me, saying, "These are the teachings that need to be spread here today."

I promised to pray for her and took my place in the bus. I was so elated, that I fell asleep as soon as the bus started moving. I woke up only when it stopped for a short halt. It was hot. I saw people with ice cream cones and went to get some. By the time I got back, the bus had left.

There was nothing to do but to hire a taxi and run after the bus. The taxi driver was an outspoken anti-Communist, and made it plain as soon as we started talking. I made my convictions equally clear, asking him whether he believed in God and had he ever heard of Bahá'u'lláh? He was not sure about God, as far as Bahá'u'lláh, Who was He? I told him a few things, just as we caught up with my bus. I quickly paid his fare and, just as quickly, he said, "These are the teachings that need to be spread here today."

As I said, this was in August 1989. In September the newspapers, radio and TV reported that Dr. Maria Ormos had paid an official visit to her colleagues in Berlin, at that time East Germany. In the beginning of October, as we Bahá'ís took care of the Bahá'í booth at the first *International Book Fair* in Budapest, the *Hungarian Communist Party* held a congress. At that congress Maria Ormos, together with party leader Rezsó Nyers and the president of the *Institute for Public Education*, Iván Vitányi, proposed the change from Communism to Socialism. On November 9, the Berlin Wall came down.

I left Hungary very soon after. Back in Canada, I had my photos developed and sent one of Maria Ormos and myself to her, with a note congratulating her on the success of her visit to Berlin.

She answered in her typical short, to-the-point, style, "Thanks for the photo, which is quite good, and the congratulations. By the way, since then I have also visited Sofia. Am looking forward to our next meeting." This was December 1989, and Bulgaria had just gone through her own changing of the guards... In April 1994 I went to see Maria Ormos, now a member of the *Hungarian Academy of Sciences*, head of the modern history department of the *University of Pécs*. I wanted to know how much reading the Peace Statement had influenced her in 1989.

"Did reading it make you propose the change?"

"Oh, it was not that."

"It did not hurt, did it?" She held up her hand, with a small slit between thumb and forefinger, that last little bit that was needed to do what she already wanted to do.

Silvana was the only one of the three Americans at the Kodály Institute to return to Hungary for another year. She was about to leave when I arrived back in May, 1988. She organized a good-bye breakfast for a few people she wanted me to meet. That is how I met Lajos and Ilona. First I have to tell who Ilona is and how she came to meet Silvana.

A young Persian couple from Vienna, Behrooz and Sussan Zarifzadeh, decided one day to visit Budapest, to see how they could be useful to the Faith in Hungary. Walking around, they saw a painter doing portraits of people. Sussan, who had always hated that kind of a thing, found herself sitting down to get her portrait done ... ("You don't like things like that? Today, for the Faith, you do.") While the artist worked, they chatted, where are they from, etc. The painter said that she often went to Vienna.

"Here is our address, when you are there next time, look us up." A petal thrown on the waters ... A few weeks pass, the phone rings at the Zarifzadeh home, it's the painter from Budapest. They go to fetch her, bring her home, they sit down to dinner. The painter turns around, looks searchingly at the wall behind her. She finds the Greatest Name.

"Is that a religious symbol?"

"Yes."

"I felt it here," she says, touching the back of her neck ... The Zarifzadehs introduced Ilona to Silvana, who in turn made us meet just before she left, to the great joy of both Ilona and me. She could now ask her questions! She had very little knowledge of German, even less of English. Behrooz and Sussan also heaved a big sigh, when they could say more than loving smiles! I will never forget the evening around the fire, when Ilona's brother and his wife talked about their concerns about Hungary's problems. I translated their thoughts and Behrooz was able give to the Bahá'í answers! He must have been terribly frustrated not to be able to talk intelligently until then! Now that he could finally hear their concerns and could express himself, he reacted with such an onrushing relief that he became physically sick. Next day he walked around pale but happy.

Ilona had been a devoted Catholic. She suffered for it when it was not easy in Hungary to be a practising Christian. She became the first Bahá'í in Szolnok, where she was an art teacher. Now, because she was in contact with these strangers, she lost her job. She found a better one in a school where she was much happier. Hungary gained her *National Spiritual Assembly*, and in April 1993, Ilona was elected to serve on it.

The other guest at Silvana's good-bye breakfast, Lajos, was busy with an English Club. He invited me to the next get-together. There I met Zsuzsi, the secretary of the Kodály Institute, and offered to help her with her English. Next time I met her, she was bicycling home from work on a very hot afternoon.

"Oh, I am so tired .... Did you hear from Lajos?"

"He called this morning. He caught me during my prayers."

"Prayer?" She did not understand the word. I put my hands together, in a gesture of praying.

"Oh, my grandmother taught me one."

"The Our Father?"

"Yes. Are you a Catholic?"

"I am a Bahá'í."

"What is that?"

"God has sent a new message to unite all religions, and bring peace to the world."

"Oh, I am so glad! I am not tired anymore." She came to visit, to get to know each other. When she seemed ready to leave, I asked whether she would like to have the English text of the Our Father.

"No, not that, I want the one you use in the morning." I gave her the Remover of Difficulties and we translated it into Hungarian together.

"Can I say it, even if I am not a believer? But if I want to say it, I AM a believer!"

My old roots in that town made it easy to meet everybody. Shoghi Effendi was so right when he advised us to take the Faith to the place from where we came. Every time I arrived in Kecskemét, I started by visiting Aunt Mici, my father's best friend's widow. She was the one who recited her husband's biblical poems in her strong, crystalline voice. During my absence in 1988, when she was 99, she died, but was revived. They gave her a pacemaker, making her the oldest pacemaker-user in Hungary. When I visited her the next time, her daughter warned me that she was mostly absent, I should not be disappointed but it was not likely that she would recognize me. As we entered her room, she looked questioningly, then gave me the sweetest smile,

"You are of the family. Yes, you are Brunó's daughter. It's wonderful to see you!" Her daughter could not believe her ears as we continued. I held her hand and said, "Aunt Mici, I am so happy that you are well, because I want to tell you about something important. What Uncle George was saying in his poems, about the world becoming mature and uniting in one world, is true. Jesus promised to come back, He did. His name now is Bahá'u'lláh, which means the Glory of God. Those who believe in Him are Bahá'ís. I am a Bahá'í." She grabbed my hand, leaning forward,

"I believe it! I proclaim it! Tell the others that I am with you."

She was 101 when she was buried. I arrived back in Hungary just in time for her funeral. The Lutheran minister said in his eulogy that Aunt Mici was always ready to answer God, without a moment's hesitation. A Calvinist minister also praised her deep faith. The coffin was driven to a village, to a Catholic cemetery where her husband rests, to be placed in the crypt, next to him. The priest said a moving prayer for unity, then invited the gathering to a repast in her honour. I had to go back to town because a meeting was held that evening at the *Toy Museum*, and accepted a ride with the Lutheran minister who was also in a rush. We did not have much time to talk but he asked enough to want to hear more. He asked me to talk about the Faith to his Bible class. In that building where I learned to walk, in that church where I sat at my mother's side, I could talk of the Promise fulfilled! I was looking forward to being there again, because they wanted to hear more.

At the *International Yurta Camp* I mentioned, I made friends with a young woman from England. She was worried about her mother, who was still mourning the death of her husband who died many years earlier. I asked whether her father ever visited her in her dreams.

"How did you know?!" She has never met anybody with whom she could talk about that. I told her that it is natural that those who loved us here want to help us from the Other Side. From there, they can do it even better. I talked about a teacher I had in elementary school, who sent me a message of love one day, when I was in great anxiety about my missing daughter. She was a good friend of my mother's, and she taught me at the time my mother died. I told Stephanie how I got that message, from a woman who practised automatic writing and received a message from my mother to comfort me. That woman received several messages, but she was not detached about them; when they did not agree with her ideas, she was disturbed. I tried to tell her to be a good mailbox, not to feel responsible for the content of the letters. She called me one evening, complained about not getting any more messages. I asked her to see if she got one while I was with her.

"If you write down what arrives." I took paper and wrote the date.

"You seem so sure," she said and she sat down at her table...

"Do you know an Aunt Ilonka?" she asked me.

"Yes."

"Are you the one Angéla is thinking of?" The answer came,

"I taught her to read and write, and am glad to communicate with her, one whose life I follow with love."

I told Stephanie that she could pray for her father, for him to help her mother to stop grieving. There was a calm, warm atmosphere around us, comforting her. I sensed that we were not alone, although we sat, just the two of us, on a bench in an empty playground.

As if my eyes were drawn to it, I looked at the school across the street. Above the gate of the new school there was a familiar name, the name of the teacher about whom I was just talking. Over the gate of the school, stood *Magyar Ilona Általános Iskola*, which means, "*The Ilona Magyar Public School*". She must have been good to many people and they must have loved her as I did, to name a new school after her.

She was one of the most important people who tried to fill the gap when my mother left me behind; some of the loving souls who were good to me, have passed out of my conscious memory, leaving only a glow of trust for my fellowmen.

One Saturday afternoon, in the early Hungarian spring, I walked to an address in search of a young man who wanted to be contacted by Bahá'ís. Suddenly the warmth of an old couple who was very kind to me popped out of the haze of forgotten memories. When I felt lonely, sad, I could walk over to their small house in a garden, beyond a white wooden gate. Their name was gone. I could not remember whether it was she or he who was a special friend, it must have been both of them. Their house stood somewhere around here, on a country path, where I was now among tall buildings.

"I am sorry that I do not remember you clearly. I only remember how good you were to me. Please come with me now..." I found the address I had, and rang the doorbell. The young man was not home, but his mother received me cordially. Yes, he had told her about meeting the Bahá'í youth from many countries who came to Kecskemét.

"I have to be honest with you, I am not a religious person, but I do believe in God. And, yes, I also believe that there is life after death. Do you?" I answered by telling her about the conversation I just had with the long-dead friends, who used to live around this place ... Ella declared her belief in Bahá'u'lláh shortly before I left for Canada.

She had just read my book, the autobiography, when another Hungarian-Canadian Bahá'í, Gale Bond visited them. Gale was holding her prayer-book and out of it a photo-post-card fell to the ground. Ella picked it up and her eye caught the name to which the old card was addressed, and exclaimed, "That is Angéla's father!" The postcard was dated August 9, 1916 and was addressed to Brunó Schmidt, in Trencsén, where he was stationed before they sent him to the Serbian front. The photo shows a group of five women and four children, the women are in black, the youngest is my mother. In the centre is my grandmother, a newspaper in her hand with the list of those who had died or were taken prisoner on the front. Among the dead was my mother's brother, husband of the sad-faced woman in the back row, father of two of the children. Among the prisoners taken on the Russian front was the husband of my aunt Irene, the one who sent the card to Brunó, to give news of Aranka. The photo was taken in the courtyard of the old family home where I was born.

I knew that photo, but had never seen that postcard before. Gale has no idea where it came from, no idea how to explain it. Neither have I. Whatever, whoever put that card on the floor for Ella to pick up and identify, we will likely never know. What I do know is that what happened to us before we met the Faith was no accident, and that whatever happens to us in the path of teaching is no accident either. To make this line of thought even clearer, I have to tell the story of my 71st birthday. I decided to celebrate it by visiting Igló and the house where I was born. To go to Igló from Kecskemét, I had to go to Budapest, and take the train next morning to Kosice, then Czechoslovakia, the Republic of Slovakia since

January 1, 1993. In Budapest I slept in the house of a niece. Marianne Széll received me with a surprise gift, a photo of Aranka, my mother, as a little girl of about four. I had never seen the picture before. It's beautiful. She is standing on an armchair, with a bouquet of flowers in her hand.

Then I took the train to Kosice, where two cousins were waiting. They had a surprise for me too, a photo of Brunó, my father, about one year old, standing on the same armchair, holding a whip in his hand. The same photographer, same position, same size of picture, with white borders both of them. The little girl holds flowers, the little boy is holding a whip. Not more than a year old, he already had the stamp on him. He was supposed to become a man, a strong one, who commands.

When he went to college, his father had a stack of postcards printed with five words: *Egyenesen állj és ne hadarj!* which means, "Stand straight and don't mumble!" Then he had to be a hero, to fight for his country. No wonder this poor little boy ended his life in an insane asylum. No wonder he helps me now to work for peace.

From Kosice I took the train to Igló, found a taxi and showed a paper with the address to the driver. When we reached it, I opened my purse and held it to him to show me how much the fare was. I do not speak Slovak. He did not speak Hungarian, so we had to use gestures. He gently put his hand over my purse, closed it and shoved it away. He gave me a birthday present!

A cousin was waiting for me in her nice new apartment. When I visited her in 1980, she had a small, very dark one room. Now she lives on the ninth floor of one of the three apartment blocks which were built on what used to be my grandmother's garden, where I aimed rotten apples at the hats of Czech soldiers, where Imu used to tell stories on Sunday afternoons, where I was playing when I heard my mother's voice on the morning she died. Now children of families from three big buildings can play in the still nice garden left of the big-big, rich one. My cousin has a sunny terrace from where she can see the most beautiful mountain-range I know, the white, snow-capped mountains of the High Tátra.

Our lunch took much longer than we expected, because she had lots of questions about my beliefs. Finally, I met a relative who wanted to hear about the Faith! That was a most beautiful birthday present!

We went to the old house. It is not old any more, it has become a beautiful fine arts gallery. Where the servants' quarters used to be, we found a concert hall. Two children were practising on the piano for that evening. The teacher came to invite us, and when she heard that it was my birthday, she gave the warmest smile. I thanked her and rushed to take the bus to Iglófured, or Spisska-Nova-Ves Kupele, to visit the scene of my two glorious summers.

The villa that stood in a forest, way above the village, is now a solid part of it. A strongly built, nice family home. It looked down on me, with the two wide windows of the main floor. That villa belonged to my father's cousin, Theobald Kregczy (Uncle Theo). I met him only by correspondence. He was taken prisoner during World War One by the Russians and never came home. When the Russian Revolution of 1917 freed him, he became a teacher in a noble Russian family and fled with them to Shanghai. They drove through the Gobi Desert, with Uncle Theo as driver and mechanic. He became husband to their lovely daughter, Nina. They lived in Calcutta when we began corresponding. He sent me a copy of our family tree.

According to the family tree, our oldest known ancestor is a Barbara Cilli born at Cilli Castle, Stiermark (now Celje in Slovenia) who married a Benigni, fighter against the Turks. The last male member of the Cilli family, Count Ulrich was murdered in 1456, in a town called today Belgrade. We learned at school that he was stabbed to death by Laszlo Hunyadi, because he, the regent for the child-king of Hungary, wanted to allow the Sultan's armies to march west against the Holy Roman Empire, just as the Crusaders were allowed to march east through Hungary when they were on their way against the Turks, to free the Holy Land.

When I got the family tree, I was already a Bahá'í, and found it remarkable that this man, considered an awful figure by our history books, would have trust for the Sultan of the Ottoman Empire. His death, hailed as a heroic act, for me became a martyrdom on the altar of broad-mindedness in an era when religious and civil laws were bent to suit the prevailing powers, not to serve justice and truth.

I looked up, greeted the villa of uncle Theo, the scene of two happy family summers, and took the bus back to Igló to catch the train, so I could continue commuting to and from Europe and North America and the places of my past, present and future.

In February 1991, I went to the first *Bahá'í Winter School of Romania*, held in Felix, near Oradea. It was the happiest Bahá'í gathering of my life. I felt that the spirit of Queen Marie of Romania, the first crowned head to bow in adoration and recommend that the people pay attention to the Bahá'í Writings, surrounded us with her spirit, humility, and love.

There I met a young Bahá'í whose nickname was Cilli. I told him about my relationship to that name. He thought for a while, then said, "Had the Turks marched against Vienna, they would have likely taken it, and Europe would have become Muslim. Bahá'u'lláh did say that all divinely revealed religions had the potential to become world religions and that it was only the opposition of certain powerful people or groups that stopped this from happening." Here he stopped, and we both wondered what results that might have brought. Then he carried on, "By that time Islam had strayed as far

291

from its original purity as did Christianity." Thus we ended our historical musings on a note of acceptance of Divine Will.

This was the first time I could talk about that forefather of mine with a Bahá'í who knew European history and with whom I could share my thoughts about that period from a Bahá'í point of view.

The bus was coming. I looked up to say good-bye to the place of my happy childhood. I took the bus, to catch the train and then the plane back to Canada. God willing, I will continue to commute between North America and Europe, between the past, the present and a bright future.

The time is ripe, thoughts are ready. It takes a small, hardly noticeable push for the walls to crumble. The many remaining walls might still look solid, but they are not. There is nothing that can hold back winter when spring arrives.

People have suffered enough to know what is worth working for, and what is not. In this age, there are no secrets.

We are building a new society. We are all on this same planet, covered by the same sky.

The sky is open, and the sky is good and just to all.

29 Martinique Revisited 1997

Zeus, my dear spiritual son who was 19 when I left Martinique in 1979, woke me one morning with a surprise phone call. I take time to get my wits together in the morning. Even if it had not been on waking, I would have taken time to realize who was calling! He was calling to ask me to visit and help revive the spirit of his Bahá'í community.

It took me three years before I was able to take that trip. I do not know how much I helped revive the spirit of the Bahá'ís of Martinique, but my visit with them revived my spirits immensely. It gave me a glimpse into some of the mysterious ways God is working to revive the whole of mankind.

Morne-des-Esses, where Zeus lives, and also little black Angéla about whom I was hoping that she could grow up with the same material advantages as other youngsters of the world, such as running water and electricity, today has impressive new homes, with hot and cold water, and refrigerators. The trouble at the moment is that those refrigerators are the old type, which cannot be easily sold in France any more because they are not self-defrosting. People, who did not grow up slowly with electrical appliances, think that their fridges are having mechanical problems when they plug up with ice. In two homes my chief contribution was to defrost the refrigerator! (A whole chapter could be added here on the shocks created by the meeting of "developed" and "underdeveloped" economics.)

What was of greatest importance to me was the realization that the spirit of the Bahá'í Writings, which were widely proclaimed there in the early seventies by a group of devoted Canadian youth, has penetrated the life of the whole island.

Soon after Bahá'u'lláh declared His mission, He wrote letters, or Tablets, to the kings and clergy of the world. He called them to get together and make peace. None heeded His advice. He said that because the rulers do not obey God, and do not use their power for what God gave it to them, their power is taken away and is given to the people. It will take time and much suffering but people will eventually grow up and use that power for the general good.

It was the pioneers in Portugal, Val Nichols and Louise Baker, who followed Shoghi Effendi's call and left for 10 Western European countries during the Second Seven Year Plan (1946-1953), who told me about Bahá'u'lláh's proclamation to the rulers of the world. They mentioned that Queen Victoria was the only one who is known to have said something about the Tablet she received. If I remember correctly, they quoted her:

"If this man is from God, time will prove him, if he is a fake, God will deal with him."

We know as a fact that Bahá'u'lláh praised Queen Victoria for abolishing slavery and instituting elected parliaments. He even revealed a special prayer for her. Shoghi Effendi reports in *The Promised Day is Come* that her response was: "If this is of God it will endure; if not it can do no harm." And, that, because of her merits, her crown will survive the others.

Two attitudes, one coming from a queen with enormous authority, shrugging her royal shoulder instead of following a command coming from God; and the second, coming from the Divine Messenger, out of His wisdom and compassion, pointing out what can be praised in the actions of a ruler with a finite mind.

Shoghi Effendi, the Guardian has said that the historians of the future will be amazed... As one who is a political scientist, and became a Bahá'í to work for world peace, I find specially amazing at this moment the Tablet Bahá'u'lláh addressed to "the Rulers of America and the Presidents of the Republics therein". He says, among other things:

"Give ear unto that which hath been raised from the Dayspring of Grandeur: 'Verily there is none other God but Me, the Lord of Utterance, the All-Knowing.' Bind ye the broken with the hands of justice, and crush the oppressor who flourisheth with the rod of the commandments of your Lord, the Ordainer, the All-Wise" (Bahá'u'lláh, *Kitáb-i-Aqdas*, p. 52).

During the First World War, 'Abdu'l-Bahá wrote letters to North Americans calling them to bring the new message of peace to the world. He said that Canada had a special future, both materially and spiritually blessed. And that by the end of this century, the Lesser Peace will dawn on the horizon of the world. This will mean the end of wars and give mankind a chance to use the human genius to build a world of harmony and prosperity for all.

In 1936, Shoghi Effendi said that a communication system, exact and instantaneous will be developed, connecting all parts of the world. We now have Internet. It can be used by everybody, good and bad alike. It takes away the ability of the bad to rule over the good. Everybody can see and hear everyone else. We can form educated opinions, accept what is valid, recognize and refuse what is wrong.

Now is the time of reckoning, now we can show how
well we have understood the messages God has sent to educate us. Moses brought laws, Krishna brought tolerance, Buddha brought detachment, Jesus brought love, Muhammad
brought science. The Báb called all believers in God to be
ready for a new message, and Bahá'u'lláh brought the teachings to unite mankind. It is not their fault that their Names
were often used by men against their fellowmen.

**Angéla, with Aimé Cesaire, still Mayor of Fort-de-France,
and called "the father of Martinique," 1997.**

In Martinique one can touch the core of human error and also of human perfection. The colonizing armies went
to Africa and brought back human beings, treating them like
cattle, while carrying the cross. That is a symbol that should
remind us of Christ's love. "Religion" comes from "religare",
tying together, tying man to God, tying men to each other. It
was often misused. Those who suffered most from this, are
the ones who can best show how it was meant to be used.
Bahá'u'lláh says that if religion separates, it is better not to
have one. But if there is no religion, inequity can reign. We
have to learn to recognize the difference.

On arrival in Fort-de-France, I was greeted by a pioneer from Nova Scotia and one from New Brunswick. She
296

took me to Michel Guilbeault, from Québec. From these three Canadians, I got a smattering of the different economic and intellectual concerns. From Michel's place, I went to pass a wonderful week with Zeus' mother, a real spiritual sister to me.

Zeus was awfully busy. He is involved in everything that can be done for moral education in the schools. All around the island, spectacles are shown which make people think. They are offered to students from preschool age to adolescence, and their parents, aimed specially at mothers. I watched one play about a Bird and a Rat. The bird was only interested in beauty, song and dance; the rat passed his time with his calculator, adding up his money. The lesson is, of course, that we need both. The children had a hilarious time watching and taking active part in the play.

Then I rented a studio in Bellefontaine, with a big terrace, overlooking the sea, and started visiting around. I went to Anse-à-l'Âne, to see the place where I used to live. The studio I was renting for 600 franks, now costs 2,800. It was elegant then, now it is neglected. In contrast, the poor dwelling I used to see below my terrace, where a big family lived, the father taking his sheep to pasture every morning, is a bit bigger. It has a smart terrace in front, and one in the back, for the family to eat comfortably in the shade. The mother recognized and invited me, told me what her children had achieved in life, their studies, their work. Their standing has clearly risen. Generally speaking, the rich have become less rich and the poor less poor. The extremes are diminishing, as Bahá'u'lláh, and the economists of today, are saying they should.

Another significant change I noticed is in the position of women. One example was a mother, who had her wedding dress ready, but changed her mind. She had eight children from the man she originally intended to marry, but she wanted to be free to bring them up the way she felt was right for them.

I always felt that the Martiniquais are kind, warm-hearted human beings, but now it struck me that they may be close to what I think Shoghi Effendi meant when he spoke of the "new race of men".

For a long time, I wanted to understand what the difference between backbiting and giving useful information is. We are supposed to be well-informed, discerning people, capable of consulting freely, of sharing knowledge correctly. Backbiting is forbidden by Bahá'u'lláh as a grievous sin. He speaks of it in the same sentence with murder and adultery. It is important to know the difference. It seems to me that the Martiniquais, generally speaking, do know it. They do not jest and tease. They give information freely, but never to tear anybody apart.

One evening, while walking by the sea, I was stopped by an elderly man. I was trying to catch the meaning of his words, when a bus driver I knew stopped to listen. I finally understood that I was being asked about my religion, and said among other things, that drinking alcohol is forbidden by Bahá'u'lláh. The younger man said, in a calm voice, "That is the problem he has," and he gave me a quizzical smile. I understood it as "Now you know why you are embarrassed listening to him."

There was so much compassion for both the other man and for me in that short sentence and the smile, that it flooded my heart with light.

People invited me to their Sunday services. In one of the noisiest ones, I took my favourite photo of this visit. A small boy clings to his mother, while she swings right-and-left, to the loudspeaker's blaring music. His face is calm, completely relaxed. His mother is a reliable skyhook for him.

These people, who were so badly treated in the past, and are even now easily exploited because they do not see when they are being manipulated, are so close to my heart. Could it be that I love them, whose ancestors were treated like cattle, with a special compassion, because I took my first steps on this earth as a refugee in a cattle-car?

30 | **Postscriptum 1999**

50 YEARS IN THE FORMATIVE AGE:
Mentalities, Genders and Generations

Presented by Angéla Szepesi to the 22nd Annual Conference of the Association for Bahá'í Studies, Montréal 24-27 September 1998.

When I offered to present a paper on these 50 years, I never imagined how difficult it would be to compose a 45-minute resumé of my thoughts and feelings about this half-a-century. I reminded myself that Shoghi Effendi had said that what is difficult takes long to do, what is impossible, takes a bit longer.

The term "Formative Age" suggests a time-span when change occurs, something new and better takes shape. What could be seen in 1921 was very different from what we can see today. The chaotic world of that year has turned into an infinitely more chaotic one by today. I shall look at the changes, their content and their direction.

The Bahá'í aim of the change is a world in order, where justice reigns. What has been unorganized, disharmonious, has to fit into a mould where parts complete each other and produce a whole.

The actors who do the changing, the finding of the ways in which things fit better, are we, simple human beings. We are parts of groups, according to birth, upbringing, temperaments, talents and shortcomings, experiences and expectations. The grouping factors I chose to look at, to try to make sense and understand the events I am most aware of are: our mentalities, the gender into which we were born and the generations to which we belong. Until recently all three were used for battlegrounds, areas of conflict.

Coming in contact with people who act and react differently from what we regard normal and right, baffle us and may make us amazed, frightened, hurt, even angry. But we are learning to become curious, and happy to learn something new. Unknown mentalities can be as varied as the plants in the fields. They all belong together.

Whether one was born a male or a female acts in a less unknown and varied manner. By-and-large, the men of most mentalities were supposed to guide, rule, dominate, and to fight against other males. Women were supposed to take care of the men, rear children and keep silent about what else they would like to do. Now men and women are learning to become partners.

The generations following each other were often filled with envy, resentment, because the others were younger or older, weaker and wiser or stronger and more foolish. We are now learning to see them as ancestors from whom we inherited good things, or descendants, inheriting the best in ourselves, giving hope for a better future.

In the historical context of the world, I see much improvement in all three fields in a relatively short time. Relationships between many different mentalities, equality between men and women seem improved, and the co-operation of old, adult, young and child members of the human family give much joy everywhere. Under the guidance of Bahá'u'lláh and His Covenant, battlegrounds are becoming orchards where delicious fruits grow. Of what I was helped to add, and specially because I am speaking at the conference of the *Association for Bahá'í Studies,* may I mention the thesis written on the Proposed World Order which earned a master's degree at *Laval University* and made Will van den Hoonard see that the Faith has become a palatable subject in academia.

My thesis advisor at *Laval University* found that Bahá'u'lláh's proposals were far ahead of what was then known in political science, but they were an historical and logical continuation of what was already known. He helped me add the necessary connections. If I were asked to suggest somebody for an award of academic excellence — in the Bahá'í perspective — I would nominate Professor Gérard Bergeron. A devoted Catholic, outspoken French-Canadian nationalist, and renowned academician, he told me not to hold back, not to hide my belief in the ultimate victory of the proposals forwarded by Bahá'u'lláh, because I owe it to the future to be sincere, because this was an unusual thesis, a normative theory.

Twenty years later, in 1988, Richard Gagnon, a younger-generation Bahá'í, earned a doctorate in the same department, with an analysis of the structure of the Bahá'í administrative order.

As the world around us is searching for the way out of the chaos, we can confidently prepare for the new challenges emerging with the Lesser Peace. I am certain that by the end of the next 50 years, 'Abdu'l-Bahá's hope for Canada's and Montréal's role will be amply fulfilled. I also think that the Aqdas will bring such a profound change to the character, behaviour and morals of the people of East and West, North and South, that Albert Einstein's remark (in his *Ideas and Opinions*) will also be realized. He said that a man of the future, of a vastly more mature age, looking back at what human beings of today were like, will be profoundly ashamed when he remembers that he belongs to the same species.

I would very much like to live in that age, but first we have still lots to do.

Glossary

(in order of appearance)

Dispensation: the historical period when the social teachings of a Manifestation are supreme. Example: Mosaic, Christian, Muhammedan Dispensations.

Manifestation: through Whom God speaks to man, or manifests Himself.

Anyuka: the name I used for my mother, diminutive of anya=mother.

Apu: the name I used for my father, diminutive of apa=father.

Imu: short for "Ilma grandmother", the name I used for my paternal grandmother.

pengoe: currency used in Hungary between the two world wars.

néni: aunt, also an older woman friend.

Bahá'u'lláh: Arabic word meaning "The Glory of God".

'Abdu'l-Bahá: Bahá'u'lláh's eldest son, appointed authority after His passing, Exemplar for Bahá'ís and the Centre of the Covenant.

Covenant: pact of God and of His Manifestations with mankind ("If you want to be happy, follow My commandments").

Shoghi Effendi: 'Abdu'l-Bahá's grandson, appointed by him as Guardian of the Bahá'í Faith

Rúhíyyih Khánum: born Mary Maxwell, wife of Shoghi Effendi.

L.S.A.: Local Spiritual Assembly, local governing body.

N.S.A.: National Spiritual Assembly, national governing body.

Universal House of Justice: supreme authority of the Bahá'í world, with its seat on Mount Carmel, above Haifa, Israël.

Knights of Bahá'u'lláh: believers who opened virgin territories for the Faith, mostly between 1953 –1963.

The Greatest Name: Allah'u'Abhá, meaning "God is the Most Glorious."

Supreme Concourse: departed souls who help those still on this earth.

Greatest Holy Leaf: Bahíyyih Khánum, Bahá'u'lláh's daughter.

Hands of the Cause: protectors of the Faith and the believers.

Ridván: Festival of Bahá'u'lláh's declaration, April 21–May 2. On April 21 of each year the Local Spiritual Assemblies are elected all over the world.

Deputize: to send somebody in one's place.

Fast: From March 2 to 21 Bahá'ís do not eat or drink between sunrise and sunset.

Remover of difficulties: Prayer revealed by the Báb: "Is there any Remover of difficulties save God? Say: Praised be God! He is God! All are His servants and all abide by His bidding." Shoghi Effendi quotes it on p. 119 of *God Passes By*, the history of the first century of the Bahá'í Era.

B.E.: Bahá'í Era. It started in A.D. 1844.

Lesser Peace: When wars will be made impossible, and begins the development toward the Golden Age of the Eternal Peace.

Aqdas: *The Kitáb-i-Aqdas*, Bahá'u'lláh's Most Holy Book.